McDonald's
Happy Meal® Toys from the Nineties

Joyce & Terry Losonsky

With Price Guide

Schiffer® Publishing Ltd
4880 Lower Valley Road, Atglen, PA 19310 USA

Every effort has been made to identify copyright holders of materials referenced in this book. Should there be omissions, the authors apologize and shall be pleased to make appropriate acknowledgments in future editions.

THIS GUIDE IS NEITHER AUTHORIZED NOR APPROVED BY THE McDONALD'S CORPORATION, OAK BROOK, ILLINOIS.

The following trademarks and service marks TM, SM and ® are owned by McDonald's Corporation, Oak Brook, Illinois 60521:

Archy McDonald, Big Mac, Birdie, Birdie the Early Bird, Birthdayland, Captain Crook, Captain (The), Chicken Nuggets, CosMc, Earlybird, Fry Girls, Fry Guys, Fry Kids, Glo-Tron, Golden Arches, The Golden Arches Logo, Grimace, Hamburglar, Happy Meal, Happy Meals, Happy Pail, Iam Hungry, Mac Tonight, Mayor McCheese, McBoo, McBunny, McCaps, McCheese, McDonald's, McDonaldland, McDonald's FT Magazine Logo, McGhost, McGoblin, McJack, McMuffin, McNugget Buddies, McPunk'n, McPizza, McWitch, MBX, Professor, Quarter Pounder, Robocakes, Ronald, Ronald McDonald, Speedee, Willie Munchright.

The following trademarks and service marks TM, SM and ® are owned by the companies indicated:

101 Dalmations, Baloo, Bambi, Donald, Ducktales, Dumbo, Benji, Faline, Huey, Luey, Louis, Scrooge, Launchpad, Snow White and the Seven Dwarfs, Talespin, Webby — Walt Disney Company.
Acme Acres, Animaniacs, Bat Duck, Bugs, Bugs Bunny, Daffy Duck, Dukes of Hazzard, Gogo Dodo, Hampton, Looney Tunes, Road Runner, Super Bugs, Sylvester, Tas-Flash, Tiny Toon, Toonsters, Tweety, Wile Coyote, Wonder Pig — Warner Bros.
Archies, The New Archies, Dino, Jughead, Reggie — Prime Designs Ltd.
Barbie, Hot Wheels, Mini-Streex, Attack Pack — Mattel Inc.
Beanie Babies, Teenie Beanie Babies — Ty, Inc.
Berenstain — S & J Berenstain.
Bibble, Corkle, Gropple, Thugger — Current Inc.
Boober, Bulldozer, Cotterpin, Doozer, Fozzie, Fraggle Rock, Gobo, Bonzo, Kermit, Mokey, Muppet Babies (The), The Great Muppet Caper, Wembly, Snoopy, Charlie Brown, Lucy, Linus, Miss Piggy, Muppet Workshop, Muppet, What-Not — Jim Henderson Productions, Inc./Henson Associates.
Coca-Cola, Diet Coke, Sprite, Minute Maid — Coca-Cola Company, Atlanta, Georgia.
Colorforms — Colorforms.
Crayola — Binney And Smith.
Commandrons, Dragonoids, Elephoids, Octopoid, Scorpoid, Poppin — Tomy.
Fievel — Universal City Studios.
Flintstones (The) — Copyright: Universal City Studios, Inc. and Amblin Entertainment.
Flintstones (The), Barney, Fred, Wilma, Betty — Trademark: Hanna-Barbera Productions Inc.
Frankentyke, Vinnie Stoker, Cleofatra, Gravedale High — NBC.
Garfield, Odie, Pooky — United Feature Syndicate Inc.
Ghostbuster, Ghostbusters, Slimer — Columbia Pictures Industries Inc.
Goomba, Koopa, Luigi, Super Mario Bros. 3, Super Mario — Nintendo of America Inc.
Hook, Rufio, Captain Hook, Peter Pan — Tri-Star Pictures Inc.
Kirk, Klingons, McCoy, Spock, Star Trek — Paramount Pictures.
Kissyfur — S. L. Colburn, Milwaukee, Wisconsin
Lego, Legoduplo — Lego Group.
Matchbox — Matchbox International.
Nascar — Jr. Maxx, Charlotte, North Carolina.
Paas — Schering-Plough.
Piggsburg Pigs, Quacker, Huff, Pighead, Portly, Puff, Rembrandt — Fox Children's Network, Inc.
Playmobil — Geobra-Brandslatter GMBH & Co.
Playmobil Characters, Stomper, Bigfoot — Schafer Mfg. Co.
Raggedy Ann, Raggedy Andy, Raggedy Ann and Andy — MacMillan Inc.
Super Mario Bros. 3, Super Mario, Goomba, Luigi, Koopa — Nintendo of America Inc.
The Friendly Skies — United Air Lines.
The Magic School Bus — Scholastic Inc., Joanna Cole and Bruce Degen.
Tom and Jerry — Turner Entertainment.

Library of Congress Cataloging-in-Publication Data

Losonsky, Joyce.
McDonald's Happy Meal toys from the nineties/Joyce and Terry Losonsky.
p. cm.
Includes index.
ISBN: 0-7643-0673-1 (pbk.)
1. McDonald's Corporation--Collectibles--Catalogs. 2. Premiums (Retail trade)--Collectors and collecting--United States--Catalogs. 3. Lunchboxes--Collectors and collecting--United States--Catalogs. I. Losonsky, Terry. II. Title.
NK6213.L6796 1998
688.7'2'093075--dc21 98-24944
CIP

Designed by Bonnie M. Hensley
Layout by Randy L. Hensley
Type set in Humanist521 BT

ISBN: 0-7643-0673-1
Printed in China
1 2 3 4

Published by Schiffer Publishing Ltd.
4880 Lower Valley Road
Atglen, PA 19310
Phone: (610) 593-1777; Fax: (610) 593-2002
E-mail: Schifferbk@aol.com
Please write for a free catalog.
This book may be purchased from the publisher.
Please include $3.95 for shipping.

In Europe, Schiffer books are distributed by
Bushwood Books
6 Marksbury Avenue
Kew Gardens
Surrey TW9 4JF England
Phone: 44 (0)181 392-8585; Fax: 44 (0)181 392-9876
E-mail: Bushwd@aol.com

Please try your bookstore first.

We are interested in hearing from authors
with book ideas on related subjects.

Acknowledgments

The authors would like to take this opportunity to express our sincere appreciation and gratitude to all our collector friends who have contributed their time and knowledge to our research. In the event of oversight, we sincerely apology for any names and familiar faces left off our overgrowing list. It takes a collector group of friends to write a comprehensive price guide on McDonald's Happy Meal Toys From the Nineties. We would like to "Thank" the following:

ADVISORY BOARD

Ken Clee
Ron & Eileen Corbett
Jimmy & Pat Futch
John & Eleanor Larsen
McDonald's Corporation
Greg & Rhonda MacClaren
Bill & Pat Poe
E. J. Ritter
Rich & Laurel Seidelman
Bill Thomas
Meredith Williams

One reason for writing this book is to share our knowledge with other collectors who enjoy the thrill of seeking out McDonald's collectibles in the family toy boxes, thrift stores, and yard sales. The thrill of finding a "new" item is a sustaining factor among collectors. Since McDonald's is located in at least one hundred countries and distributes millions of toys every week, there are enough collectibles for all of us. Our desire to accurately record the history of McDonald's collectibles is the driving force behind our books, because understanding the history of the past provides insight into the future.

We would like to extend a special "hug" to our children and our families for their love and patient help over the last thirty years of collecting. To our children: Andrea, Natasha, Nicole, and Ryan and to children everywhere, we thank them for providing the incentive to visit McDonald's frequently. To our families: Stephen and Ann Zurko, Frank and Nancy Losonsky, Steve and Linda Zurko, Max Zurko, Phil and Alana Losonsky, Chris and Toni Losonsky and Aunt Ursula Shows, we sincerely thank them for all their encouragement and help over the years. We extend a heartfelt "Thanks" to the many McDonald's employees who over the years have fulfilled our request for items, especially for their cheerful, friendly, helpful, polite manners extended to collectors around the world. To Chris and Betsy, Kevin and Judy, the McDonald's owner/operators (O/O) and crew everywhere who say with a smile, "May I take your order, please?" we would like to express sincere appreciation. On behalf of all collectors, we expressly want to "Thank" McDonald's Corporation, Oak Brook, Illinois, for their assistance!

Lastly, a very special "Thank you and Hug" are extended to the many wonderful collector friends who have helped us in various ways over the last thirty years of collecting, from offering advice to sending material or photographs. These special friends have encouraged us to develop, update, and expand this book and our upcoming books. We wish to acknowledge assistance from the following individuals:

Helen Farrell - McDonald's Archives
Lois Dougherty - McDonald's Archives
Laura Kleiner - McDonald's Archives
George Griggs - Director/Field Marketing
Kathy List - Marketing/McDonald's
Wilma Weir - Marketing/McDonald's
Sam Apkarian
Dave Archer
Kathy Arne
Ron & Ethel Bacon
Linda Bailey
Richard & Crystal Banyon
Tom & Bonnie Becker
Terry Beedie
Becky Berger
Tom Borton
Bill & Marie Boyce
Harvey & Cleo Bradstreet
Bob & Mary Ann Brown
Sidney & Jeanne Bruce
Gerald & Helen Buchholz
Bert & Carolyn Buckler
Mark Carder
Carl & Rosemary Carlson
Maynard Carney
Karen Cavanaugh
Jim Challenger
Scott Chandler
Jim & Sally Christoffel
Ann Marie Clark
John & Brenda Clark
Kathy Clark
Judy Clark
Marilyn Clulow
Mark Coleman
David Cunningham
Clint Deale
Marvinette Dennis
Nate Downs
Darrell & Robyn Duncan
Gail Duzak
David Epstein
Gordon & Kath Fairgrieve
Leslie Fein
Fred Fiedler
Marjorie Fontana
Mike & Deanna Fountaine
Mike & Kathy Franze
Bonnie & Cheri Garnett
Jim & Linda Gegorski
Kay Geva
Brian Gildea
Mark & Carol Gillette
Bob & Gretchen Gipson
Lance Golba
Cindy Gore
Steve Gould
Pat & Martha Gragg
Shirley Graulich
Nick Graziano
Gary & Teena Greenberg
Chuck Gustafson
David Hale
Roberta Harris
Gary & Judy Heald
Gary & Shirley Henriques
Ed Hock
Roger Hordines
Sharon Iranpour
Steven & Ann Jackson
Dave Johnson
Brian Jones
Anne King
Joyce Klassen
Robert Lanier
Jerry Ledbetter
Pat Lonergan
Kent Longmire
Darrell Lulling
Lee Marsh
Thomas & Frankie Massey
Bob McClintock
Bill & Betty McCormick
Glen & Kathleen McElwee
Janet McGuire
Art McManis
Victor Medcalf
Don Metiva
George Miller
Howard Morris
Julius & Margaret Mortvedt
Stanley Mull
Pat Multz
Beulah Murphy
Rene & Anne Marie Naim
Steve & Margie Nation
Steven Jr. & Rebecca & Rachel Nation
Tom & Terry Nelson
Jim & Cooky Oberg
Harry Oberth
Roger Olshanski
Tom & Teresa Olszeski
Joe & Dolly Pascale
Mark Patterson
Garnett Pennington
Mark & Jane Petzel
Janet Phillips
Joe & Carol Pierce
Ray Podraza
Larry & Maynuella Poli
Edward & Jean Pomeroy
Jean Pomeroy
Mike Portzline
Charles & Connie Prater
Ron & Jane Prussiano
Fred Rauch
Jimmy Renella
Russell & Marie Rinehart
Alyce Roberts
Tom & Kathy Robusto
Natalie Royer
Ed Ruby
Chris & Julie Rucho
Emma Rush
Doug & Debbie Ryan
Barbara Saitta
Essie Saunders
Ed & Sharon Scarbrock
Pat Sentell
Bob Serighino
Jim Silva
Trudy Slaven
Scott Smiles
Dan Smith
Jerry & Lorraine Soltis
Rich & JoLyn Stack
Lorie Steele
Julie Stegeman
Peggy Stockard
David Stone
Richard & Marge Taibi
Debbie Taylor
Nigel Thomas
John & Virginia Thompson
Robert & Jackie Thompson
Ray & Dorothy Tognarelli
Frances Turey
Gary & Jill Turner
Lee Turpin
Dave Tuttle
Kees & Conny Versteeg
Taylor & Cindy Wagen
Lloyd & Nancy Washburn
Fred & Elaine Waterman
Ted Waters
Toni Welsh
Gary & Karen Wenzlaff
Robert Wilkey
Don Wilson
Jim & Rosalie Wolfe
Mike & Mary Ann Wooten
Ron & Eldra Word
Frank Work
Claire Zabo
Frank Zamarripa

Joyce and Terry Losonsky can be reached at:

7506 Summer Leave Lane
Columbia, Maryland 21046-2455
Tel: USA 1-410-381-3358
FAX: USA 1-410-381-1852
E-mail: JoyceUSA@aol.com

Introduction

Welcome to the world of McDonald's Happy Meal toy collecting in the nineties! The Happy Meal and Happy Meal toys, jingles, logos, slogans, and convention themes reflect an image of what America has experienced in the last forty-three years — McDonald's toy collecting is Americana at its best! The 1990s continued the era of McDonald's Happy Meal toys in grand style. From its beginning with the Barbie/Hot Wheels promotion through two Teenie Beanie Babies Happy Meal promotions, this decade represents the epitome of fast food toy collecting. McDonald's has become an American institution producing the "gastronomical glue" which binds parents to children and grandparents to grandchildren in a common experience, all enjoying McDonald's food and collecting Happy Meal toys.

Some collectors want to collect only Happy Meal character toys from the nineties, others seek only Disney toys, while still others prefer only Garfield, Batman, Barbie, Hot Wheels, or Beanie Babies. The wishes and desires of the collectors are as infinite as the toys themselves; the common thread is the collecting for fun theme.

McDonald's has tried and repeated many toy themes, slogans, logos, and trademarks throughout its forty-three year history and, as always, McDonald's collectibles from the nineties provide many examples of each. If we asked a group of McDonald's customers what an advertising slogan is, they'd probably reply, "Just another way to get me to buy a product." While that is true for some, for McDonald's collectors, a slogan or trademark means much more. Identification of toys, slogans, logos, jingles, and convention themes is one of the best ways to date an advertising collectible! The age of an item, its condition, its rarity, and general distribution data on the item all tend to influence price. Everyone seems to want to know, "What is it worth?" They don't necessarily want to sell the item, they just want to have that warm, fuzzy feeling of knowing the item they possess has value. But in the end, price is determined between what amount a buyer is willing to pay and what amount the seller is willing to take. Prices of McDonald's items are constantly changing—up and down, regionally and globally—based on supply and demand.

"Where did it all start and where is it going?" is another common question among collectors. Before fully exploring the world of McDonald's Happy Meal Toys from the Nineties, whether they are the Teenie Beanie Babies, 101 Dalmations, or latest Disney toys, an understanding of the impressive history of the McDonald's success story is necessary. The following Losonsky Lists are provided to aid in the identification of items and to document the history of McDonald's toys, jingles, logos, slogans, and convention themes through the years. The lists are followed by helpful information for using this book and then a brief overview of McDonald's formative period during its first four decades (for a more detailed description of McDonald's early years, please see Joyce and Terry Losonsky's companion books, *McDonald's® Pre-Happy Meal® Toys from the Fifties, Sixties, and Seventies* and *McDonald's® Happy Meal® Toys from the Eighties*, also available from Schiffer Publishing).

Losonsky's Identification Guides to McDonald's Collectibles

Losonsky List #1: Jingles and Slogans

1950s

1953 - "McDonald's HAMBURGERS...THERE'S ONE NEAR YOU!"

1955 - "Speedee" corporate logo
1955-62 - "Speedee, the Hamburger Man"

1957 - "COAST to COAST"

1959 - "HOME OF AMERICA'S 'GOODEST' HAMBURGER"
1959 - "ALL AMERICAN MEAL only 45 cents"

1960s

1960 - "Look for the Drive-in with the Arches"
1960 - Speedee says: "Look for me at McDonald's speedee drive -ins"
1960-65 - "Look for the Golden Arches" jingle
1960s - "McDonald's Speedee drive-ins - often imitated, never duplicated"
1960s - "Those who know—Go to McDonald's"

1961 - YOUR KIND OF PLACE
1961 - THE ALL AMERICAN MEAL - still only 45 cents

1962 - "Go for Goodness at McDonald's"
1962 - "...the Drive-in with the arches"
1962 - "...way of life coast to coast" (repeated)
1962 - "EVERYBODY'S FAVORITE Coast to Coast"
1962 - Home of America's Favorite Hamburger
1962 - Home of...America's Favorite Hamburgers... still only 15 cents

1963 - "Meet Ronald McDonald"
1963 - "EVERYBODY'S FAVORITE Coast to Coast" (repeated)

1964 - "Look for THE DRIVE-IN WITH THE (GOLDEN) ARCHES"
1964 - "Come as you are and eat in your car—it's always fun for the family to eat at McDonald's from coast-to-coast, McDonald's sells the most! " ("coast-to-coast" repeated)
1964 - "Come as you are and eat in your car"
1964 - ALL AMERICAN MEAL only 47 cents

1965 - "McDonald's—where quality starts fresh every day - look for the Golden Arches"
1965 - "The Sky's The Limit"

1966-68 - "Ronald McDonald and His Flying Hamburger"

1967 - "McDonald's is Our Kind of Place"
1967 - "Look For The Golden Arches - The Closest Thing To Home"
1967 - Welcome to McDonald's...The Closest Thing To Home

1968 - "McDonald's is Your Kind of Place" (modified & repeated)
1968 - "The Customer is #1...What have you done lately for the Customer?"

1969 - "You Deserve a Break Today - So Get Up and Get Away to McDonald's"
1969 - "The Challenge of Success"

1970s

1970 - "You Deserve A Break Today - So get Up And Get Away To McDonald's" (repeated)

1971 - "You Deserve A Break Today - So get Up And Get Away To McDonald's" [repeated]
1971 - "Success and Then Some"
1971 - "Grab a Bucket & Mop"

1972 - "Don't Forget to Feed the Wastebasket"
1972 - "Let's Face It"

1973 - "You Deserve a Break Today" (abbreviated ad)

1974 - "You Deserve A Break Today We're Close By...Right on Your Way"
1974 - "McFavorite Clown"

1975 - "Two All-Beef Patties Special Sauce"
1975-79 - "We Do It All For You"
1975 - "Two all beef patties special sauce lettuce cheese pickles onions on asesameseed bun"

1976 - "You, You're the One"
1976 - "The Challenging World of Number One"

1978 - "Keep Your Eyes on Your Fries"
1978 - "When We Work At It—It Works"
1978 - "Happy Meals Tickle My Tummy"

1979 - "Nobody Can Do It Like McDonald's Can"

1980s

1980 - "Our World...Today, Yesterday and Tomorrow"

1981 - "You Deserve a Break Today" (repeated)

1982 - "McDonald's and You" (Camp Nippersink)
1982 - "Delivering the Difference"

1983 - "McDonald's and You" (repeated)

1984 - "It's a Good Time for the Great Taste of McDonald's"
1984 - "When the USA Wins You Win"
1984 - "One of a Kind"

1985 - "Large Fries for Small Fries"
1985 - "The Hot Stays Hot and the Cool Stays Cool"

1986 - "Back To Our Future"

1987 - "McKids"

1988 - "Good Time, Great Taste of McDonald's"
1988 - "Good Time, Great Taste, That's Why This is My Place"
1988 - "Sharing the Dream"
1988 - "McKids" (repeated)

1990s

1990 - "Food, Folks, and Fun"
1990 - "Call to Action, Customer Satisfaction"

1991 - "Do You Believe in Magic?"
1992 - "What You Want Is What You Get [at McDonald's Today]"
1992 - "Together, we've got what it takes"

1993 - "McWorld"

1994 - "Great Expectations"

1995 - "Have You Had Your Break Today?"

1996 - "QSC and Me"

1997 - "My McDonald's"
1997 - "did somebody say McDonald's?"

1998 - "did somebody say McDonald's?" (repeated)

1998 - "Where the World's Best Come Together" (Olympics, 1998)
1998 - "Made for You"
1998 - "Made for You...At the Speed of McDonald's"
1998 - "the value of GOLD"

Losonsky List #2: Sign Identification

1948

1948 - Speedee is the McDonald brothers Company Symbol

1950s

1953 - Speedee sign with Single Arch and Speedee holding 15 cent sign

1955-62 - Speedee, the Hamburger Man

1957 - Double Arch replaces Single Arch with Speedee

1958 - ONE HUNDRED MILLION sold

1960s

1960 - 400 HUNDRED MILLION sold

1961 - 500 HUNDRED MILLION sold

1962 - 700 HUNDRED MILLION sold
1962 - Bisected arches M replaces "Speedee"
1962-63 - Bisected Arches with Half Arrow Head

1963 - ONE BILLIONTH Hamburger Served
1963 - Bisected Arches within a Ship's Wheel
1963 - Double Arches with "McDonald's Hamburgers" signs replace Single Arch signs with "McDonald's Hamburgers"

1964 - Over ONE BILLION SOLD

1966 - TWO BILLION SERVED

1967 - FOUR BILLION SERVED
1968 - Over 4 Billion Served
1968 - Billions served on signs
1962-68 - Bisected Arches replaces Speedee

1969 - "Billions Served" sign changed to "5 Billion Served"

1970s

1972 - 10th & 11th BILLION HAMBURGERS SOLD

1974 - 15th BILLIONTH SERVED

1976 - 20 BILLION SERVED

1978 - 25 BILLION SERVED

1979 - 30 BILLION SOLD

1980s

1983 - 45 BILLION SOLD

1984 - 50 BILLION SERVED

1985 - 55 BILLION SERVED

1986 - More Than 60 Billion Served

1987 - 65 BILLION SERVED

1988 - 70 BILLION SERVED

1989 - 75 BILLION SERVED

1990s

1990 - 80 BILLION SERVED

1992 - 90 BILLION SERVED

1992 - Signs changed to "McDonald's"

1995 - Signs on highways changed to Arches only (no McDonald's name)

1997 - 99 BILLION SERVED

Losonsky List #3: Character Introduction/Redesigns

1955

1955-62 - Speedee character introduction

1960s

1963 - Ronald McDonald as Regional Spokesman - Bisected arches
1963-68 - Ronald McDonald with bisected arches costume

1964 - Archy McDonald (October - December)

1966 - Ronald McDonald as National Spokesman - bisected arches (October)

1969 - Ronald McDonald's costume changed to even pockets (no bisected arches)

1970s

1970 - Ronald McDonald introduced in McDonaldland (January)
1970 - Evil Grimace introduced on TV (Nov./Dec.)
1970 - Hamburglar introduced on TV (Nov./Dec.)
1970 - Mayor McCheese introduced on TV (Nov./Dec.)
1970 - Captain Crook introduced on TV (Nov./Dec.)
1970 - The Professor introduced on TV (Nov./Dec.)
1970 - Big Mac introduced on TV (Nov./Dec.)
1970 - Gobblins introduced on TV (Nov./Dec.)

1971 - Evil Grimace with four arms officially introduced
1971 - Hamburglar with unusual nose officially introduced
1971 - Mayor McCheese officially introduced
1971 - Captain Crook with skull and cross bones and green hair officially introduced
1971 - The Professor with long hair officially introduced
1971 - Big Mac officially introduced
1971 - Gobblins officially introduced

1973 - Evil Grimace redesigned to Grimace (two arms)
1973 - Hamburglar redesigned to long pointed nose
1973 - Mayor McCheese redesigned
1973 - Captain Crook redesigned
1973 - The Professor redesigned
1973 - Big Mac redesigned

1973 - Uncle O'Grimacey introduced

1973-81 - Ronald redesigned - Pockets have black lines

1974 - Grimace still called: The Grimace
1974 - Hamburglar still called: The Hamburglar

1975 - The Captain Crook's hair is no longer green

1979 - The Happy Meal Guys appear and disappear

1980s

1981 - Birdie, the Early Bird introduced

1982 - The Professor is redesigned
1982 - Gobblins were renamed the French Fry Guys
1982 - Design change of Captain Crook

1983 - McNugget Buddies introduced
1983 - (French) Fry Guys redesigned
1983 - Captain Crook redesigned to "The Captain"

1985 - Fry Girls redesigned

1987 - Mac Tonight introduced
1987 - Ronald redesigned (January)
1987 - Grimace redesigned again (January)
1987 - Birdie, the Early Bird redesigned (January)
1987 - Hamburglar redesigned to pudgy face, smiling character (January)

1988 - CosMc - The little space alien joins McDonaldland

1990s

1997 - Flubber (Disney/McDonald's) introduced

1998 - "Iam Hungry" computer animated character introduced

Helpful Information for Using this Book

Pricing

Note: Mint Price Range Only Listed for All Items

MINT - mint price value listed - Mint in the package range listed. $5.00-8.00 = Mint in the Package price range. The price range listed is for MINT IN THE PACKAGE.

LOOSE -Loose toys are 50% less than the low mint value listed. $2.50 = 50% off lowest price = Loose value. Damaged, chipped, or broken toys tend to have little value with a collector.

$—— - indicates no definitive price has been established for the item.

The real value of any collectible is what a buyer is willing to pay. This value may exceed the stated mint in the package (MIP) range. Likewise, since McDonald's makes millions of toys, value may be over inflated based on regional markets. Price ranges vary by regions, since some toys were distributed in specific regional markets.

Name and Numbering System

Premium Names - The premiums are listed by the names on the packaging whenever possible.

Box Names - The boxes were named by the authors with the accompanying identifying numbering system. Whenever possible, the names came from the front panel where the words "Happy Meal" are displayed.

Number System - The numbering system reflects the **country of origin/country of distribution,** followed by the first two letters of the Happy Meal or **first two letters of the Happy Meal** name or the generic representation of the Happy Meal items. The two letters are followed by the **year of distribution**, followed by a **numerical listing of the items**. The authors intention is to reflect a different alphabetical/numerical listing for each and every item distributed.

Example: USA Ci7909 = CIRCUS WAGON HAPPY MEAL, 1979

USA = Country of distribution/origin
Ci = [Ci] rcus Wagon Happy Meal
79 = Year of distribution
09 = Numerical listing of item

Example: USA Dt8865 = DUCK TALES I HAPPY MEAL, 1988

USA = Country of distribution/origin = USA
Dt = [D] uck [T] ales I Happy Meal, 1988
88 = Year of distribution
65 = Numerical listing of an item: Translite

Numerical Designator - Last two numbers of identification code.

BAG-Happy M	30-33
BANNER	27
BOX-Happy M	10-13
BUTTON	50
CEILING DANGLER	41
COUNTER CARD	42
COUNTER MAT	60
CREW Refer sheet	43
CREW POSTER	44
DISPLAY	26
HEADER CARD	62
LUG-ON	63
MESSAGE C INSERT	61
PIN	95
REGISTER TOPPER	45
TABLE TENT	56
TOYS	1-8
TRAYLINER	55
TRANSLITE/SM	64
TRANSLITE/LG	65

Whenever conflict in selecting the alphabetical/numerical designator arose, the first letter of the first two names of the Happy Meal was used and/or the generic alphabetic representation of the item was used. For example, Michael Jordan/Fitness Fun Happy Meal, 1992 and/or Fitness Fun/Michael Jordan Happy Meal is noted as Mj. Likewise, some Happy Meal promotions were repeated over the years. These were consistently assigned alphabetic listings: Attack Pack becomes Ap; Barbie becomes Ba; Batman becomes Bt; Cabbage Patch becomes Cp; Funny Fry Friends becomes Ff; Halloween becomes Ha; Hot Wheels becomes Hw; Tonka becomes Tk and so on. As time progresses, it is hoped these alpha/numeric listings will become standardized. The authors apologize for all past inconsistencies in developing a system which identifies each and every item with a separate alpha/numeric label. A Cross/Numbering listing can be found in the back of this text.

McDonald's Collecting Language

Hm = Happy Meal
MIP = Mint in Package
MOC = Mint on Card
MOT = Mint on Tree/plastic holder
Nd = No date on item
NP = Not packaged

Clean-up week - Open time period following a Happy Meal when no specific designed toy is distributed. The stock room backlog is given out.

Counter card - advertising or customer information card or board which sits on the counter.

Counter mat - advertising mat which sits on the counter; used in early years.

Display - advertising medium which holds/displays the toys being promoted and distributed during a specific time frame. These range from older bubble type to cardboard fold-up type. These are displayed in stand-up Ronald McDonald in the lobby.

Generic - item such as a box or a toy not specifically associated with a specific theme Happy Meal or promotion. The item(s) may be used in several different promotions over a period of time.

Header card - used in older Happy Meal promotions as advertising on top of the permanent display or ceiling dangler to display Happy Meal boxes or toys.

Insert card - advertising card within/along with the premium packaging.

Lug-on - sign added to the menu board.

McDonaldland - imaginary place where all the McDonald's cast of characters live and play; a playland area; a place in the hearts of children.

National - all stores in the USA distribute the same Happy Meal at the same time; supported with national advertising.

Register Topper - advertising item placed on the top of registers.

Regional - geographical distribution was limited to specific cities, states, stores, or marketing areas.

Self-liquidator - item intended to be sold over the counter which may or may not be included in the Happy Meal box.

Table tent - rectangle shaped advertising sign placed on the tables and counters in the lobby.

Translite - advertising transparent sign used on overhead or drive-through menu boards to illustrate the current promotion.

U-3 - under the age of 3 premiums; specifically designed for children under the age of 3. Packaging is typically in zebra stripes around the outside of the package. The colors of the stripes vary.

In the Beginning...

The Fifties

Ray Kroc, the founder of McDonald's, opened his first store in Des Plaines, Illinois on April 15, 1955 and the history of McDonald's began to unfold. Kroc was fifty-two years old at the time, a salesman for milk shake machines who saw a "golden" opportunity in the successful drive-thru restaurants originally opened in California by Dick and Marice (Mac) McDonald in the late 1940s. Simplistically, Ray Kroc franchised the McDonald's Speedee Service System in 1955 and began constructing buildings using red and white candy striped tile walls and yellow neon arches going through the roof — thus the Golden Arches were born. It was Ray Kroc's vision of serving reasonably priced hamburgers, shakes, and french fries to the ever-growing population that propelled McDonald's into a legendary business of the twentieth century.

The first menu at the Des Plaines store was a check-off sheet with a limited selection of 15 cent hamburgers, 10 cent fries, and 20 cent milk shakes. It was the "All American Meal" for only 45 cents per person! The menu was promoted by the company symbol of "Speedee," the little hamburger man, and both speedy service and speedy growth soon followed. By the following year a dozen McDonald's restaurants were added in Illinois and California, and in 1959 the 100th McDonald's restaurant opened in Fond du Lac, Wisconsin.

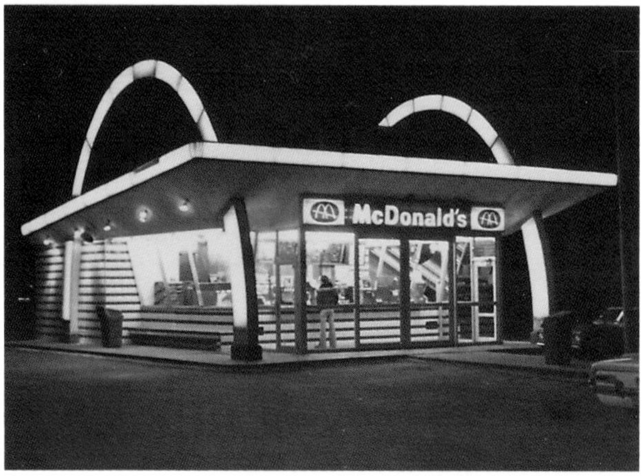

The Sixties

In 1960, "Look for the Golden Arches" jingle initiated McDonald's radio advertising and the sounds of McDonald's calling were heard all around the country. Willard Scott became the symbol of Ronald McDonald, making his first public debut in Washington D.C. in October, 1963, and the Filet-O-Fish sandwich was officially added to the menu in 1964, priced at 24 cents. In Ohio regional markets, the Archy McDonald logo was used for a limited time, along with the extremely successful Filet-O-Fish advertising. By 1966, McDonald's had become a national name and was voted "the growth company" of the year.

The Big Mac sandwich arrived in 1968, an item destined to be a dominant force in the fast food market for the next thirty years. The Big Mac Attack had begun! Along with the Big Mac sandwich, the Hot Apple Pie was added to the menu at the opening of the 1,000th McDonald's restaurant in Des Plaines, Illinois.

The Seventies

"The best is yet to come" became McDonald's motto in the 1970s — certainly a prophetic statement! In 1970, McDonaldland was created, the home of Ronald McDonald and his colorful cast of characters: Big Mac, The Hamburglar, Grimace, Mayor McCheese, The Professor, The Gobblins, and Captain Crook. The characters, whose appearance would change little over the years, added another level of appeal to McDonald's concept and generated smiles wherever they appeared.

In 1972, the Quarter Pounder was added to the menu in conjunction with the opening of the 2,000th McDonald's restaurant in Des Plaines, Illinois. The breakfast menu was initially tested in California and instituted in all locations by 1976.

In the seventies, the Happy Meal concept was tested and promoted nationally; at the same time the Barrel of Fun "rolled" into the stores. McDonald's advertising focused on children and the "Collect All" theme began to take root. The sprout was green and rapidly growing with the introduction of the Circus Wagon Happy Meal in 1979. Ronald McDonald's theme ushered in the generation of fast food consumers and collectors alike.

The Eighties

"You Deserve a Break Today" advertising slogan quickly caught the attention of the mobile food market in the early 1980s. During this decade, McDonald's doubled in size, from 40 Billion Hamburgers sold to 80 Billion; the "Green and Growing" theme was a reflection of reality. While the introduction of the Happy Meal concept led to the tremendous growth of the lunch menu, American consumers were instantly drawn to McDonald's breakfast menu of the eighties as well.

McDonald's was becoming more things to more people, and national advertising pointed the way! Specifically, the advertising tied to national movie ventures such as *Star Trek*, *E.T.*, and *The Muppets* was the most successful. Customers flocked to McDonald's as long as quality, service, value, and cleanliness were evident. The organization rode a steady course in the eighties until competition started to erode the burger field. This challenge was met with an increase in the national advertising budget, which proved successful at first.

The impact of playland parks, outside and inside, would be felt for decades to come. The restaurants of the eighties expanded to include drive-thru service, which increased business tremendously. By the end of the decade, more customers were being served through the drive-thru than inside the restaurants. Americans were on the move, requiring quick and accurate menu orders. "Nobody can do it like McDonald's can" national advertising slogan wrapped up the eighties; during this decade, nobody could.

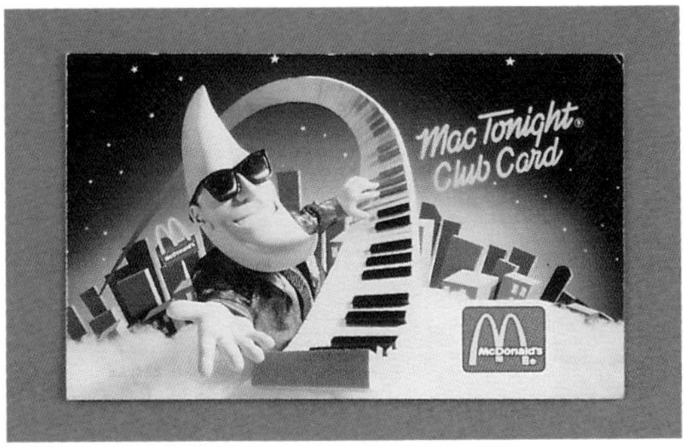
Mac Tonight® Club Card

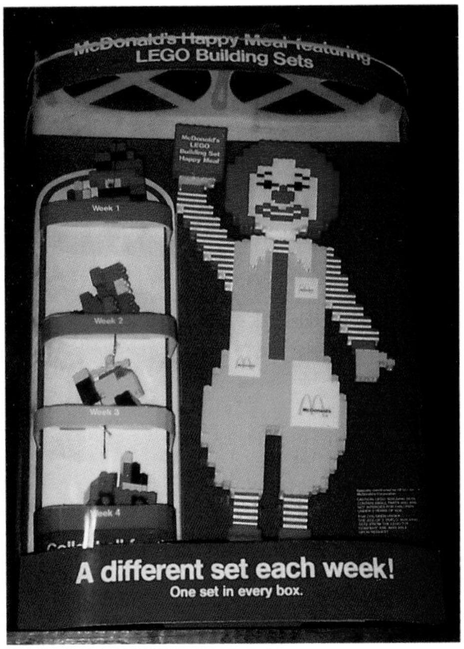
McDonald's Happy Meal featuring LEGO Building Sets
Week 1
Week 2
Week 3
Week 4
A different set each week!
One set in every box.

27

The Nineties

In the decade of the nineties, McDonald's began to experience a shake-out in the fast food industry. Competition in the USA was met with national promotions costing vast sums of money. The company slowly came to realize they could not do fifty-two weeks of continuous promotions and continue to be effective week after week. Instead, McDonald's chose to creatively advertise "The Magic Moment," the emotional experience that sets them apart from their competition. They knew it all had to do with reasonably priced food selections along with "Quality, Service, Value and Cleanliness," the basics of Ray Kroc's original approach. The Happy Meal toy was an important instrument to increase sales, but the eroding consumer confidence was also an important consideration.

In the early nineties, McDonald's experimented with shorter messages in an attempt to reach specific marketing segments by using the cornerstone of Americana: TV advertising. Men were reached through extensive advertising at major sporting events; women through television advertising, and children through the Saturday morning cartoon advertising. When this advertising failed to sufficiently increase business at the local level, McDonald's tried the colossal approach and spent much too much money advertising such items as the Arch Deluxe sandwich. McDonald's soon realized that customers, on the whole, were not going to McDonald's to lose or gain weight — they were going to McDonald's for convenience, quality, value, service and cleanliness. McDonald's in the early nineties was striving to be all things to all people, a surely impossible feat. This period of confusion in the leadership of the company led to a re-evaluation of the focus. The secret of McDonald's success over time has been their attention to detail and their willingness to try new approaches to old problems, which was the essence of Ray Kroc's original vision. Put, quite simply, "Nobody can do it like McDonald's can."

This refocusing led to a varied selection of Happy Meal products being given and sold in the stores. At times, the number of products sold in the stores exceeded the number of items on the food menu. The restaurants of the nineties were expanding in some markets and shrinking in others; expansion efforts led to double and triple Drive-Thru windows in some markets, McStop and McSnack operations in others. Newly constructed restaurants were trying to blend in with the surroundings, while the McDonald's signs were raised higher on poles to attract the mobile expressway traffic. The name "McDonald's" was being dropped from the signs, with the Golden Arches prominently displayed solo. Playgrounds were expanded in many operations to attract and entertain the younger generation of Happy Meal customers. At the dinner hour, McDonald's playgrounds were smoothing the transition for parents, as mothers and fathers made the switch from professional work role to parental role.

On the character front, Ronald McDonald was portrayed as a magical clown in the early 1990s. He was a humorous character who lived in both the fantasy world and the real world. Jack Doepke assumed the role from Squire Fridell in 1990. This position as "the television Ronald" or simply "Ronald McDonald" had been solidified through the eighties. Commercials during the 1990s focused on the "Fun" of Ronald and McDonald's. During the 1990s, Ronald was portrayed in funny situations advertising the upcoming Happy Meal promotion; he was always shown to be nice because he shared his fries. He was smart because he figured out a way to catch Hamburglar and get the hamburgers back; he was magical because he made an "M" with his fingers or bounced up to the moon on a pogo stick. In a sense, he was portrayed as more than a magical clown, he was a "real" clown who could do magical tricks. In the late 1990s, Ronald McDonald is still being portrayed as the leader of McDonaldland and a magical friend to kids everywhere. Anything can happen when Ronald is around. Ronald makes magical events unfold, as McDonald's builds a "strong bridge" to the twenty-first century. Naturally, the bridge to the twenty-first century is a double arch bridge, reflecting the "Golden Arches."

Heading into the twenty-first century, Ronald McDonald still resides in McDonaldland but is at home anywhere he goes. He appears intelligent and sensitive, but always clown-like. He can do nearly anything, including feats of computer magic. His favorite food is still hamburgers, and his favorite people are still children. During late 1995 and early 1996, Ronald McDonald went through a short-lived transition to an adult sports (pool playing) Ronald, in an attempt to appeal to adults. This adult advertising focus was quickly dropped and Ronald McDonald sensibly returned to being the "McFriendliest" fellow in town who appeals to children worldwide.

McDonald's memorabilia collectors began to organize and formed a National McDonald's Collectors Club in 1990; the club is growing geometrically in membership each year. By 1997, and continuing with the 1998 Teenie Beanie Happy Meal frenzy, collector demand escalated the demand for McDonald's collectibles in the nineties. Although noteworthy, the overriding principle of "value" established "over a period of time" seemed to disappear with the Teenie Beanie Babies promotions, since demand for the first Teenie Beanie Babies Happy Meal exceeded supply in many markets. McDonald's made a sincere effort not to erode consumer confidence by increasing the production of the second Teenie Beanie Babies Happy Meal promotion 88 per cent. Towards the end of the nineties, McDonald's demonstrated their true professionalism in product development, product advertising, price containment, and food value by offering the second Teenie Beanie Happy Meal toys both with and without a Happy Meal purchase. McDonald's continues to be a lighthouse beacon viewed from a Golden Arch bridge to the twenty-first century.

1990

Barbie/Hot Wheels I Test Market Happy Meal, 1990
Beach Toy II "Collect All 8" Happy Meal, 1990
Berenstain Bear Books Happy Meal, 1990
Camp McDonaldland Happy Meal, 1990
Dink the Little Dinosaur Happy Meal, 1990
From the Heart/Valentine Happy Meal, 1990
Fry Benders Happy Meal, 1990
Funny Fry Friends II "Collect All 8" Happy Meal, 1990
Halloween '90 Happy Meal, 1990
Hats Happy Meal, 1990
I Like Bikes Happy Meal, 1990
Jungle Book I Happy Meal, 1990
McDonaldland Carnival Happy Meal, 1991/1990
McDonaldland Dough Happy Meal, 1990
McDrive Thru Crew/McFarmland Test Market HM, 1991/90
Peanuts Happy Meal, 1990
Rescuers Down Under Happy Meal, 1990
Sports Ball Happy Meal, 1991/1990
Super Mario 3 Nintendo Happy Meal, 1990
Tale Spin Happy Meal, 1990
Tom & Jerry Band Happy Meal, 1990
Turbo Macs II Happy Meal, 1990
USA Generic Promotions, 1990

- **"Food, Folks, and Fun" (May) jingle**
- **35th Anniversary of McDonald's**
- **11th National O/O convention held**
- **"Call to Action, Customer Satisfaction" - O/O advertising theme**
- **1st National McDonald's Collectors Club meeting**

Barbie/Hot Wheels I Test Market Happy Meal, 1990

Boxes:

❑ ❑ USA Ba9020 **Hm Box - Barbie in Concert/Garage**, 1990. $125.00-175.00

❑ ❑ USA Ba9021 **Hm Box - Movie Star/Road Race**, 1990. $125.00-175.00

Premiums: Barbie Doll with Paper Diorama

❑ ❑ USA Ba9001 **Barbie Doll: Movie Star,** 1990, Pink Dress with finger hole in base/Paper Dressing Room Diorama. $100.00-150.00+

❑ ❑ USA Ba9002 **Barbie Doll: In Concert,** 1990, Black Dress standing on wht circle base/Paper Concert Diorama. $100.00-150.00+

❑ ❑ USA Ba9003 **Barbie Doll: Tea Party,** 1990, Pink Dress standing on white circle base/Paper Tea Party Diorama. $100.00-150.00+

❑ ❑ USA Ba9004 **Barbie Doll: Moonlight Ball,** 1990, Pink Gown with finger hole in base/Open Red Star Outline on Crown/ Red Star is NOT Totally Filled in/Diorama. $100.00-150.00+

Premiums: Hot Wheel Cars

❑ ❑ USA Hw9011 **Set 1 Corvette,** 1990, Wht with Red Stripe. $75.00-100.00+

❑ ❑ USA Hw9012 **Set 2 Ferrari,** 1990, Red. $75.00-100.00+

❑ ❑ USA Hw9013 **Set 3 Hot Bird,** 1990, Sil with Pin Stripe. $75.00-100.00+

❑ ❑ USA Hw9014 **Set 4 Camaro Z-28,** 1990, Turq with Blu Stripe, 1990. $75.00-100.00+

❑ ❑ USA Ba9026 **Display/Premiums**, 1990. $350.00-500.00++

❑ ❑ USA Ba9064 **Translite/Sm**, 1990. $75.00-100.00

❑ ❑ USA Ba9065 **Translite/Lg**, 1990. $100.00-125.00

Comments: Regional Distribution: USA Test Market - July 1990 in Savannah, Georgia. Premium markings - "Mattel Inc 1989 Arco China." Same premiums were sold in retail stores. MIP must include paper backdrop. Barbie Moonlight Ball with a total red star on crown is NOT the McDonald's premium. Total red star on crown Barbies were sold in retail stores. Auction prices realized for the Barbie Test mint in package range from $185.00-240.00 each. Not enough transactions to validate increasing book price quote. **Prices for loose Barbie figurines range from $15.00-25.00. Star on hair of Moonlight Ball figurines is outlined in red with a white center.** Moonlight Ball figurines sold in retail stores had star fully enclosed in red. **If the Moonlight Ball's star has a red center, the figurine was retail purchased and not given out by McDonald's.**

Ba9021

Ba9020

BA9001

Ba9002

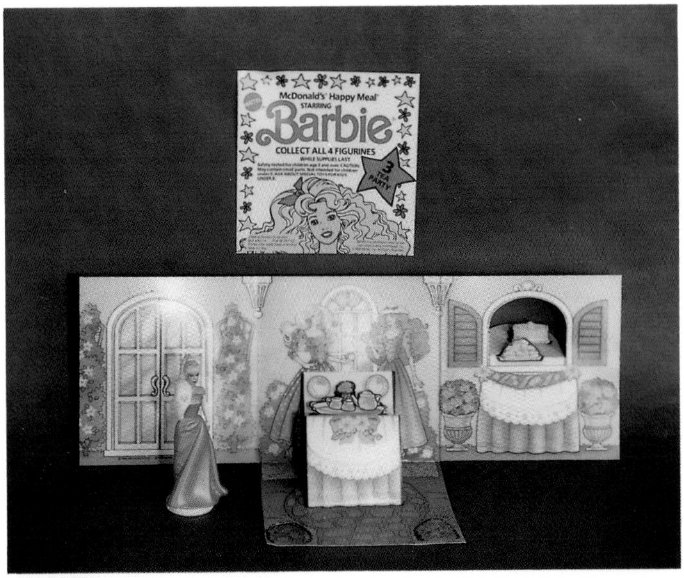

BA9003

Hw9013

Hw9014

Ba9003

Ba9004

Hw9011

Hw9012

Beach Toy II "Collect All 8" Happy Meal, 1990

Bags:

❑ ❑ USA Be9085 **Hm Bag - Grimace with Tube**, 1989. $2.00-3.00

❑ ❑ USA Be9086 **Hm Bag - Hamburglar with Ball**, 1989. $2.00-3.00

❑ ❑ USA Be9087 **Hm Bag - Ronald with Stars/Sand Castle**, 1989. $2.00-3.00

❑ ❑ USA Be9088 **Hm Bag - Ronald with Treasure Chest**, 1989. $2.00-3.00

Be9085

Be9086

Be9087

Be9088

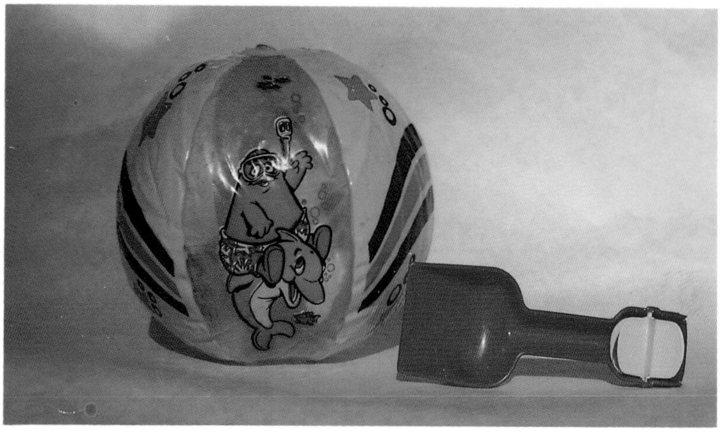

Be9072 Be9075

Premiums:

- ❑ ❑ USA Be9071 **Set 1 Fry Kid Super Sailor,** 1989, Red-Purp Catamaran/Yel Sail. $1.00-1.50
- ❑ ❑ USA Be9074 **Set 2 Sand Pail with Grimace,** 1989, Clear Plastic Pail/Yel Lid-Handle. $1.00-1.50
- ❑ ❑ USA Be9072 **Set 3 Grimace Bouncin Beach Ball,** 1989, Yel-Blu-Grn. $1.00-1.50
- ❑ ❑ USA Be9075 **Set 4 Birdie with Shovel/Sand,** 1989, Red with Yel Sand Propeller. $1.00-1.50
- ❑ ❑ USA Be9073 **Set 5 Ronald Fun Flyer,** 1989, Inflatable Turq-Org Ring. $1.00-1.50
- ❑ ❑ USA Be9076 **Set 6 Fry Kids Sand Castle Pail,** 1989, Clear Plastic/Red Lid-Handle. $1.00-1.50
- ❑ ❑ USA Be9070 **Set 7 Birdie Seaside Submarine,** 1988, Pink-Blu Inflatable. $1.00-1.50
- ❑ ❑ USA Be9077 **Set 8 Ronald Squirt Gun Rake,** 1989, Blu-Grn. $1.00-1.50

- ❑ ❑ USA Be9041 **Ceiling Dangler/Sets 1-4,** 1989. $20.00-25.00
- ❑ ❑ USA Be9042 **Ceiling Dangler/Sets 5-8,** 1989. $20.00-25.00
- ❑ ❑ USA Be9064 **Translite/Sm,** 1989. $5.00-10.00
- ❑ ❑ USA Be9065 **Translite/Lg,** 1989. $10.00-15.00

Comments: National Distribution: USA - June 1-28, 1990. "Collect All 8" printed on the MIP package. USA Be9070-73 = USA Bt8970-73, Beach Toy I "Collect All 4" Happy Meal, 1989, loose out of package.

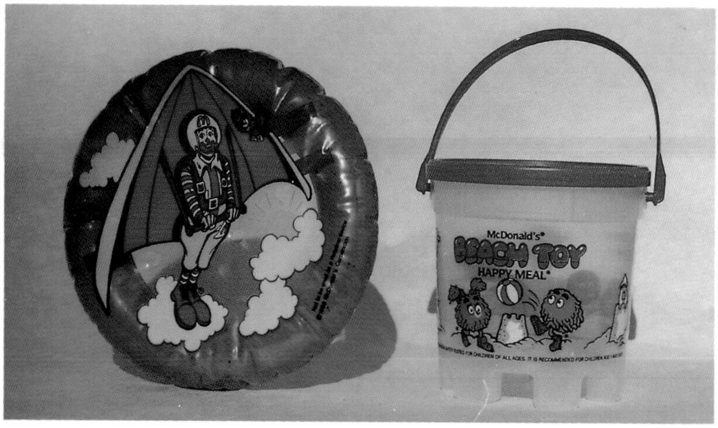

Be9073 Be9076

Be9070 Be9077

Be9071

Be9065

Berenstain Bear Books Happy Meal, 1990

Boxes & Bags:

❑ ❑ USA Bb9040 **Hm Box - Sharing Brings Good Things,** 1989. $1.00-2.00

❑ ❑ USA Bb9041 **Hm Box - Teamwork Saves the Day,** 1989. $1.00-2.00

❑ ❑ USA Bb9042 **Hm Box - Thank Goodness ...Bears,** 1989. $1.00-2.00

❑ ❑ USA Bb9043 **Hm Box - What to Do Depends on You,** 1989. $1.00-2.00

❑ ❑ USA Bb9044 **Hm Bag - Teamwork Saves the Day,** 1989. $15.00-20.00

❑ ❑ USA Bb9045 **Hm Bag - What to Do Depends on You,** 1989. $15.00-20.00

Premiums: Books

❑ ❑ USA Bb9025 **Book: Life with Papa,** 1990, Storybook. $2.00-3.00

❑ ❑ USA Bb9026 **Activity Book: Life with Papa,** 1990, Activity Book. $2.00-3.00

❑ ❑ USA Bb9027 **Book: Attic Treasure,** 1990, Storybook. $2.00-3.00

❑ ❑ USA Bb9028 **Activity Book: Attic Treasure,** 1990, Activity Book. $2.00-3.00

❑ ❑ USA Bb9029 **Book: Substitute Teacher,** 1990, Storybook. $2.00-3.00

❑ ❑ USA Bb9030 **Activity Book: Substitute Teacher,** 1990, Activity Book. $2.00-3.00

❑ ❑ USA Bb9031 **Book: Eager Beavers,** 1990, Storybook. $2.00-3.00

❑ ❑ USA Bb9032 **Activity Book: Eager Beavers,** 1990, Activity Book. $2.00-3.00

❑ ❑ USA Bb9064 **Translite/Sm,** 1990. $5.00-10.00

❑ ❑ USA Bb9065 **Translite/Lg,** 1990. $10.00-15.00

Comments: National Distribution: USA - January 26-February 22, 1990. Two bags were test marketed in South Bend, Indiana.

Bb9041

Bb9042

Bb9043

Bb9040

Bb9044 Bb9045

Bb9026 Bb9028 Bb9030 Bb9032

Bb9025 Bb9027 Bb9029 Bb9031

Bb9065

Camp McDonaldland Happy Meal, 1990

Boxes & Bags:

❑ ❑ USA Cm9010 **Hm Box - At the Lake,** 1989. $1.00-2.00

❑ ❑ USA Cm9011 **Hm Box - Camping out,** 1989. $1.00-2.00

❑ ❑ USA Cm9012 **Hm Box - Nature Walk,** 1989. $1.00-2.00

❑ ❑ USA Cm9013 **Hm Box - Playtime at Camp,** 1989. $1.00-2.00

❑ ❑ USA Cm9014 **Hm Bag - Playtime/ Tug-Of-War,** 1989. $15.00-20.00

❑ ❑ USA Cm9015 **Hm Bag - Nature Walk**, 1989. $15.00-20.00

U-3 Premium:

❑ ❑ USA Cm9005 **U-3 Collapsible Cup/Ronald,** 1989, 2p Red Cup with Lid. $2.00-3.00

Premiums:

❑ ❑ USA Cm9000 **Set 1 Grimace Canteen,** 1989, 2p Blu with Yel Top. $2.00-2.50

❑ ❑ USA Cm9001 **Set 2 Birdie Camper/Mess Kit,** 1989, 3p Grn with Org Handle. $2.00-2.50

❑ ❑ USA Cm9002 **Set 3 Fry Kid Utensils,** 1989, 3p Turq Fk/Yel Sp/Purp Kn with 5 Bandaids. $2.00-2.50

❑ ❑ USA Cm9006 **Set 3 Fry Kid Utensils,** 1989, 3p Turq Fk/Yel Sp/Purp Kn without 5 Bandaids. $2.00-2.50

❑ ❑ USA Cm9003 **Set 4 Collapsible Cup/Ronald,** 1989, 2p Red Cup with Lid. $2.00-3.00

❑ ❑ USA Cm9004 **Fry Kid Utensils,** 1989, 3p Yel Fk/Blu Sp/Grn Kn without Bandaids. $2.00-2.50

❑ ❑ USA Cm9050 **Button,** 1990, Camp McDonaldland Hm. $3.00-5.00

❑ ❑ USA Cm9064 **Translite/Sm**, 1989. $5.00-10.00

❑ ❑ USA Cm9065 **Translite/Lg**, 1989. $10.00-15.00

Comments: National Distribution: USA - April 27-May 24, 1990. USA Cm9003 = USA Cm9005, loose out of package. USA Cm9004 was distributed during clean-up weeks in 1990 and 1991.

Cm9010 Cm9011

Cm9012 Cm9013

Cm9014 Cm9015

Cm9000 Cm9001 Cm9003

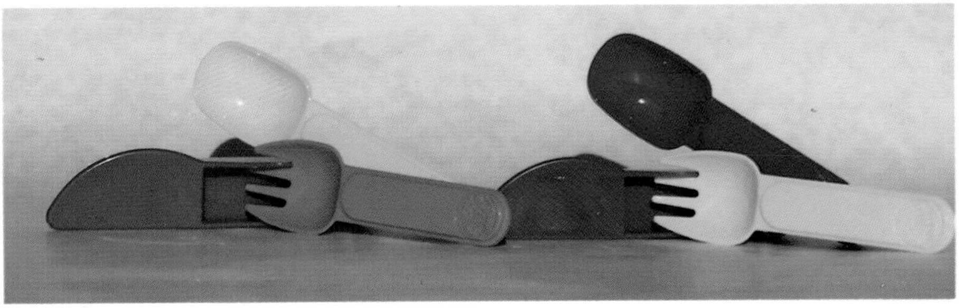

Cm9002 Cm9004

Cm9005

Cm9050

Cm9065

Dink the Little Dinosaur Happy Meal, 1990

Box:

❏ ❏ USA Di9010 **Hm Box - Dink/Toys**, 1990. $10.00-15.00

Premiums: Dinosaur Figurine and Diorama (MIP: $15.00-20.00; Loose: $2.00-4.00)

❏ ❏ USA Di9000 **Set 1 Crusty the Turtle,** 1989, Grn with Blu/Grn Shell with Diorama. $15.00-20.00

❏ ❏ USA Di9001 **Set 2 Amber the Dinosaur,** 1989, Beige Body with Diorama. $15.00-20.00

❏ ❏ USA Di9002 **Set 3 Scat the Alligator,** 1989, Grn Body with Diorama. $15.00-20.00

❏ ❏ USA Di9003 **Set 4 Shyler the Dinosaur,** 1989, Grn Body with Diorama. $15.00-20.00

❏ ❏ USA Di9004 **Set 5 Flapper the Tridactyl,** 1989, Brn Body with Diorama. $15.00-20.00

❏ ❏ USA Di9005 **Set 6 Dink the Dinosaur,** 1989, Grn Body with Diorama. $15.00-20.00

❏ ❏ USA Di9064 **Translite/Sm,** 1990. $15.00-25.00

❏ ❏ USA Di9065 **Translite/Lg,** 1990. $20.00-30.00

Di9010

Di9002 Di9004

Di9000 Di9001 Di9003 Di9005

Di9002

Di9065

Comments: Regional Distribution: USA - August 1990 in Oklahoma/Texas test markets. Premium markings "1989 Ruby-Spears Inc China Sv." MIP must include diorama. Loose Dinks range from $2.00-4.00 each without the diorama.

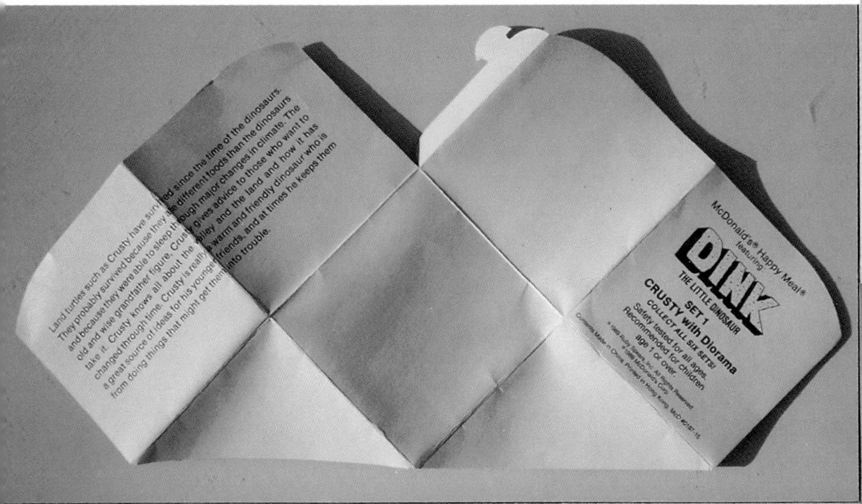

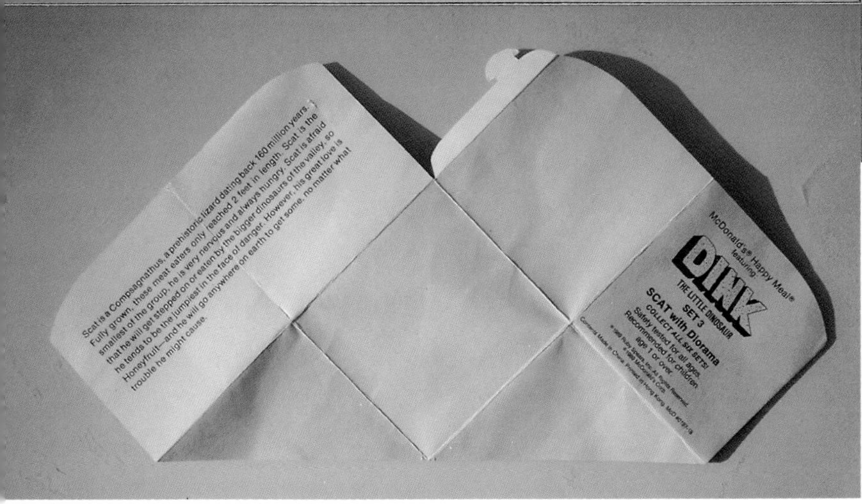

From the Heart/Valentine Happy Meal, 1990

Box:

❑ ❑ USA Fr9010 **Hm Box - Play Matchmaker**, 1989. $2.00-3.00

Premiums: Valentines

❑ ❑ USA Fr9001 **Valentine - Frosting Cake,** 1990, Chocolate/ Scratch & Sniff. $2.00-3.00

❑ ❑ USA Fr9002 **Valentine - Hot Chocolate,** 1990, Cinnamon/ Scratch & Sniff. $2.00-3.00

❑ ❑ USA Fr9064 **Translite/Sm**, 1990. $15.00-25.00

❑ ❑ USA Fr9065 **Translite/Lg,** 1990. $20.00-30.00

Comments: Regional Distribution: USA - February 2-February 14, 1990 in southern United States.

Fr9010

Fr9001 Fr9002

Fb9010

Fr9065

Fb9004 Fb9003

Fb9002 Fb9005 Fb9001

Fb9001 Fb9003 Fb9002 Fb9004

Fry Benders Happy Meal, 1990

Box:

❑ ❑ USA Fb9010 **Hm Box - Fry Bender Cut-Outs/Help Roadie Find the Clubhouse**, 1990. $2.00-3.00

U-3 Premium:

❑ ❑ USA Fb9005 **U-3 Tunes - on Red Skateboard with Music Box.** $15.00-20.00

Premiums:

❑ ❑ USA Fb9001 **Free Style - on Roller Skates**, 2p. $5.00-7.00

❑ ❑ USA Fb9002 **Froggy - wearing Red Scuba Diver's Tanks**, 2p. $5.00-7.00

❑ ❑ USA Fb9003 **Grand Slam - holding Baseball Glove,** 2p. $5.00-7.00

❑ ❑ USA Fb9004 **Roadie - on Bicycle,** 2p. $5.00-7.00

❑ ❑ USA Fb9064 **Translite/Sm**, 1990. $8.00-12.00

❑ ❑ USA Fb9065 **Translite/Lg**, 1990. $10.00-15.00

Comments: Regional Distribution: USA - September 7-October 4, 1990 and March-April 1991. Used during clean-up week in many areas.

Fb9065

Fry Benders blue book.

Funny Fry Friends II "Collect All 8" Happy Meal, 1990

Boxes:

☐ ☐ USA Ff9015 **Hm Box - Cool Day at School**, 1989.$1.00-2.00

☐ ☐ USA Ff9016 **Hm Box - City Sights**, 1989. $1.00-2.00

☐ ☐ USA Ff9017 **Hm Box - Ski Holiday,** 1989. $1.00-2.00

☐ ☐ USA Ff9018 **Hm Box - Snowy Day Play**, 1989. $1.00-2.00

U-3 Premiums:

☐ ☐ USA Ff9009 **U-3 Little Darling,** 1989, Cow Girl/Yel. $5.00-7.00

☐ ☐ USA Ff9010 **U-3 Lil' Chief,** 1989, Indian Chief/Org Chief Hat. $5.00-7.00

Premiums:

☐ ☐ USA Ff9001 **Set 1 Hoops,** 1989, Purple Kid wearing Sweat-band holding Basketball. $4.00-5.00

☐ ☐ USA Ff9002 **Set 2 Rollin Rocker,** 1989, Yel Girl with Head Phones with Skates. $4.00-5.00

☐ ☐ USA Ff9003 **Set 3 Matey,** 1989, Red Kid with Pirate Hat. $4.00-5.00

☐ ☐ USA Ff9004 **Set 4 Gadzooks,** 1989, Blu Kid with Eyeglasses. $4.00-5.00

☐ ☐ USA Ff9005 **Set 5 Tracker,** 1989, Blu Kid with Safari Hat with Snake. $4.00-5.00

☐ ☐ USA Ff9006 **Set 6 Zzz's,** 1989, Turq Kid with Sleeping Cap with Bear. $4.00-5.00

☐ ☐ USA Ff9007 **Set 7 Too Tall,** 1989, Grn Kid with Clown Hat. $4.00-5.00

☐ ☐ USA Ff9008 **Set 8 Sweet Cuddles,** 1989, Pnk Kid with Baby Bonnet with Bottle. $4.00-5.00

☐ ☐ USA Ff9026 **Display/Premiums**, 1989. $85.00-110.00

☐ ☐ USA Ff9045 **Register Topper/2 Types**, 1989. $7.00-10.00

☐ ☐ USA Ff9064 **Translite/Sm**, 1989. $5.00-8.00

☐ ☐ USA Ff9065 **Translite/Lg**, 1989. $10.00-15.00

Comments: National Distribution: USA - December 22, 1989-January 18, 1990.

Ff9015 Ff9016

Ff9017 Ff9018

Ff9002

Top: Ff9009 Ff9004 Ff9005 Ff9008

Bottom: Ff9010 Ff9001 Ff9002 Ff9003 Ff9006 Ff9007

Ff9026

Ha9055 Ha9056 Ha9057

Ha9065

Ff9045

Ff9065

Halloween '90 Happy Meal, 1990

Premiums: Halloween Pails

❑ ❑ USA Ha9055 **Pumpkin,** 1986, Day Glo Pail/Org/Neon Color. $1.00-2.00

❑ ❑ USA Ha9056 **Ghost,** 1986, Glow-In-The-Dark Pail/Wht. $1.00-2.00

❑ ❑ USA Ha9057 **Witch,** 1986, Day Glo Pail/Grn/Neon Color. $1.00-2.00

❑ ❑ USA Ha9064 **Translite/Sm**, 1990. $4.00-5.00

❑ ❑ USA Ha9065 **Translite/Lg**, 1990. $8.00-10.00

Comments: National Distribution: USA - October 5-25, 1990.

Hats Happy Meal, 1990

Premiums: Vacuum Formed Hats

❑ ❑ USA Ht9000 **Birdie - Derby Hat,** 1990, Grn with Fry Guy/ Ronald on Bottom Mold. $12.00-15.00

❑ ❑ USA Ht9001 **Fry Guy - Safari Hat,** 1990, Org with 2 Fry Guys on Bottom Mold. $12.00-15.00

❑ ❑ USA Ht9002 **Grimace - Construction Hat,** 1990, Yel with Hamb/Prof on Bottom Mold. $12.00-15.00

❑ ❑ USA Ht9003 **Ronald - Fireman Hat,** 1990, Red with Fry Guy/Birdie on Bottom Mold. $12.00-15.00

❑ ❑ USA Ht9064 **Translite/Sm**, 1990. $25.00-35.00

❑ ❑ USA Ht9065 **Translite/Lg**, 1990. $35.00-50.00

Comments: Regional Distribution: USA - September 7-October 4, 1990 in parts of Alabama, Georgia, Florida, and Louisiana. Hats without the bottom molds are selling for $7.00-10.00.

Ht9003 Ht9002 Ht9001 Ht9000

Ht9003 Ht9002 Ht9001 Ht9000

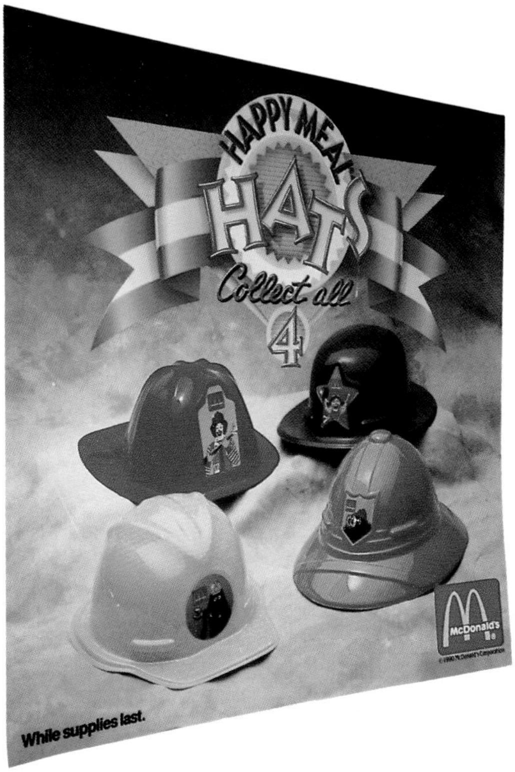

Ht9065

Comments: Limited Regional Distribution: USA - July 1990 in Northern Illinois and South Carolina. USA "Collect All 4" does not include a water bottle, like nationally distributed I Like Bikes Happy Meal in Europe.

119030

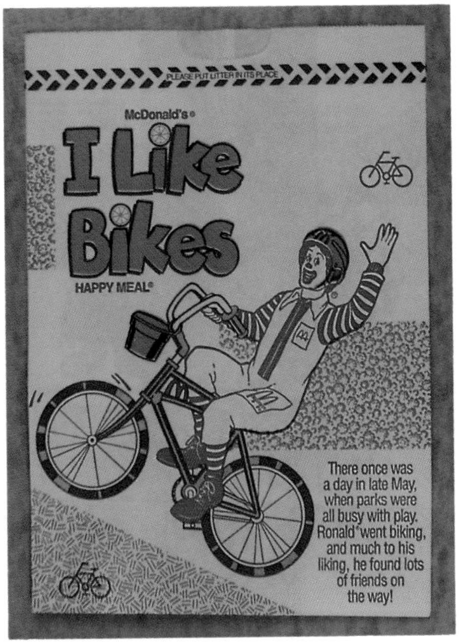

119031

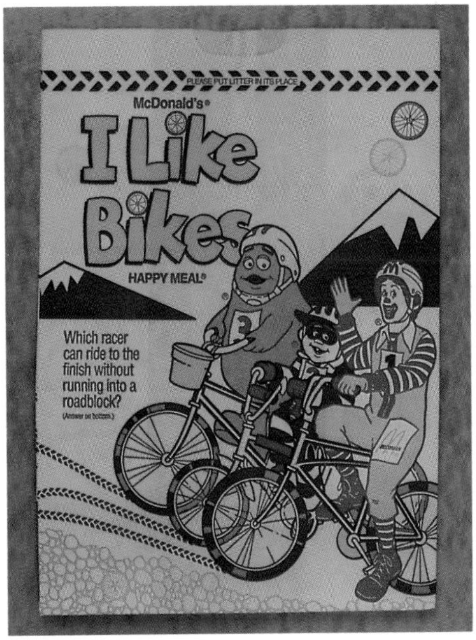

I Like Bikes Happy Meal, 1990

Bags:

❑ ❑ USA 119030 **Hm Bag - Ronald on a Bike** "There Once Was a Day", 1990. $15.00-20.00

❑ ❑ USA 119031 **Hm Bag - Ronald/Hamburglar/Grimace on Bike** "Which Racer Can Ride", 1990. $15.00-20.00

Premiums:

❑ ❑ USA 119000 **Spinner,** 1989, 1p Birdie on Red Plane/1p/Yel Spinner. $5.00-10.00

❑ ❑ USA 119001 **Horn,** 1989, 1p Org/Blu Fry Guy Horn. $5.00-10.00

❑ ❑ USA 119002 **Mirror,** 1990, 1p 6" Rear View Grim Mirror. $5.00-10.00

❑ ❑ USA 119003 **Bike Basket,** 1989, 4p Yel/Ron Basket/Lid/2 Straps. $75.00-100.00+

❑ ❑ USA 119026 **Display/Premiums,** 1990. $250.00-350.00+

❑ ❑ USA 119064 **Translite/Sm**, 1990. $25.00-40.00

❑ ❑ USA 119065 **Translite/Lg**, 1990. $35.00-50.00

119003

I Like Bikes blue book.

Jungle Book I Happy Meal, 1990

Boxes:

- ❑ ❑ USA Ju9010 **Hm Box - Baloo the Bear**, 1989. $2.00-4.00
- ❑ ❑ USA Ju9011 **Hm Box - Hidden Animal/Tiger**, 1989. $2.00-4.00
- ❑ ❑ USA Ju9012 **Hm Box - Kaa the Snake**, 1989. $2.00-4.00
- ❑ ❑ USA Ju9013 **Hm Box - King Louie the Orangutan**, 1989. $2.00-4.00

U-3 Premiums:

- ❑ ❑ USA Ju9004 **U-3 Junior the Elephant,** 1989, Grey Elephant Sitting. $7.00-8.00
- ❑ ❑ USA Ju9005 **U-3 Mowgli the Boy,** 1989, Boy in Grn Clay Pot. $7.00-8.00

Premiums:

- ❑ ❑ USA Ju9000 **Set 1 Baloo,** 1989, Gry Bear. $3.00-4.00
- ❑ ❑ USA Ju9001 **Set 2 King Louie,** 1989, Org Orangutan. $3.00-4.00
- ❑ ❑ USA Ju9002 **Set 3 Kaa,** 1989, Grn Snake. $3.00-4.00
- ❑ ❑ USA Ju9003 **Set 4 Shere Khan,** 1989, Org Tiger. $3.00-4.00
- ❑ ❑ USA Ju9026 **Display with Premiums**, 1989. $50.00-60.00
- ❑ ❑ USA Ju9041 **Dangler**/Baloo/King Louie/Kaa/Shere Khan/ Each, 1989. $7.00-10.00
- ❑ ❑ USA Ju9050 **Button/Crew**, 1989. $4.00-7.00
- ❑ ❑ USA Ju9051 **Mug/Plastic**, 1989, the Bare Necessities. $2.00-4.00
- ❑ ❑ USA Ju9052 **Key Chain,** 1989, the Bare Necessities. $2.00-3.00
- ❑ ❑ USA Ju9064 **Translite/Sm**, 1989. $8.00-10.00
- ❑ ❑ USA Ju9065 **Translite/X-0 Graphic/Lg**, 1989. $25.00-35.00
- ❑ ❑ USA Ju9095 **Pin**, 1989, the Bare Necessities/Square Shaped. $3.00-4.00

Comments: National Distribution: USA - July 6-August 2, 1990. Premium markings - "Disney China."

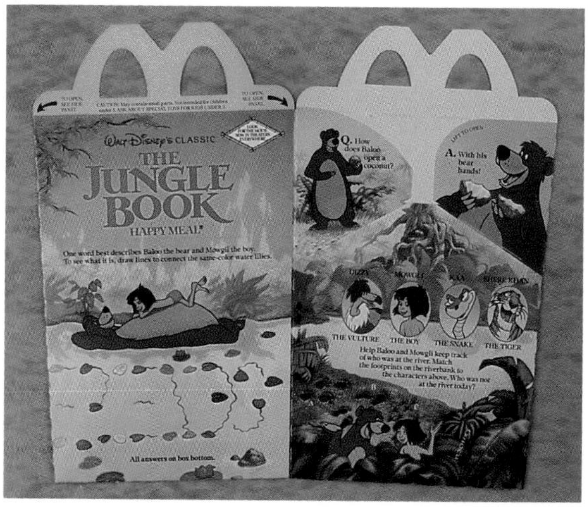

Ju9010

Ju9011

Ju9012

Ju9013

Ju9050

Ju9051

Ju9004 Ju9005

Ju9052

Ju9064

Ju9000 Ju9001 Ju9002 Ju9003

Ju9026

McDonaldland Carnival Happy Meal, 1991/1990

Box:

❑ ❑ USA Ca9010 **Hm Box - Ronald on Train,** 1990.
$2.00-3.00

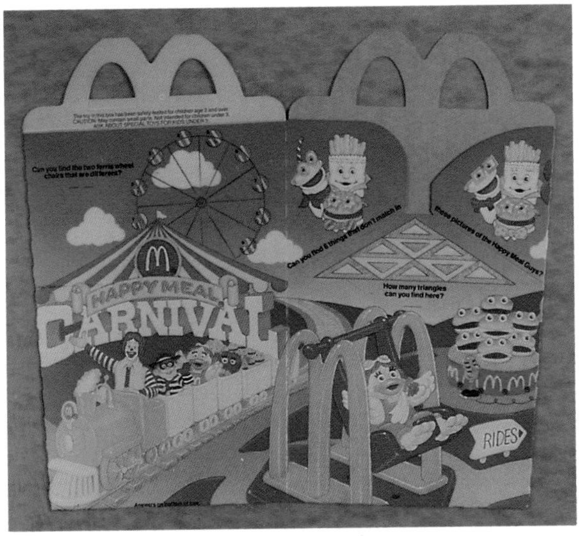

Ca9010

U-3 Premium: (MIP: $12.00-15.00; Loose: $7.00-10.00)
❑ ❑ USA Ca9004 **U-3 Grimace,** 1990, on Purp Rocker/Floater. $12.00-15.00

Premiums:
❑ ❑ USA Ca9000 **Birdie on Orange/Red Swing**, 1990, 5p. $4.00-5.00
❑ ❑ USA Ca9001 **Grimace on Red/Yellow Turn-Around**, 1990, 5p. $4.00-5.00
❑ ❑ USA Ca9002 **Hamburglar on Purple Ferris Wheel**, 1990, 5p. $4.00-5.00
❑ ❑ USA Ca9003 **Ronald on Green Teeter Totter**, 1990, 4p. $4.00-5.00

❑ ❑ USA Ca9064 **Translite/Sm**, 1990. $8.00-10.00

❑ ❑ USA Ca9065 **Translite/Lg**, 1990. $10.00-20.00

Comments: Regional Distribution: USA - September 7-October 4, 1990 and March-April 1991.

Ca9004

Ca9000 Ca9001 Ca9002 Ca9003

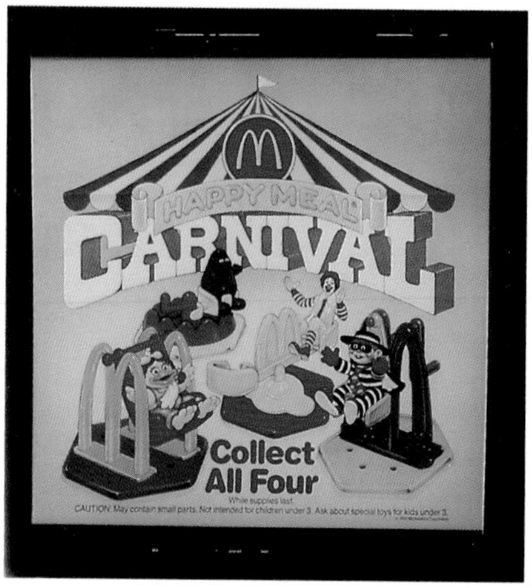

Ca9065

McDonaldland Dough Happy Meal, 1990

Boxes:
❑ ❑ USA Do9010 **Hm Box - Hoop to it,** 1990. $2.00-4.00

❑ ❑ USA Do9011 **Hm Box - Tic-Tac-Toe,** 1990. $2.00-4.00

Premiums: Play Doh Containers With Mold
❑ ❑ USA Do9000 **Red Dough with Red Ronald Star Mold,** 1990, Red Top Red Dough. $4.00-5.00

❑ ❑ USA Do9001 **Yellow Dough with Red Ronald Square Mold,** 1990, Yel Top Yel Dough. $4.00-5.00

❑ ❑ USA Do9002 **Green Dough with Green Fry Girl Octagon Mold,** 1990, Grn Top Grn Dough. $4.00-5.00

❑ ❑ USA Do9003 **Blue Dough with Green Fry Guy Hexagon Mold,** 1990, Blu Top Blu Dough. $4.00-5.00

❑ ❑ USA Do9004 **Purple Dough with Purple Grimace Square Mold,** 1990, Purp Top Purp Dough. $4.00-5.00
❑ ❑ USA Do9005 **Orange Dough with Purple Grimace Triangle Mold,** 1990, Org Top Org Dough. 4.00-5.00
❑ ❑ USA Do9006 **Pink Dough with Yellow Birdie Heart Mold,** 1990, Pnk Top Pnk Dough. $4.00-5.00

❑ ❑ USA Do9007 **White Dough with Yellow Birdie Circle Mold,** 1990, Wht Top Wht Dough. $4.00-5.00

❑ ❑ USA Do9064 **Translite/Sm**, 1990. $8.00-10.00

❑ ❑ USA Do9065 **Translite/Lg**, 1990. $10.00-20.00

Comments: Regional Distribution: USA - September 7-October 4, 1990 in southern states. Eight different molds were distributed in dough containers. Molds listed may not match the specific color dough. A total of eight colors and eight molds were distributed.

Do9010

Do9011

Do9000 Do9001 Do9002 Do9003

Do9004 Do9005 Do9006 Do9007

Md9001 Md9003 Md9002 Md9000

Do9065

McDonaldland Dough blue book.

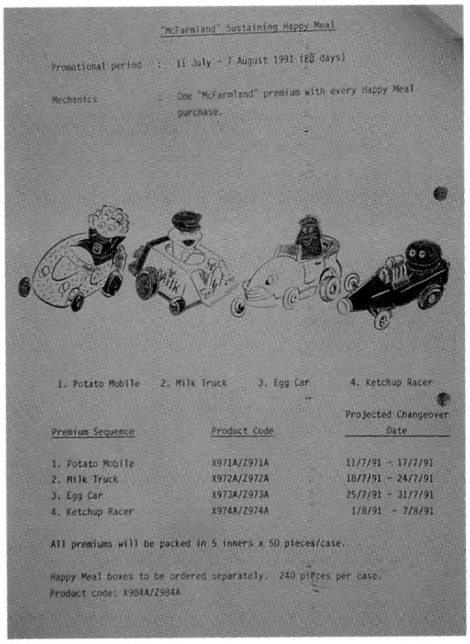

"McFarmland" Sustaining Happy Meal

Promotional period : 11 July - 7 August 1991 (28 days)

Mechanics : One "McFarmland" premium with every Happy Meal purchase.

1. Potato Mobile 2. Milk Truck 3. Egg Car 4. Ketchup Racer

Premium Sequence	Product Code	Projected Changeover Date
1. Potato Mobile	X971A/Z971A	11/7/91 - 17/7/91
2. Milk Truck	X972A/Z972A	18/7/91 - 24/7/91
3. Egg Car	X973A/Z973A	25/7/91 - 31/7/91
4. Ketchup Racer	X974A/Z974A	1/8/91 - 7/8/91

All premiums will be packed in 5 inners x 50 pieces/case.

Happy Meal boxes to be ordered separately. 240 pieces per case.
Product code: X984A/Z984A

Peanuts Happy Meal, 1990

Boxes:

❏ ❏ USA Pe9010 **Hm Box - County Fair**, 1989. $1.00-2.00

Pe9010

McDrive Thru Crew/McFarmland Test Market Happy Meal, 1991/1990

Premiums: (MIP: $12.00-35.00; Loose: $10.00-25.00)

❏ ❏ USA Md9000 **Fries in Potato Speedster,** 1990, Pull Back Friction Car. $15.00-20.00

❏ ❏ USA Md9001 **Hamburglar in Ketchup Racer,** 1990, Pull Back Friction Car. $20.00-35.00

❏ ❏ USA Md9002 **McNugget in Egg Roadster,** 1990, Pull Back Friction Car. $12.00-15.00

❏ ❏ USA Md9003 **Shake in Milk Carton Zoomer,** 1990, Pull Back Friction Car. $12.00-15.00

Comments: Regional Distribution: USA - September 7-October 4, 1990 in Illinois and Ohio regions. Distributed again in 1991 as McFarmland during July 11-August 7, 1991 in parts of Ohio.

☐ ☐ USA Pe9011 **Hm Box - E-I-E-I-O**, 1989. $1.00-2.00
☐ ☐ USA Pe9012 **Hm Box - Field Day**, 1989. $1.00-2.00
☐ ☐ USA Pe9013 **Hm Box - Hoe down**, 1989. $1.00-2.00

U-3 Premiums:
☐ ☐ USA Pe9004 **U-3 Charlie Brown's Egg Basket**, 1989, 1p/Cb with Basket. $5.00-6.00
☐ ☐ USA Pe9005 **U-3 Snoopy's Potato Sack,** 1989, 1p Snoopy with Sack. $5.00-6.00

Premiums:
☐ ☐ USA Pe9000 **Set 1 Snoopy's Hay Hauler,** 1989, 3p/Snoopy/Turq Wagon/Yel Hay. $2.50-3.50

☐ ☐ USA Pe9001 **Set 2 Charlie Brown's Seed Bag/Tiller,** 1989, 3p/Red-Blu Tiller/Yel Sack. $2.50-3.50
☐ ☐ USA Pe9002 **Set 3 Lucy's Apple Cart,** 1989, 3p/Lucy/Grn Wheeelbar/Red Apples. $2.50-3.50
☐ ☐ USA Pe9003 **Set 4 Linus' Milk Mover,** 1989, 3p/Linus/Org Mover/Gry Milk Can. $2.50-3.50

☐ ☐ USA Pe9026 **Display/Premiums**, 1989. $90.00-100.00
☐ ☐ USA Pe9064 **Translite/Sm**, 1989. $10.00-15.00
☐ ☐ USA Pe9065 **Translite/Lg**, 1989. $15.00-20.00

Comments: National Distribution: USA - March 30-April 26, 1990. Premium markings - "United Feat. Synd. China."

Pe9013

Pe9011

Pe9012

Pe9000 Pe9001 Pe9002 Pe9003

Pe9004 Pe9005

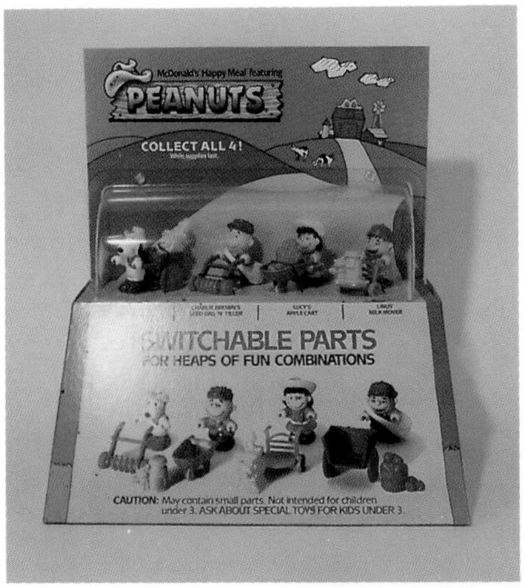

Pe9026

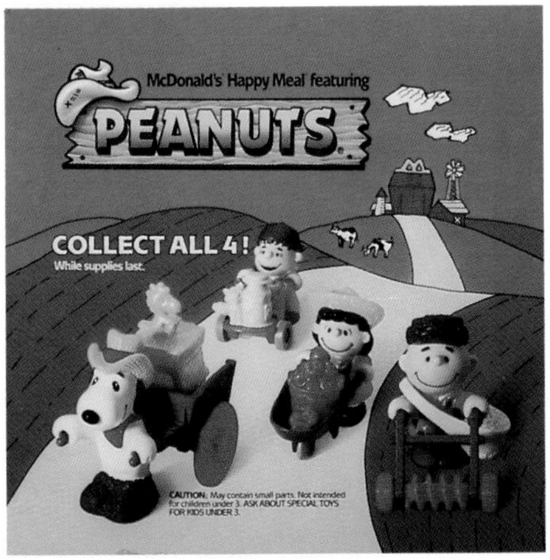

Pe9065

Rescuers Down Under Happy Meal, 1990

Boxes:

❑ ❑ USA Re9010 **Hm Box - Eagle/Bernard/Miss Bianca**, 1990. $1.00-2.00

❑ ❑ USA Re9011 **Hm Box - Fireflies/To Light the Night**, 1990. $1.00-2.00

❑ ❑ USA Re9012 **Hm Box - Lizard/Frank the Frill-Necked**, 1990. $1.00-2.00

❑ ❑ USA Re9013 **Hm Box - Rope/McLeach the Villain/Top Secret**, 1990. $1.00-2.00

U-3 Premium:

❑ ❑ USA Re9004 **U-3 Bernard,** 1990, On Piece of Yellow Cheese/Rubber. $4.00-5.00

Premiums:

❑ ❑ USA Re9000 **Bernard & Bianca,** 1990, Grn Camera/Yel Label. $3.00-4.00

❑ ❑ USA Re9001 **Jake,** 1990, Orange Camera/Grn Label. $3.00-4.00

❑ ❑ USA Re9002 **Cody,** 1990, Clear Camera/Blu Label. $3.00-4.00

❑ ❑ USA Re9003 **Wilbur,** 1990, Purp Camera/Pnk Label. $3.00-4.00

❑ ❑ USA Re9050 **Button**, 1990, Rescuers Down Under/Rectangle. $3.00-5.00

❑ ❑ USA Re9064 **Translite/Sm**, 1990. $4.00-5.00

❑ ❑ USA Re9065 **Translite/Lg**, 1990. $10.00-15.00

Comments: National Distribution: USA - November 30-December 27, 1990. Disney promotion in conjunction with the movie release. All premiums came polybagged.

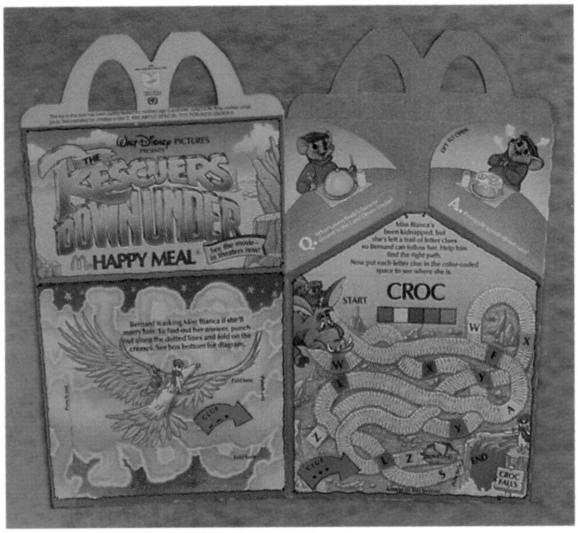

Re9010

Re9011

Re9012

Re9013

Re9050

Re9065

Re9004

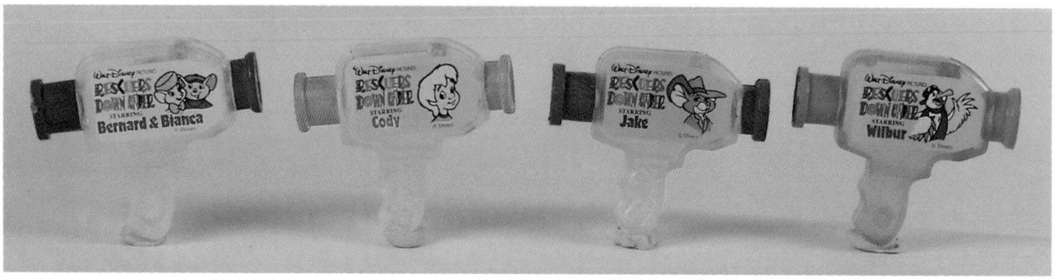

Re9000 Re9001 Re9002 Re9003

Sports Ball Happy Meal, 1991/1990

Box:

❑ ❑ USA Sp9035 **Hm Box - Ronald at Bat/10 Things**, 1990. $2.00-3.00

Premiums:

❑ ❑ USA Sp9025 **Baseball,** 1989, Wht with Red Stitching/Soft with Large Red M. $3.00-4.00

❑ ❑ USA Sp9026 **Basketball,** 1989, Org with Blk Seams/Soft with Large Blk M. $3.00-4.00

❑ ❑ USA Sp9027 **Football, 1989, Yellow with Red Lacing**/Soft with Large Red M. $3.00-4.00

❑ ❑ USA Sp9028 **Soccer Ball,** 1989, Red/Yel/Soft with Small Yel M. $3.00-4.00

❑ ❑ USA Sp9042 **Counter Card with Premiums**, 1990. $35.00-50.00

❑ ❑ USA Sp9064 **Translite/Sm**, 1990. $15.00-25.00

❑ ❑ USA Sp9065 **Translite/Lg**, 1990. $20.00-30.00

Comments: Regional Distribution - September 7-October 4, 1990 and March/April 1991. The premium tags had "M-B Sales, Oakbrook, Il - 1989." Note: the MIP package cards are dated 1990 and football is yellow.

Sp9035

Sp9025 Sp9026 Sp9027 Sp9028

Sp9042

Sp9065

Summer Surprise Happy Meal, 1990

Bags:

❑ ❑ USA Ss9030 **Hm Bag - Ronald's Good Time Meal**, 1989. $1.00-1.25

❑ ❑ USA Ss9031 **Hm Bag - McDonald's Hm/Ronald**, 1990. $1.00-1.25

❑ ❑ USA Ss9050 **Button**, 1990, Neon Grn/$1.99 Hm. $2.00-3.00

❑ ❑ USA Ss9051 **Button**, 1990, Neon Red/$1.99 Hm. $2.00-3.00

❑ ❑ USA Ss9064 **Translite/Sm**, 1990, a Smile in Every Box. $4.00-5.00

❑ ❑ USA Ss9065 **Translite/Lg**, 1990, a Smile in Every Box. $7.00-10.00

Comments: Regional Distribution: USA - Summer 1990.

Ss9031

Ss9051 Ss9050

Ss9065

Super Mario 3 Nintendo Happy Meal, 1990

Boxes:

❑ ❑ USA Su9010 **Hm Box - Desert Land**, 1990. $1.00-2.00

❑ ❑ USA Su9011 **Hm Box - Island World**, 1990. $1.00-2.00

❑ ❑ USA Su9012 **Hm Box - Pipe Land**, 1990. $1.00-2.00

❑ ❑ USA Su9013 **Hm Box - Sky Land**, 1990. $1.00-2.00

Su9012

Su9013

U-3 Premium:

❑ ❑ USA Su9005 **U-3 Super Mario,** 1990, Standing Mario with Blu Jeans & Red Shirt. $4.00-5.00

Premiums:

❑ ❑ USA Su9001 **Set 1 Mario,** 1990, Spring Loaded Mario Pops up. $2.50-3.00

❑ ❑ USA Su9002 **Set 2 Luigi,** 1990, Luigi Zooms Around. $2.50-3.00

❑ ❑ USA Su9003 **Set 3 Goomba,** 1990, Goomba Flips. $2.50-3.00

❑ ❑ USA Su9004 **Set 4 Koopa,** 1990, Standing/Hops. $2.50-3.00

Su9005 Su9001 Su9002 Su9003 Su9004

❑ ❑ USA Su9026 **Display/Premiums**, 1990. $85.00-100.00

❑ ❑ USA Su9041 **Dangler**/Each, 1990. $8.00-12.00

❑ ❑ USA Su9050 **Button**, 1990, Nintendo Hm. $3.00-5.00

❑ ❑ USA Su9055 **Trayliner**, 1990. $1.00-2.00

❑ ❑ USA Su9064 **Translite/Sm**, 1990. $8.00-12.00

❑ ❑ USA Su9065 **Translite/Lg/X-0 Graphic**, 1990. $25.00-40.00

❑ ❑ USA Su9066 **Translite/Lg**, 1990. $10.00-20.00

❑ ❑ USA Su9095 **Pin,** 1990, Super Mario with Yel Hm Box. $3.00-5.00

Su9026

Comments: National Distribution: USA - August 3-30, 1990. Premium markings - "1989 Nintendo of America Inc. China."

Su9041

Su9010 Su9011

Su9050

Su9055

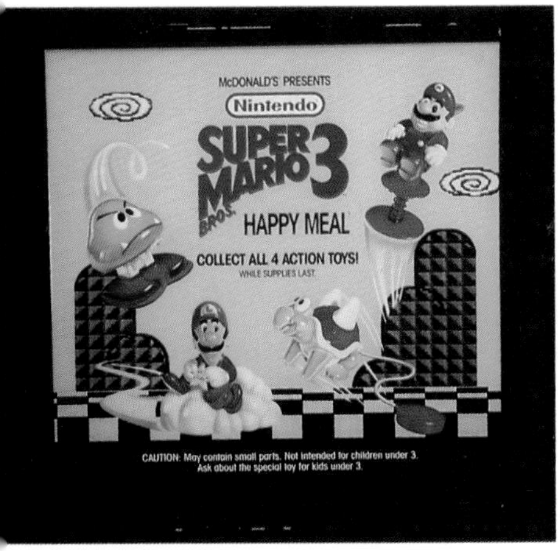

Su9064

Su9095

Tale Spin Happy Meal, 1990

Boxes:

❏ ❏ USA Ta9010 **Hm Box - Higher for Hire**, 1990.
$2.00-3.00

❏ ❏ USA Ta9011 **Hm Box - Louies**, 1990.
$2.00-3.00

❏ ❏ USA Ta9012 **Hm Box - Pirate Island**, 1990.
$2.00-3.00

❏ ❏ USA Ta9013 **Hm Box - Sea Duck**, 1990.
$2.00-3.00

Ta9010 Ta9011

Ta9012 Ta9013

U-3 Premiums:

❏ ❏ USA Ta9005 **U-3 Baloo's Seaplane,** 1990, Org Soft Plastic/Rubber.
$4.00-5.00

❏ ❏ USA Ta9006 **U-3 Wildcat's Flying Machine,** 1990, Grn Soft Plastic/Rubber.
$4.00-5.00

Ta9006 Ta9005

Ta9026

Premiums:
- ☐ ☐ USA Ta9001 **Baloo's Seaplane,** 1990, Org-Gld Die Cast Metal. $1.00-1.50
- ☐ ☐ USA Ta9002 **Kit's Racing Plane,** 1990, Org-Gld Die Cast Metal. $1.00-1.50
- ☐ ☐ USA Ta9003 **Molly's Biplane,** 1990, Grn-Red Die Cast Metal. $1.00-1.50
- ☐ ☐ USA Ta9004 **Wildcat's Flying Machine,** 1990, Grn-Red Die Cast Metal. $1.00-1.50

- ☐ ☐ USA Ta9026 **Display/Premiums**, 1990. $75.00-100.00
- ☐ ☐ USA Ta9041 **Ceiling Dangler**/Each, 1990. $5.00-7.00
- ☐ ☐ USA Ta9064 **Translite/Sm**, 1990. $5.00-10.00
- ☐ ☐ USA Ta9065 **Translite/Lg**, 1990. $10.00-15.00

Comments: National Distribution: USA - November 2-29, 1990. Premium markings "Disney Kh China" or "Disney Ch China" or Disney Wm China."

Ta9041

Ta9001

Ta9002

Ta9065

Ta9003

Ta9004

Tom & Jerry Band Happy Meal, 1990

Bags:
- ☐ ☐ USA To9030 **Hm Bag - Tom & Jerry/Large Wht bag with Friends Playing Instruments**, 1989. $2.00-3.00
- ☐ ☐ USA To9031 **Hm Bag - Tom & Jerry/Small Wht bag with More Yel #2 Bag**, 1990. $4.00-5.00

U-3 Premium: (MIP: $7.00-10.00; Loose: $2.00-3.00)
- ☐ ☐ USA To9004 **U-3 Droopy,** 1989, Dog without Microphone. $7.00-10.00

Premiums:
- ☐ ☐ USA To9000 **Set 1 Tom with Keyboard,** 1989, 4p Tom/ **Grn Keyboard with 2 Legs.** $10.00-15.00
- ☐ ☐ USA To9001 **Set 2 Droopy with Mike,** 1989, 3p Droopy with **2p Black Mike.** $10.00-15.00

☐ ☐ USA To9002 **Set 3 Jerry with Drums,** 1989, 2p Tom with **Drum.** $7.00-10.00

☐ ☐ USA To9003 **Set 4 Spike with Bass,** 1989, 2p Spike with **Wht Bass.** $7.00-10.00

☐ ☐ USA To9064 **Translite/Sm**, 1989. $12.00-15.00

☐ ☐ USA To9065 **Translite/Lg**, 1989. $15.00-25.00

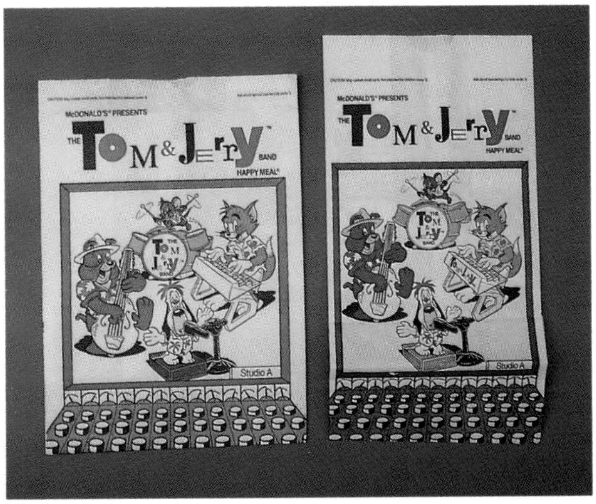

To9030 To9031

To9004 To9000 To9001 To9002 To9003

To9065

Comments: National Distribution: USA - September 2-October 4, 1990. Premium markings "1989 Simon Marketing China"; Los Angeles, California test market - January 1990. Regional Distribution: USA Hawaiian Islands, 1990.

Turbo Macs II Happy Meal, 1990

U-3 Premium:

☐ ☐ USA Tu9024 **U-3 Ronald,** 1988, Ronald/Rubber/Insert Card. $5.00-8.00

Premiums:

☐ ☐ USA Tu9000 **Birdie in Pink Car**, 1988, Red Hair/Lg Yel Arches. $3.50-4.50

☐ ☐ USA Tu9001 **Grimace in White Car**, 1988, Lg Red M on Front of Car. $3.50-4.50

☐ ☐ USA Tu9002 **Hamburglar in Yellow Car**, 1988, Lg Red M on Front of Car. $3.50-4.50

☐ ☐ USA Tu9003 **Ronald in Red Car with NO Teardrop under Eyes**, 1988, Lg Yel M on Front of Car. $3.50-4.50

☐ ☐ USA Tu9065 **Translite/Lg**, 1988, Ron/No Teardrop. $15.00-25.00

Comments: Limited Regional Distribution: USA - September 7-October 4, 1990. In 1990 Turbo Macs Happy Meal was redistributed using the 1988 box and 1988 cars with the large arches. Each MIP came with an insert card.

Tu9024

Tu9000 Tu9001 Tu9002 Tu9003

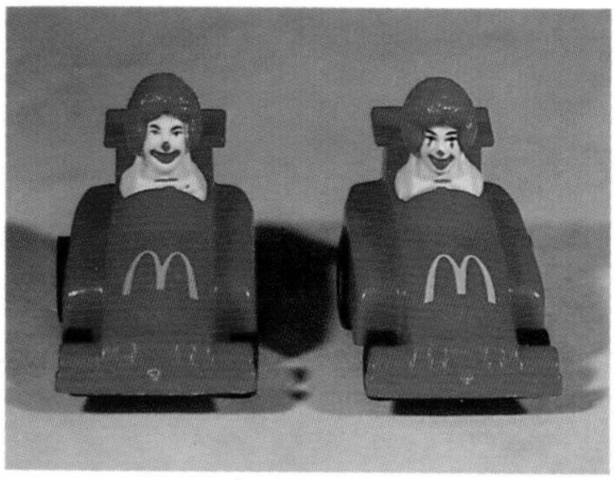

Tu9003

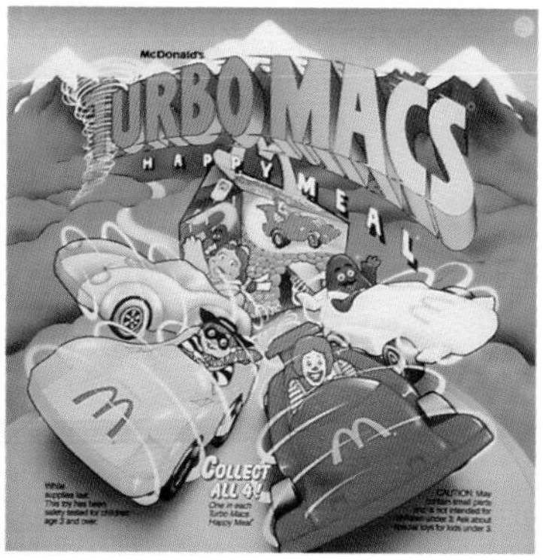

Tu9065

Ge9001

Ge9002

Ge9012 Ge9013

Ge9065

USA Generic Promotions, 1990

- ❑ ❑ USA Ge9001 **Hm Bag - Kid's Combo Meal**, 1990. $.25-.50
- ❑ ❑ USA Ge9002 **Beef Taco Hm**, 1990, Happy Meal/Adv Sign. $2.00-4.00
- ❑ ❑ USA Ge9065 **Translite/Lg**, 1990, Kid's Combo Meal. $4.00-5.00

- ❑ ❑ USA Ge9004 **Fun Times Magazine: Vol. 12 No. 1 Issue 1, 1990** $1.00-2.00
- ❑ ❑ USA Ge9005 **FTM: Vol. 12 No. 2 Issue 2, 1990.** $1.00-2.00
- ❑ ❑ USA Ge9006 **FTM: Vol. 12 No. 3 Issue 3, 1990.** $1.00-2.00
- ❑ ❑ USA Ge9007 **FTM: Vol. 12 No. 4 Issue 4, 1990.** $1.00-2.00
- ❑ ❑ USA Ge9008 **FTM: Vol. 12 No. 5 Issue 5, 1990.** $1.00-2.00
- ❑ ❑ USA Ge9009 **FTM: Vol. 12 No. 6 Issue 6, 1990.** $1.00-2.00
- ❑ ❑ USA Ge9010 **FTM: Vol. 12 No. 6 Special Issue, 1990.** $2.00-2.50

- ❑ ❑ USA Ge9011 **Calendar: Ronald McDonald Colorful Year in Virginia**. Regional state calendar. $5.00-7.00

- ❑ ❑ USA Ge9012 **Ornament: Miss Bianca, Stuffed Mouse, 3" High/"Rescuers Down Under."** $4.00-6.00
- ❑ ❑ USA Ge9013 **Ornament: Bernard, Stuffed Mouse, 3" High/"Rescuers Down Under."** $4.00-6.00

Comments: Regional Distribution: USA - 1990 and during clean-up weeks. Bernard and Miss Bianca stuffed ornaments were given free with the purchase of Gift Certificates in the stores.

Moscow McDonald's opened with world press in 1990. The idea that McDonald's was located in the Soviet Union awakened customers to the realization that McDonald's was a safe haven (even in the Soviet Union), reaffirming the widely held belief that the Golden Arches served as a familiar and universal safe haven landmark. Recyclable packaging continued with the phasing out of Styrofoam containers. McDonald's stressed the relationship between food sources and the environment as the emphasis was placed on a Global Relationship. Lastly, "Food, Folks and Fun" was the advertising slogan selected to promote family gatherings. McJobs, a special program to hire and develop disabled persons as employees won immediate approval and Ray Kroc, posthumously, was selected by *LIFE* magazine as one of the Most Important Americans of the 20th Century.

The 11th National O/O Convention was held in Las Vegas, Nevada on May 7-11th. The theme was: "Call to Action, Customer Satisfaction."

McDonald's collectors from afar met in Freemont, Ohio in 1990 to form the National McDonald's Collectors Club.

1991

101 Dalmatians Happy Meal, 1991
Alvin and the Chipmunks Happy Meal, 1991
Barbie/Hot Wheels II Happy Meal, 1991
Breakfast Happy Meal, 1991
Connectibles/McDonaldland Connectible Vehicles HM, 1991
Crazy Vehicles Happy Meal, 1991
Discover the Rain Forest Happy Meal, 1991
Friendly Skies HM, 1995/1994/1993/1992/1991
Good Morning Happy Meal, 1991
Gravedale High Happy Meal, 1991
Halloween '91/McBoo Bags/Buckets Happy Meal, 1991
Hook Happy Meal, 1991
McCharacters on Bikes/McDonaldland on Wheels HM, 1991
McDino Changeables Happy Meal, 1991
McDonaldland Circus Parade HM, 1993/1992/1991
Mighty Mini Happy Meal, 1991
Muppet Babies III Happy Meal, 1992/1991
Nature's Helper Happy Meal, 1991
Piggsburg Pigs Happy Meal, 1991
Pizza Happy Sack Happy Meal, 1991
Stencil/Space/Crayons Generic Happy Meal, 1991
Sports Ball Happy Meal, 1991
Super Looney Tunes Happy Meal, 1991
Tiny Toon Adventures I/Flip-cars/Happy Meal, 1991
Wacky Glasses Promotion, 1991
USA Generic Promotions, 1991

- **"Do You Believe in Magic?" jingle**
- **United Airlines and McDonald's take to the skies with Happy Meals in flight**

101 Dalmatians I Happy Meal, 1991

Boxes:

☐ ☐ USA On9110 **Hm Box - Barn**, 1991. $2.00-3.00

☐ ☐ USA On9111 **Hm Box - Dog's Leashes,** 1991. $2.00-3.00

☐ ☐ USA On9112 **Hm Box - Piano**, 1991. $2.00-3.00

☐ ☐ USA On9113 **Hm Box - Staircase**, 1991. $2.00-3.00

Premiums:

☐ ☐ USA On9100 **Set 1 Pogo the Dog,** 1990, Dalmation Standing. $3.00-4.00

☐ ☐ USA On9101 **Set 2 Lucky the Pup,** 1990, Wht/Blk Dalmation Pup with Red Collar. $3.00-4.00

☐ ☐ USA On9102 **Set 3 Colonel/Sgt. Tibbs,** 1990, Sheep Dog with Cat. $3.00-4.00

☐ ☐ USA On9103 **Set 4 Cruella Devilla,** 1990, Yel/Blk Villainess. $3.00-4.00

☐ ☐ USA On9126 **Display with Premiums**, 1991. $85.00-100.00

☐ ☐ USA On9164 **Translite/Sm**, 1991. $10.00-15.00

☐ ☐ USA On9165 **Translite/Lg**, 1991. $12.00-20.00

Comments: National Distribution: USA - July 5 - August 1, 1991. Note the new smaller box size. No U-3 given.

On9110 On9111

On9112 On9113

On9100 On9101 On9102 On9103

On9126

On9165

Alvin and the Chipmunks Happy Meal, 1991

Bag:

❑ ❑ USA AI9130 **Hm Bag - Alvin with Target Store Coupon on bag**, 1990. $2.00-3.00

U-3 Premium:

❑ ❑ USA AI9105 **U-3 Alvin,** 1990, Leaning on a Jukebox/Rubber. $15.00-20.00

Premiums:

❑ ❑ USA AI9101 **Alvin,** 1990, 2p/Red Alvin with **Blu Guitar.** $20.00-25.00

❑ ❑ USA AI9102 **Brittney,** 1990, 2p/Pnk Brit with **Grn Jukebox.** $15.00-20.00

❑ ❑ USA AI9103 **Simon,** 1990, 2p/Yel Simon with **Pnk Movie Camera.** $15.00-20.00

❑ ❑ USA AI9104 **Theodore,** 1990, 2p/Turq/Yel Theo with **Rap Machine.** $15.00-20.00

❑ ❑ USA AI9108 **Target Coupon**, 1990. $.50-1.00

❑ ❑ USA AI9127 **Counter Card with Premiums**, 1990. $85.00-100.00

❑ ❑ USA AI9164 **Translite/Sm**, 1990. $12.00-20.00

❑ ❑ USA AI9165 **Translite/Lg**, 1990. $20.00-25.00

Comments: Regional Distribution: USA - March 8-April 12, 1991 - Texas. Premium markings "Kh China 1990 M-B Sales" or "1990 Bagdasarian Prod China" or "Dy China." Auction prices have increased premium price. Loose figurines without the guitar and camera sell for $4.00-5.00 each.

AI9130

AI9105

AI9101 AI9102 AI9103 AI9104

AI9108

Above: AI9127

Barbie/Hot Wheels II Happy Meal, 1991

Boxes:

☐ ☐ USA Ba9170 **Hm Box - At Home**, 1991. $1.00-2.00

☐ ☐ USA Ba9171 **Hm Box - On Stage**, 1991. $1.00-2.00

☐ ☐ USA Ba9172 **Hm Box - Cruising**, 1991. $1.00-2.00

☐ ☐ USA Ba9173 **Hm Box - Racers**, 1991. $1.00-2.00

U-3 Premiums:

☐ ☐ USA Ba9148 **U-3 Costume Ball,** 1991, Pnk Long Dress/Holding Purp Mask. $3.00-5.00

☐ ☐ USA Ba9149 **U-3 Wedding Midge,** 1991, Wht Gown/Pnk Flowers/Purp Ribbon. $3.00-5.00

☐ ☐ USA Ba9163 **U-3 Tool Set,** 1991, Plastic/Yel Wrench/Red Hammer/2p. $2.00-3.00

Premiums: Barbie Dolls

☐ ☐ USA Ba9140 **#1 Barbie: All American,** 1991, Short Blu Dress/Reebok Sneakers. $3.00-5.00

☐ ☐ USA Ba9141 **#2 Barbie: Costume Ball,** 1991, Pnk Long Dress/Holding Purp Mask. $3.00-5.00

☐ ☐ USA Ba9142 **#3 Barbie: Lights/Lace,** 1991, Pnk Ballerina Dress/Purp Stand. $3.00-5.00

☐ ☐ USA Ba9143 **#4 Barbie: Happy Birthday,** 1991, Blk Barbie/Pnk Long Dress. $3.00-5.00

☐ ☐ USA Ba9144 **#5 Barbie: Hawaiian Fun,** 1991, Pnk Wrap/Sea Shell Base. $3.00-5.00

☐ ☐ USA Ba9145 **#6 Barbie: Wedding Day Midge,** 1991, Wht Gown/Pnk Flowers/Purp Ribbon/Brn Hair. $3.00-5.00

☐ ☐ USA Ba9146 **#7 Barbie: Ice Capades,** 1991, Purp Dress/Wht Ice Skates. $3.00-5.00

☐ ☐ USA Ba9147 **#8 Barbie: My First Barbie,** 1991, Spanish Barbie/Purp-Wht Long Dress. $3.00-5.00

Premiums: Hot Wheel Cars

☐ ☐ USA Hw9155 **#1 '55 Chevy - yellow,** 1991. $3.00-4.00

☐ ☐ USA Hw9156 **#2 '63 Corvette - green,** 1991. $3.00-4.00

☐ ☐ USA Hw9157 **#3 '57 T Bird - turquoise,** 1991. $3.00-4.00

☐ ☐ USA Hw9158 **#4 Camaro Z-28 - purple,** 1991. $3.00-4.00

☐ ☐ USA Hw9159 **#5 '55 Chevy - white,** 1991. $3.00-4.00

☐ ☐ USA Hw9160 **#6 '63 Corvette - black,** 1991. $3.00-4.00

☐ ☐ USA Hw9161 **#7 '57 T Bird - red,** 1991. $3.00-4.00

☐ ☐ USA Hw9162 **#8 Camaro Z-28 - orange,** 1991. $3.00-4.00

☐ ☐ USA Ba9126 **Display/Premiums**, 1991. $125.00-175.00

☐ ☐ USA Ba9150 **Button**, 1992, Ask Me about Today's HM. $4.00-5.00

☐ ☐ USA Ba9164 **Translite/Sm**, 1991. $15.00-25.00

☐ ☐ USA Ba9165 **Translite/Lg**, 1991. $20.00-30.00

☐ ☐ USA Ba9183 **Trayliner**, 1991. $1.00-2.00

Comments: National Distribution: USA - August 2-28, 1991. USA Ba9141 and USA Ba9148 as well as USA Ba9145 and USA Ba9149 are the same, loose out of package. USA Ba9145 was produced (very limited Regional Distribution) with blonde hair and with the nationally distributed brown hair version.

Ba9170 Ba9171

Left to right: Ba9172 Ba9173

Ba9149 Ba9148

Left to right: Ba9148, Ba9149, Ba9140, Ba9141, Ba9143, Ba9142, Ba9144, Ba9145, Ba9146, Ba9147

Ba9126

Ba9140 Ba9141 Ba9142 Ba9143

Ba9150

Ba9144 Ba9145 Ba9146 Ba9147

Ba9165

Ba9163

Top row: Hw9156 Hw9158 Hw9160 Hw9161
Bottom row: Hw9155 Hw9157 Hw9159 Hw9162

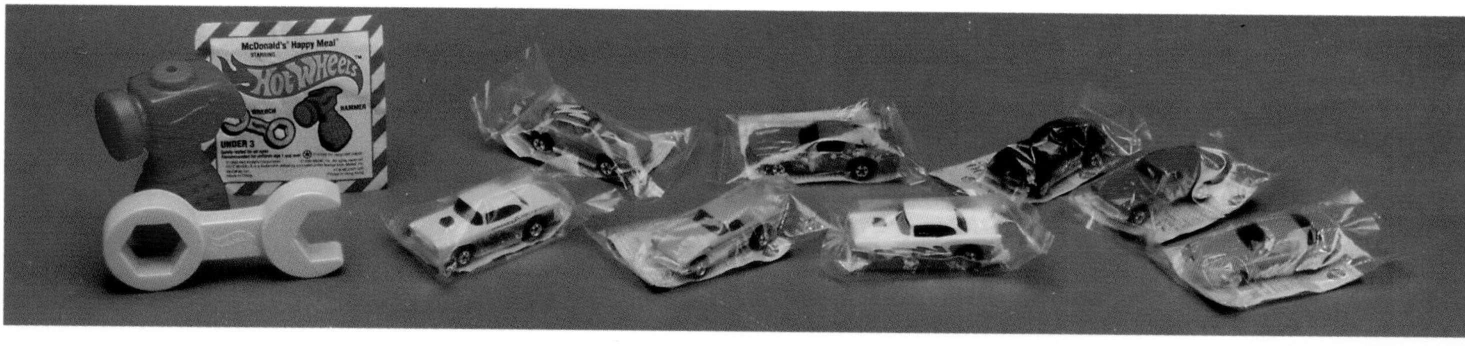

Breakfast Happy Meal, 1991

Premium:

❑ ❑ USA Br9101 **Squeeze Bottle, 1991**, Minute Maid Logo. $2.00-2.50

❑ ❑ USA Br9150 **Button**, 1987, Try Our O.J. $7.00-10.00

❑ ❑ USA Br9164 **Translite/Sm**, 1991. $4.00-6.00

Comments: Regional Distribution: USA - 1991 in the Summer/Fall in northeastern United States. Button was issued in 1987 and worn again during 1991 promotion. During 1995-1998, the Breakfast Happy Meal was being used regionally.

Br9101

Br8750

Br9164

Connectibles/McDonaldland Connectible Vehicles Happy Meal, 1991

Premiums:

❑ ❑ USA Co9100 **Birdie on a Blue/Pink/Yellow Tricycle**, 1990, 2p. $4.00-5.00

❑ ❑ USA Co9101 **Grimace in a Red Wagon**, 1990, 2p. $4.00-5.00

❑ ❑ USA Co9102 **Hamburglar in a Green/Yellow Airplane**, 1990, 2p. $4.00-5.00

❑ ❑ USA Co9103 **Ronald in a Yellow/Red Soapbox Racer**, 1990, 2p. $4.00-5.00

Comments: Limited Regional Distribution: USA - August 29-September 5, 1991 during clean-up week. MIP insert cards are dated "1991." No specific Happy Meal boxes or bags were given with these premiums. Name changed to "McDonaldland Connectible Vehicles," based on blue book information from McDonald's archives.

Co9100 Co9101 Co9102 Co9103

Crazy Vehicles Happy Meal, 1991

Premiums:

❑ ❑ USA Cr9101 **Birdie in Pink/Yellow/Purple Airplane**, 1990, 3p. $2.50-4.00

❑ ❑ USA Cr9102 **Grimace in Green/Yellow/Orange Car**, 1990, 3p. $2.50-4.00

❑ ❑ USA Cr9103 **Hamburglar in Yellow/Blue/Purple Train**, 1990, 3p. $2.50-4.00

❑ ❑ USA Cr9104 **Ronald in Red/Yellow/Blue Buggy Car**, 1990, 3p. $2.50-4.00

Comments: Limited Regional Distribution: USA during clean-up week - August 29-September 5, 1991.

Cr9101 Cr9102 Cr9103 Cr9104

Di9125 Di9126

Di9128 Di9127

Discover the Rain Forest Happy Meal, 1991

Bag:

❑ ❑ USA Di9130 **Hm Bag - Discover**, 1991. $1.00-2.00

Premiums: Activity Books

❑ ❑ USA Di9125 **Set 1 Sticker Safari,** 1991, 12 Pages/14 Stickers. $2.00-3.00

❑ ❑ USA Di9126 **Set 2 Paint it Wild,** 1991, with Paint Brush/Pallet/16 Pages. $2.00-3.00

❑ ❑ USA Di9127 **Set 3 Ronald in the Jewel,** 1991, of the Amazon Kingdom/16 Pages. $2.00-3.00

❑ ❑ USA Di9128 **Set 4 Wonders in the Wild,** 1991, 16 Pages. $2.00-3.00

❑ ❑ USA Di9164 **Translite/Sm**, 1991. $4.00-5.00

❑ ❑ USA Di9165 **Translite/Lg**, 1991. $5.00-8.00

Comments: National Distribution: USA - September 6-October 3, 1991.

Di9130

Di9165

Friendly Skies Happy Meal, 1998 - 1991

Boxes:

❑ ❑ USA Fr9110 **Hm Box: 1991 - Toy in this Box**/6 1/2" x 6 1/2" x 2". $10.00-15.00

❑ ❑ USA Fr9111 **Hm Box: 1991 - Ronald Toy Inside**/5 1/4" x 5 1/4" x 2". $10.00-15.00

❑ ❑ USA Fr9114 **Hm Box: 1991 - Grimace Toy Inside**/5 1/4" x 5 1/4" x 2". $10.00-15.00

❑ ❑ USA Fr9115 **Hm Box: 1993 - Windows to the World/ Snack Pack**/5 1/4" x 5 1/4" x 2". $4.00-7.00

Premiums:

❑ ❑ USA Fr9101 **1991: Ronald in White 747 Airplane.** $8.00-10.00

❑ ❑ USA Fr9102 **1991: Grimace in White 747 United Airplane.** $8.00-10.00

❑ ❑ USA Fr9403 **1994: Ronald in Grey 747 United Airplane.** $7.00-8.00

❑ ❑ USA Fr9404 **1994: Grimace in Grey 747 United Airplane.** $7.00-8.00

❑ ❑ USA Fr9405 **1995: Airplane in a Red Airplane Hangar,** dated 1994, Gry Airplane/Blu Hangar with Red Roof/Yel Door/2p. $8.00-10.00

❑ ❑ USA Fr9606 **1996: Stuffed Grey Plane,** dated 1995, Stuffed Gry/Blu Airplane. $8.00-10.00

❑ ❑ USA Fr9707 **1997: Luggage Carrier With Birdie in Red Car,** dated 1996, Sticker Sheet with Grey Luggage Carrier/ Red-Yel-Blu Luggage/3p + Sticker Sheet. $8.00-10.00

❑ ❑ USA Fr9708 **1997: Ronald in Red Cargo Truck**, dated 1996, red truck/Grey Top with United Logo. $8.00-10.00

❑ ❑ USA Fr9112 **Napkin Packet,** 1991. $2.00-3.00

❑ ❑ USA Fr9126 **Display**, 1992, with 1 Box. $65.00-80.00

❑ ❑ USA Fr9141 **Ceiling Dangler,** 1992, with 2 Ron Premiums/ with 3 Boxes. $65.00-75.00

❑ ❑ USA Fr9150 **Button**, 1993, United Friendly Skies Now Flying from Chicago! $7.00-10.00

❑ ❑ USA Fr9155 **Trayliner, 1993, Ron with Chars.** $1.00-2.00

Fr9111 Fr9110

❑ ❑ USA Fr9156 **Trayliner, 1993, Runway Funway.** $1.00-2.00

Comments: National Distribution: USA - October 10-December 1991 and in 1992/1993/1994/1995/1996/1997. The promotion was given on selected United flights throughout the USA. Initially, boxes came in two sizes and there were four different boxes.

Fr9115

Fr9104 Fr9103 Fr9102 Fr9101

Fr9105 Fr9416

Fr9606

Fr9708 Fr9707

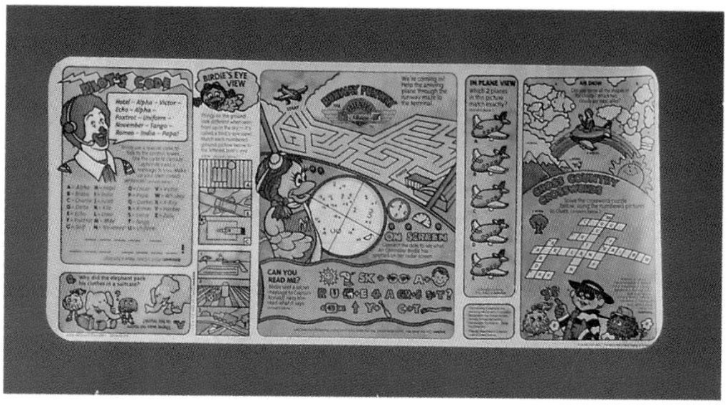

Fr9155

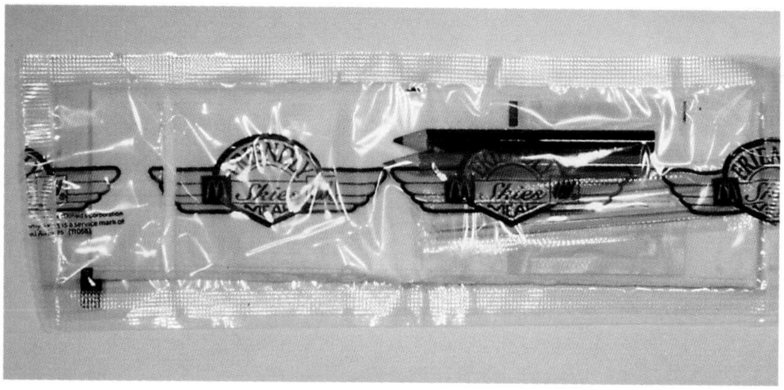

Fr9112

Fr9141

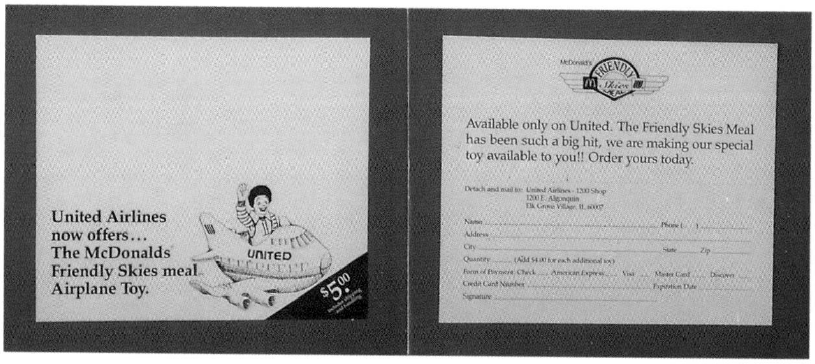

Fr9150

Good Morning Happy Meal, 1991

Bag:

❑ ❑ USA Go9130 **Hm Bag - Good Morning**, 1990. $1.00-2.00

U-3 Premium:

❑ ❑ USA Go9154 **U-3 Cup - Ronald with Bunny,** 1990, Rising Sun Birds/Not Wrapped. $1.00-1.50

Premiums:

❑ ❑ USA Go9150 **Toothbrush - Ronald,** 1989, Ronald Getting out of Bed. $2.00-3.00

❑ ❑ USA Go9151 **Clock - Ronald Flying,** 1989, Clock Hands Propellers. $1.00-1.50

❑ ❑ USA Go9152 **Cup - Ronald with Bunny,** 1990, Rising Sun Birds/4 Oz. Juicy Juice. $1.00-1.50

❑ ❑ USA Go9153 **Comb,** 1990, 5 Section Fry Kids Comb. $1.00-1.50

❑ ❑ USA Go9164 **Translite/Sm**, 1990. $4.00-5.00
❑ ❑ USA Go9165 **Translite/Lg**, 1990. $5.00-8.00

Comments: National Distribution: USA - January 4-31, 1991. A 2 ounce can of juice was substituted for the 4 ounce carton in some New England promotions. USA Go9152 = USA Go9154; they were distributed loose, with no packaging.

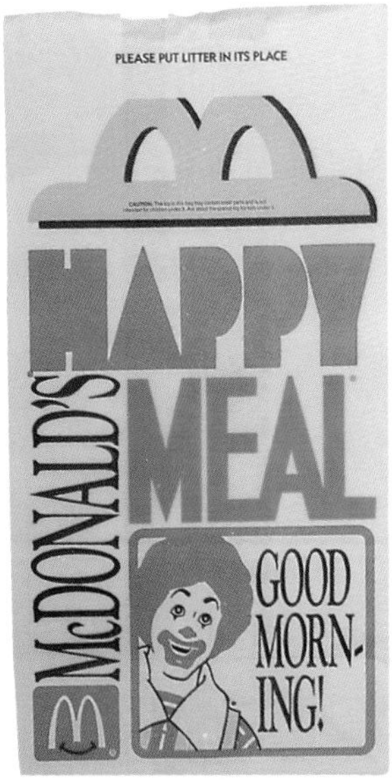

Go9130

Gravedale High Happy Meal, 1991

Bag:
❑ ❑ USA Gr9130 **Hm Bag - Crossword Puzzle**, 1991. $1.00-2.00

U-3 Premium:
❑ ❑ USA Gr9105 **U-3 Cleofatra,** 1991, Yel Girl with Org Pony Tails. $4.00-5.00

Premiums:
❑ ❑ USA Gr9101 **Set 1 Frankentyke,** 1991, Grn Monster with Movable Tongue. $4.00-5.00
❑ ❑ USA Gr9102 **Set 2 Sid/Invisible Kid,** 1991, Purp Figure with Movable Arms/Legs. $4.00-5.00

❑ ❑ USA Gr9103 **Set 3 Vinnie Stoker,** 1991, Casket with Rotating Man. $4.00-5.00
❑ ❑ USA Gr9104 **Set 4 Cleofatra,** 1991, Yel Girl with Org Pony Tails. $4.00-5.00

❑ ❑ USA Gr9164 **Translite/Collect All 4/Sm**, 1991. $7.00-10.00
❑ ❑ USA Gr9165 **Translite/Collect All 4/Lg,** 1991. $10.00-15.00
❑ ❑ USA Gr9166 **Translite/Collect All 3/Lg,** 1991. $10.00-15.00
❑ ❑ USA Gr9167 **Translite/Collect All 3/Sm**, 1991. $10.00-15.00

Comments: Regional Distribution: USA March 14-April 11, 1991. Premium markings - "NBC China." USA Gr9105 U-3 = USA Gr9104, loose out of package. Happy Meal was released during Easter 1991 and did not receive wide distribution.

Go9150 Go9151 Go9152 Go9153

Gr9130

Go9164

Gr9105 Gr9101 Gr9102 Gr9103 Gr9104

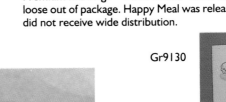

Gr9165

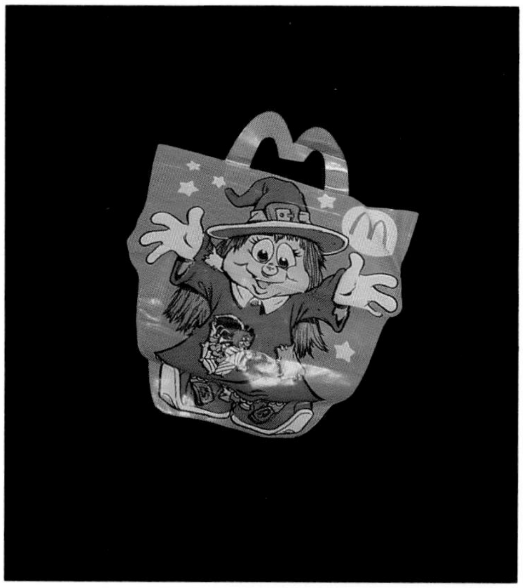
Ha9100

Gr9167
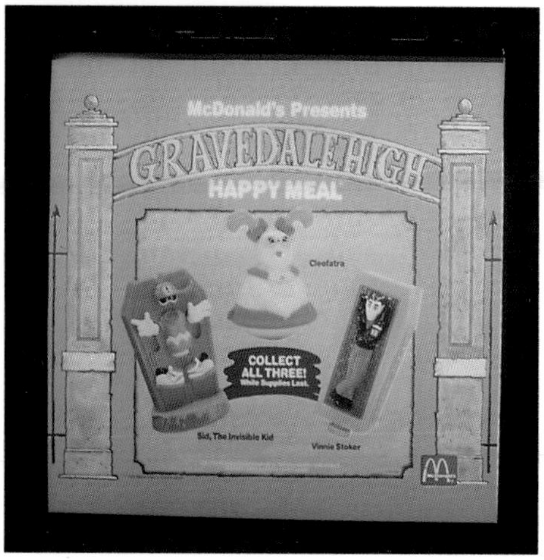

Ha9101

Halloween '91/McBoo Bags/Buckets Happy Meal, 1991

Premiums: Halloween Bags

- ❑ ❑ USA Ha9100 **McBoo Witch Bag,** 1991, Grn Vinyl Bag with Org Handle. $.50-1.00
- ❑ ❑ USA Ha9101 **McBoo Ghost Bag,** 1991, Purp Vinyl Bag with Yel Handles. $.50-1.00
- ❑ ❑ USA Ha9102 **McBoo Monster Bag,** 1991, Org with Pnk Handles, Skin Glows. $.50-1.00

Premiums: Halloween Pails With Sticker

- ❑ ❑ USA Ha9103 **McPunk'n,** 1986, Pail with Blk Arches Handle with "Made in USA Sticker." $2.00-3.00
- ❑ ❑ USA Ha9104 **Ghost,** 1986, Glow-In-The-Dark Pail/Blk Arches Handle with "Made in USA Sticker." $2.00-3.00
- ❑ ❑ USA Ha9105 **Witch,** 1986, Day-Glo Pail with Blk Arches Handle with "Made in USA Sticker." $2.00-3.00
- ❑ ❑ USA Ha9106 **McBoo,** 1986, Pail with Blk Arches Handle with "Made in USA Sticker." $2.00-3.00
- ❑ ❑ USA Ha9107 **McGoblin,** 1986, Pail with Blk Arches Handle with "Made in USA Sticker." $2.00-3.00

- ❑ ❑ USA Ha9141 **Ceiling Dangler**/1 Bag, 1991, Take off with a HM Today! $7.00-10.00
- ❑ ❑ USA Ha9164 **Translite/Sm**, 1991. $5.00-8.00
- ❑ ❑ USA Ha9165 **Translite/Lg**, 1991. $8.00-10.00

Comments: National Distribution: USA - October 11-October 31, 1991. Happy Meal also called McBoo Bags/Buckets Happy Meal, 1991. Bags have glow in the dark features. In some regional markets, Halloween Buckets were substituted for the national promotion.

Ha9102

Ha9106 Ha9107 Ha9105 Ha9104

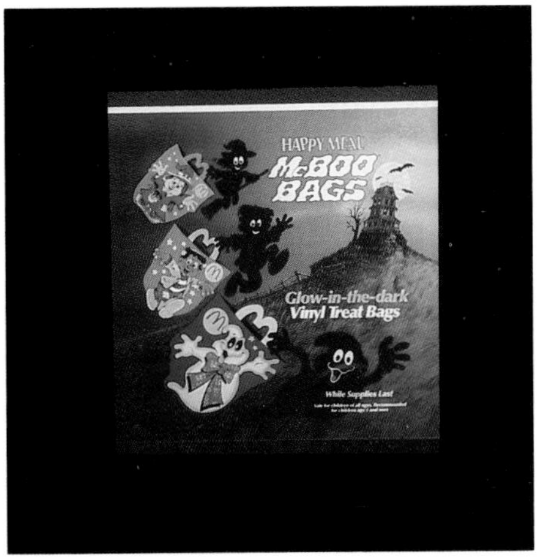

Ha9165

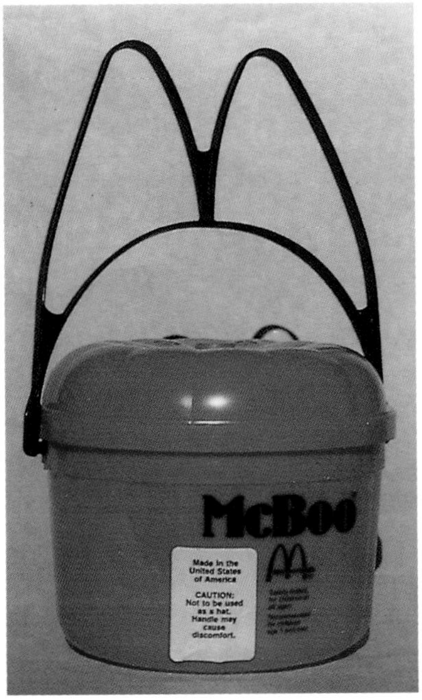

Ha9106

Ha9141

Hook Happy Meal, 1991

Boxes:

- ☐ ☐ USA Ho9110 **Hm Box - Jolly Roger**, 1991. $1.00-2.00
- ☐ ☐ USA Ho9111 **Hm Box - Never Tree**, 1991. $1.00-2.00
- ☐ ☐ USA Ho9112 **Hm Box - Pirate Town**, 1991. $1.00-2.00
- ☐ ☐ USA Ho9113 **Hm Box - Wendy's London House**, 1991. $1.00-2.00

Premiums:

- ☐ ☐ USA Ho9100 **Peter Pan,** 1991, on Purp Raft with Wheels/Floats/3p. $2.50-3.00
- ☐ ☐ USA Ho9101 **Mermaid,** 1991, Blu Mermaid/Wind up/Swims in Water/1p. $2.50-3.00
- ☐ ☐ USA Ho9102 **Hook,** 1991, Capt Hook in Blu Pirate Ship/3p. $2.50-3.00
- ☐ ☐ USA Ho9103 **Rufio,** 1991, Boy Floating on Grn/Purp Rubber Barrels-Squirts/1p. $1.50-2.00

- ☐ ☐ USA Ho9126 **Display/Premiums**, 1991. $75.00-100.00
- ☐ ☐ USA Ho9164 **Translite/Sm**, 1991. $8.00-10.00
- ☐ ☐ USA Ho9165 **Translite/Lg**, 1991. $10.00-15.00

Comments: National Distribution: USA - December 13-January 9, 1992. Smaller style Happy Meal box was introduced in 1990. Hook Happy Meal emphasized McDonald's successful teaming with a large national corporation: Disney. Indiana Jones videos were sold on a national scale. Promotions and promotional items were solidly entrenched with current movies and themes.

Ho9110 Ho9111

Ho9112 Ho9113

Ho9100 Ho9101 Ho9102 Ho9103

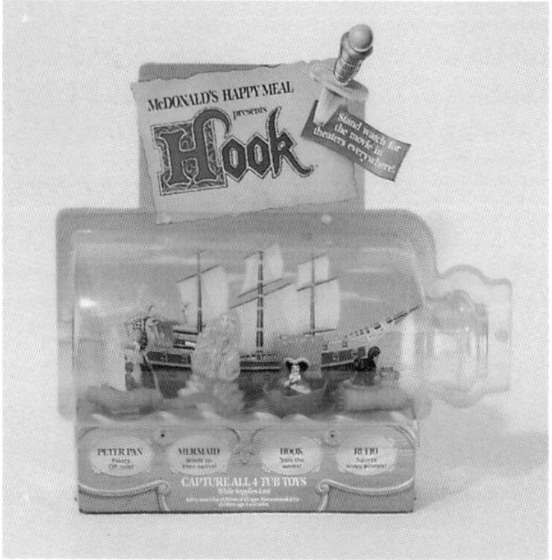

Ho9126

Ho9165

McCharacters on Bikes/McDonaldland on Wheels Happy Meal, 1991

Premiums:

❑ ❑ USA Bi9101 **Birdie on Pink Bike**, 1990, Blue Wheels. $3.00-4.00

❑ ❑ USA Bi9102 **Grimace on Blue Bike**, 1990, Green Wheels. $3.00-4.00

❑ ❑ USA Bi9103 **Hamburglar on Yellow Bike**, 1990, Red Wheels. $5.00-7.00

❑ ❑ USA Bi9104 **Ronald on Red Bike**, 1990, Yellow Wheels. $3.00-4.00

Comments: Limited Regional Distribution: USA - August 29-September 6, 1991 during clean-up week. No "McDonaldland" Happy Meal boxes or bags given with these premiums. Note: bikes are similar to "Muppet Kids '89" bikes, but are not the same. Bikes dated 1989. Note: picture with McCharacters on bikes connected has bike parts interchanged.

Bi9104 Bi9101 Bi9102 Bi9103

Bi9104

Bi9102

Bi9103

Bi9101

Premiums:

❑ ❑ USA Mc9100 **Happy Meal-O-Don,** 1990, Red Hm Box/Red Dino. $1.00-2.00
❑ ❑ USA Mc9101 **Quarter Pound Cheese-O-Saur,** 1990, QP/Turq Dino. $1.00-2.00
❑ ❑ USA Mc9102 **McNuggets-O-Saurus, 1990,** Yel Chick McNug Box/Grn Dino. $1.00-2.00
❑ ❑ USA Mc9103 **Hot Cakes-O-Dactyl,** 1990, Wht Hot Cakes Cont/Purp Dino. $1.00-2.00
❑ ❑ USA Mc9104 **Big Mac-O-Saurus Rex,** 1990, Big Mac/Org Dino. $1.00-2.00
❑ ❑ USA Mc9105 **Fry-Ceratops,** 1990, French Fries/Yel Dino. $1.00-2.00
❑ ❑ USA Mc9106 **McDino Cone,** 1990, Ice Cream Cone/Blu Dino. $1.00-2.00
❑ ❑ USA Mc9107 **Tri-Shake-Atops,** 1990, Shake/Pink Dino. $1.00-2.00

❑ ❑ USA Mc9126 **Display with Premiums/Motion**, 1991. $75.00-100.00
❑ ❑ USA Mc9164 **Translite/Sm**, 1991. $4.00-5.00
❑ ❑ USA Mc9165 **Translite/Lg**, 1991. $8.00-10.00
❑ ❑ USA Mc9166 **Translite/Lg/X-O Graphic**, 1991. $15.00-20.00
❑ ❑ USA Mc9195 **Pin**, 1990, Org Dino/McDino Changeables. $3.00-4.00

Comments: National Distribution: USA - May 24-June 20, 1991.

McDONALDLAND ON WHEELS HAPPY MEAL®

This promotion consists of four McDonaldland figurines riding on colorful tricycles.

All characters/cycle parts are fully interchangeable and interconnectable with each other to produce a cycle made for one, two, three or four.

This novel idea not only offers great playvalue but also emphasizes McDonald's fun and action.

Children will play for hours!

- Ronald McDonald
- Birdie, the Early Bird
- Grimace
- Hamburglar

For further information contact: Simon Marketing Inc., Phone: (213) 553-4460, Fax: (213) 553-2319
Note: Final design subject to revision.

McDino Changeables Happy Meal, 1991

Bag:

❑ ❑ USA Mc9115 **Hm Bag - 2 McDinos**, 1991. $1.00-2.00

U-3 Premiums:

❑ ❑ USA Mc9108 **U-3 Bronto Cheeseburger,** 1990, Rubber/Burger with Org Dino. $4.00-5.00
❑ ❑ USA Mc9109 **U-3 Small Fry-Ceratops,** 1990, Rubber/Wht Ff/Grn Dino with **Yel Arches.** $4.00-5.00
❑ ❑ USA Mc9110 **U-3 Small Fry-Ceratops,** 1990, Rubber/Wht Ff/Grn Dino with **Red Arches.** $4.00-5.00

Mc9115

Mc9108

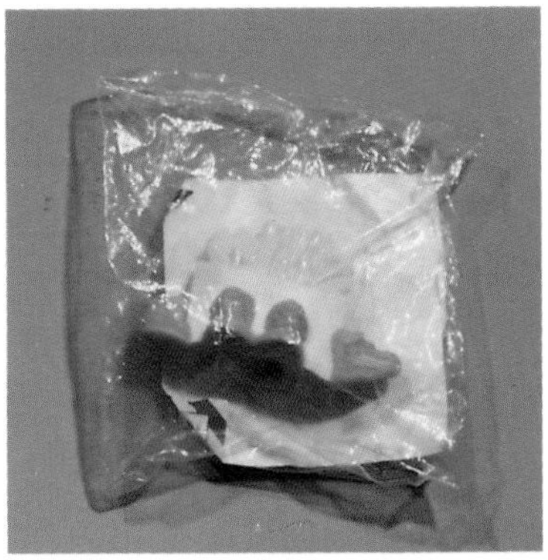

Mc9109

Mc9110

Top row: Mc9108, Mc9101, Mc9103, Mc9106
Bottom row: Mc9110, Mc9100, Mc9102, Mc9104, Mc9105, Mc9107

Mc9126

Mc9165

Mc9195

McDonaldland Circus Parade Happy Meal, 1993/1992/1991

Bag:

❑ ❑ USA Ci9130 **Hm Bag - Circus/Ronald as Ringmaster,** 1990. $1.00-1.50

Premiums:

❑ ❑ USA Ci9101 **Set 1 Ronald,** 1989, Ringmaster/Car with Ronald McDonald. $3.00-4.00

❑ ❑ USA Ci9102 **Set 2 Birdie,** 1989, Bareback Rider. $3.00-4.00

❑ ❑ USA Ci9103 **Set 3 Fry Guy,** 1989, Elephant Trainer. $3.00-4.00

❑ ❑ USA Ci9104 **Set 4 Grimace,** 1989, with Calliope. $3.00-4.00

❑ ❑ USA Ci9164 **Translite/Sm**, 1989. $8.00-10.00

❑ ❑ USA Ci9165 **Translite/Lg**, 1989. $10.00-15.00

❑ ❑ USA Ci9166 **Window Decal,** 1989. $4.00-5.00

Comments: Regional Distribution: USA - March 14-April 11, 1991 and 1992/1993 during clean-up weeks.

Ci9130

Ci9165

Ci9104 Ci9102 Ci9103 Ci9101

Mighty Mini Happy Meal, 1991

Box & Bag:
❑ ❑ USA Mi9110 **Hm Box - Desert Scene with Mini Cars,** 1990. $2.00-3.00
❑ ❑ USA Mi9130 **Hm Bag - Mighty Mini 4x4,** 1990. $1.00-2.00

U-3 Premium:
❑ ❑ USA Mi9104 **U-3 Pocket Pickup,** 1990, Blu with Blk Tires/ Rubber. $4.00-5.00

Premiums:
❑ ❑ USA Mi9100 **Set 1 Dune Buster VW,** 1990, Pnk with Long Twist Crank. $2.00-3.00
❑ ❑ USA Mi9101 **Set 2 Li'l Classic T Bird,** 1990, Yel with Long Twist Crank. $2.00-3.00
❑ ❑ USA Mi9102 **Set 3 Cargo Climber Van,** 1990, Org with Long Twist Crank. $2.00-3.00
❑ ❑ USA Mi9103 **Set 4 Pocket Pickup,** 1990, Red with Long Twist Crank. $2.00-3.00

❑ ❑ USA Mi9164 **Translite/Sm**, 1990. $5.00-10.00
❑ ❑ USA Mi9165 **Translite/Lg**, 1990. $10.00-20.00

Comments: Regional Distribution: USA - March 14-April 11, 1991. Distributed in California, Washington, Pennsylvania and parts of New England.

Mi9111

Mi9130

Mi9110

Mi9104 Mi9100 Mi9101 Mi9102 Mi9103

Mi9164

Muppet Babies III Happy Meal, 1992/1991

Bag:
❑ ❑ USA Mu9130 **Hm Bag - Race to the Finish,** 1990. $2.00-3.00

Premiums:
❑ ❑ USA Mu9100 **Fossie on Red Wagon**, 1990. $2.00-4.00
❑ ❑ USA Mu9101 **Gonzo in Green Airplane**, 1990. $2.00-4.00
❑ ❑ USA Mu9102 **Kermit on Yellow Racer**, 1990. $2.00-4.00
❑ ❑ USA Mu9103 **Miss Piggy on Blue Tricycle**, 1990. $2.00-4.00

❑ ❑ USA Mu9164 **Translite/Sm**, 1990. $5.00-10.00
❑ ❑ USA Mu9165 **Translite/Lg**, 1990. $10.00-20.00

Comments: Regional Distribution: USA - March 8-April 12, 1991 and 1992 during clean-up weeks. Premium markings "Ha! 1990 China." No U-3. All sets recommended for children age one and over.

Mu9130

Mu9103 Mu9100 Mu9101 Mu9102

Mu9165

Nature's Helpers Happy Meal, 1991

Bag:
❑ ❑ USA Na9130 **Hm Bag - Sun/Garden/What Things**, 1990. $1.00-1.50

U-3 Premiums:
❑ ❑ USA Na9105 **U-3 Garden Rake with NO Seed Packet,** 1990, Yel with Molded M and Worm Pic/No Seeds 1p. $4.00-5.00

Premiums: Gardening Tools
❑ ❑ USA Na9100 **Double Digger,** 1990, Grn/with Cucumber Seeds & "Why Trees/Veggies?" Flyer 2p. $1.00-1.25
❑ ❑ USA Na9101 **Bird Feeder,** 1990, with "Why Birds?" Flyer Grn/Wht/Org 3p. $1.00-1.50
❑ ❑ USA Na9102 **Water Can,** 1990, with "Why Flowers?" Flyer/ Blu with Yel Top 1p. $1.00-1.25
❑ ❑ USA Na9103 **Terrarium,** 1990, with Coleus Seeds/ "How..World.." Flyer/Grn Base/Dome 2p. $1.00-1.50
❑ ❑ USA Na9104 **Rake,** 1990, Yel with Marigold Seeds 1p. $1.00-1.25

❑ ❑ USA Na9164 **Translite/Sm**, 1990. $4.00-5.00
❑ ❑ USA Na9165 **Translite/Lg**, 1990. $8.00-10.00

Comments: National Distribution: USA - April 12-May 16, 1991.

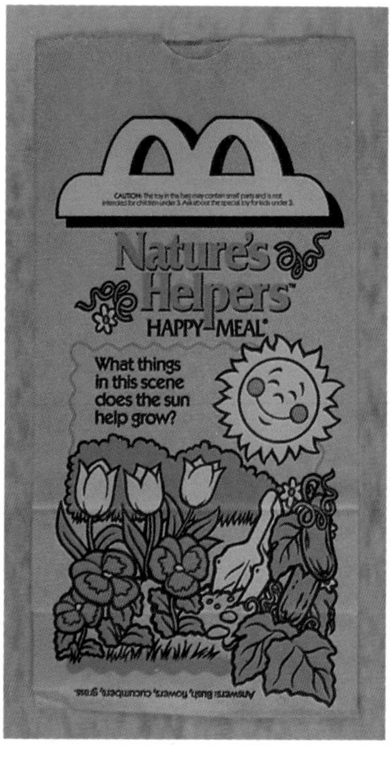

Na9130

Na9105 Na9100 Na9101 Na9102 Na9103

Na9165

Piggsburg Pigs Happy Meal, 1991

Bag:
❑ ❑ USA Pg9130 **Hm Bag - Piggsburg Pigs**, 1990. $1.00-1.50

Premiums:
❑ ❑ USA Pg9100 **Set 1 Portly/Pig Head,** 1990, on Brn Cycle with Grn Side Car. $3.00-5.00
❑ ❑ USA Pg9101 **Set 2 Piggy/Quackers,** 1990, on Brn Crate Racer. $3.00-5.00
❑ ❑ USA Pg9102 **Set 3 Rembrandt,** 1990, in Red Barnyard Hot Rod. $3.00-5.00
❑ ❑ USA Pg9103 **Set 4 Huff/Puff,** 1990, on Yel/Brn Catapult 2p. $3.00-5.00

❑ ❑ USA Pg9164 **Translite/Sm**, 1990. $15.00-20.00
❑ ❑ USA Pg9165 **Translite/Lg**, 1990. $20.00-25.00

Comments: Regional Distribution: USA - March 14-April 11, 1991 in Florida. No U-3. All sets for age one and over. Premium markings - "1990 Fox Ch's Net Inc China."

Pg9100 Pg9101 Pg9102 Pg9103

Pg9130

Pg9165

Pizza Happy Sack Happy Meal, 1991

Bag:
❑ ❑ USA Pi9130 **Hm Bag - "Welcome to My Pizza Party"** McD#90-043, 1989. $10.00-15.00

Premium:
❑ ❑ USA Pi9101 **Hamburglar Figurine,** Nd, 2 1/2" Hamburglar Standing/ Rubber. $20.00-25.00

Comments: Regional Distribution: USA - 1990 and May 1991 in Connecticut and parts of New England. Generic toys could have been given. The test market was supposed to have included a 2 1/2" rubber Hamburglar figurine.

Pi9130

Pi9101

Stencil/Space/Crayons Generic Happy Meal, 1991

Bags:
❑ ❑ USA St9130 **Hm Bag - Ronald with Raised Right Hand Small Bag**, 1990. $.50-1.00
❑ ❑ USA St9131 **Hm Bag - Ronald with Raised Right Hand/ #12 Bag**, 1990. $.50-1.00
❑ ❑ USA St9132 **Hm Bag - Ronald in Spaceship "What Kind of Ship..."/Brown**, 1990. $.50-1.00
❑ ❑ USA St9133 **Hm Bag - Ronald in Spaceship "What Kind of Ship..."/White**, 1990. $.50-1.00

Premiums:
❑ ❑ USA St9101 **Stencil - Grimace,** 1991, Purple with Box 4 Crayons/Blu/Grn/Red/Yel. $1.00-1.50
❑ ❑ USA St9102 **Stencil - Ronald,** 1991, Red with Box 4 Crayons/Blu/Grn/Red/Yel. $1.00-1.50

❑ ❑ USA St9150 **Badge/Crew**, 1991, Build Your Own Hm. $4.00-5.00

Comments: Regional Distribution: USA - 1991. Clean-up week Happy Meal - generic stencils given.

St9130 St9131

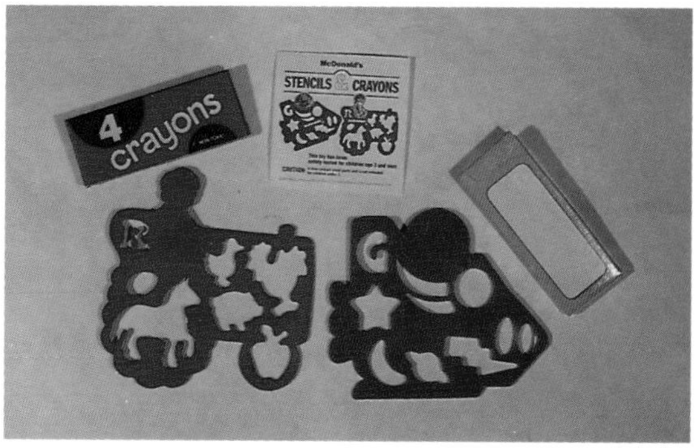

St9102 St9101

Sports Ball Happy Meal, 1991

Premiums:
❑ ❑ USA Sp9155 **Baseball,** 1989, Wht with Red Stitching/Soft with Large Red M. $2.00-3.00
❑ ❑ USA Sp9156 **Basketball,** 1989, Org with Blk Seams/Soft with Large Blk M. $2.00-3.00
❑ ❑ USA Sp9157 **Football - Brown with Yel Lacing**. 1989, Soft with Large Yel "M". $2.00-3.00
❑ ❑ USA Sp9158 **Soccer Ball,** 1989, Red/Yel/Soft with Small Yel M. $2.00-3.00

Comments: Regional Distribution: USA - August/September 1991. Some test areas included Kansas City, Indiana/New England areas. Note: the same test market premiums were regionally issued during clean-up week September 1991. The Premium "tags" had "M-B Sales All New Material" and not "Oak Brook, Il." Note the different colors of the football: brown (1991) versus yellow.

Top row: Sp9155, Sp9157
Bottom row: Sp9156, Sp9158

Super Looney Tunes Happy Meal, 1991

Bag:
❑ ❑ USA Su9130 **Hm Bag - Maze**, 1991. $.50-1.00

U-3 Premium:
❑ ❑ USA Su9105 **U-3 Bat Duck,** 1991, Rocking in His Batmobile. $3.00-4.00

Premiums:
❑ ❑ USA Su9101 **Bugs Bunny/Superbugs,** 1991, with Red/Blu Batman Costume. $2.00-3.00

❑ ❑ USA Su9102 **Tasmanian Devil/Taz-Flash,** 1991, with Red Devil Suit. $2.00-3.00
❑ ❑ USA Su9103 **Petunia Pig/Wonder Pig,** 1991, with Red/Wht/Blu Wonder Woman Suit. $2.00-3.00
❑ ❑ USA Su9104 **Daffy Duck/Bat Duck,** 1991, with Blu/Grey Batman Suit. $2.00-3.00

❑ ❑ USA Su9126 **Display/Premiums**, 1991. $85.00-100.00
❑ ❑ USA Su9164 **Translite/Sm**, 1991. $7.00-10.00
❑ ❑ USA Su9165 **Translite/Lg**, 1991. $10.00-15.00
❑ ❑ USA Su9195 **Pin**, 1991, Bugs/Super Looney Tunes. $3.00-5.00

Comments: National Distribution: USA - November 8-December 5, 1991.

Su9130

Su9105 Su9101 Su9102 Su9103 Su9104

Su9126

Su9165

Tiny Toon Adventures I/Flip-cars/Happy Meal, 1991

Boxes:
❑ ❑ USA Ti9110 **Hm Box - Acme Acres General Store,** 1990. $1.00-2.00
❑ ❑ USA Ti9111 **Hm Box - Forest**, 1990. $1.00-2.00
❑ ❑ USA Ti9112 **Hm Box - Looniversity**, 1990. $1.00-2.00
❑ ❑ USA Ti9113 **Hm Box - Wacky Land,** 1990. $1.00-2.00

U-3 Premiums:
❑ ❑ USA Ti9105 **U-3 Gogo Dodo in Wht Bath Tub**, 1990, Soft Rubber. $3.00-4.00
❑ ❑ USA Ti9106 **U-3 Plucky Duck in Red Boat**, 1990, Soft Rubber. $3.00-4.00

Premiums:
❑ ❑ USA Ti9101 **Babs Bunny in Phone/Plucky Duck in Speed Boat**, 1990. $1.50-2.50
❑ ❑ USA Ti9102 **Buster Bunny in Carrot/Elmira in Wagon**, 1990. $1.50-2.50
❑ ❑ USA Ti9103 **Montana Max in Grn Car/Gogo Dodo in Bath Tub**, 1990. $1.50-2.50
❑ ❑ USA Ti9104 **Hampton Pig in Hero Sandwich/Dizzy Devil in Amp**, 1990. $1.50-2.50

❑ ❑ USA Ti9126 **Display/Premiums**, 1990. $65.00-75.00
❑ ❑ USA Ti9164 **Translite/Sm**, 1990. $4.00-5.00
❑ ❑ USA Ti9165 **Translite/X-0 Graphic/Lg**, 1990. $15.00-25.00

Comments: National Distribution: USA - February 8-March 7, 1991. Premium markings "1990 Warner Bros."

Ti9105

Ti9106

Ti9101 Ti9102 Ti9103 Ti9104

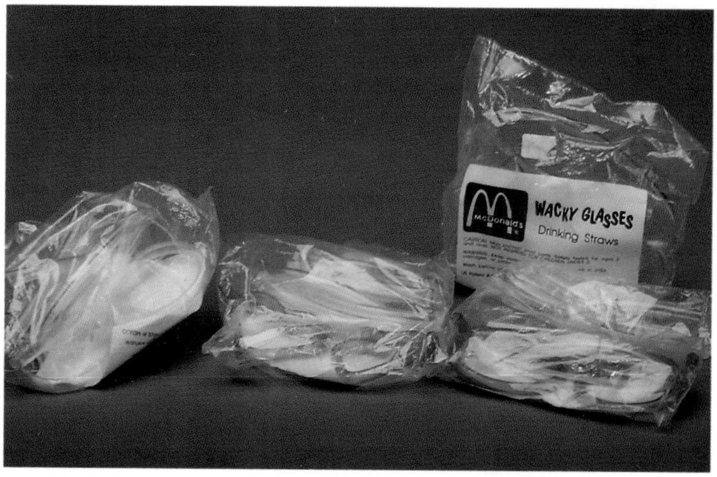

Wa8504 Wa8503 Wa8502 Wa8501

Ti9126

Ti9165

Wacky Glasses Promotion, 1991

Premiums: Seeing Glasses

❑ ❑ USA Wa9101 **Glasses - Plastic drinking straws interwoven - Blue.** $15.00-20.00

❑ ❑ USA Wa9102 **Glasses - Plastic drinking straws interwoven - Clear.** $15.00-20.00

❑ ❑ USA Wa9103 **Glasses - Plastic drinking straws interwoven - Red.** $15.00-20.00

❑ ❑ USA Wa9104 **Glasses - Plastic drinking straws interwoven - Yellow.** $15.00-20.00

Comments: Regional Distribution: USA - 1991 during clean-up weeks. Paper insert says, "US PATENT ...SANSOM INC. PHILA., PA. MADE IN MEXICO." Unconfirmed distribution sites and exact dates. Distributed in parts of Indiana. Originally thought to be distributed in 1985; additional research indicates only 1991.

USA Generic Promotions, 1991

In 1991, the Fun Times Magazine advertising focus was changed from elementary children to pre-teens. Issues were named and not numbered, causing major distribution confusion.

❑ ❑ USA Ge9101 **FTM: 1991-Feb/Mar - Kids Around the World.** $1.00-1.50

❑ ❑ USA Ge9102 **FTM: 1991-Apr/May - Kids/Environ/Earth Can Be Saved.** $1.00-1.50

❑ ❑ USA Ge9103 **FTM: 1991-Jun/Jul - Kids/Games "Summer's Here."** $1.00-1.50

❑ ❑ USA Ge9104 **FTM: 1991-Aug/Sep - Kids Talk "Can Gorilla's Talk?"** $1.00-1.50

❑ ❑ USA Ge9105 **FTM: 1991-Oct/Nov - Kids Collect.** $1.00-1.50

❑ ❑ USA Ge9106 **FTM: 1991-Dec/Jan - Making Holidays Magical/Crafts.** $1.00-1.50

❑ ❑ USA Ge9107 **1991 Calendar: Ronald McDonald House - A Celebration/Spirit of Children.** $2.00-3.00

☐ ☐ USA Ge9108 **1991 Calendar: Ronald McDonald Dino Fun - Facts.** $2.00-3.00

☐ ☐ USA Ge9109 **1991 Calendar: Ronald McDonald Coloring Calendar Fun With The Holidays .** $2.00-3.00

☐ ☐ USA Ge9110 **1991 Cup, Plate, Bowl Set.** $7.00-10.00

Comments: Regional Distribution: USA - 1991.

Ge9110

1992

Back to the Future Happy Meal, 1992
Barbie/Hot Wheels Mini-Streex III Happy Meal, 1992
Batman I Happy Meal, 1992
Behind the Scenes/Explore the Arts Happy Meal, 1992
Cabbage Patch Kids/Tonka Happy Meal, 1992
Crayon Sketch Happy Meal, 1992
Crayon Squeeze Bottle Happy Meal, 1992
Fitness Fun/Michael Jordan Happy Meal, 1992
Halloween '92 Happy Meal, 1992
Mystery of the Lost Arches Happy Meal, 1992
Nature's Watch Happy Meal, 1992
Potato Head Kids II Happy Meal, 1992
Real Ghostbusters II Happy Meal, 1992
Tiny Toon Adventures II Happy Meal, 1992
Water Games Happy Meal, 1992
Wild Friends Happy Meal, 1992
Yo, Yogi! Happy Meal, 1992
Young Astronauts II Happy Meal, 1992
USA Generic Promotions, 1992

- **"What You Want Is What You Get [at McDonald's Today]" jingle**
- **12th National O/O Convention**
- **"Together, we've got what it takes" - O/O Convention theme**

Back to the Future Happy Meal, 1992

Boxes:

☐ ☐ USA Bk9210 **Hm Box - Drive Through Dinocity**, 1991. $1.00-2.00

☐ ☐ USA Bk9211 **Hm Box - Hill Valley Hotel,** 1991. $1.00-2.00

Bk9210 Bk9211

❑ ❑ USA Bk9212 **Hm Box - Make a Drawbridge**, 1991. $1.00-2.00

❑ ❑ USA Bk9213 **Hm Box - Make a Roman Temple**, 1991. $1.00-2.00

Premiums:

❑ ❑ USA Bk9201 **Doc's Delorean Car,** 1991, 1p/Grey/Blu Car with Doc Hanging out Window. $2.00-2.50

❑ ❑ USA Bk9202 **Marty's Hoverboard,** 1991, 1p/Marty on Pink Hvbrd. $2.00-2.50

❑ ❑ USA Bk9203 **Verne's Junkmobile,** 1991, 1p/Verne on Pnk/Red/Grn/Blue Wheels. $2.00-2.50

❑ ❑ USA Bk9204 **Einstein's Traveling Train,** 1991, 1p/Blu Train with Red Wheels. $2.00-2.50

❑ ❑ USA Bk9226 **Display with Premiums**, 1991. $15.00-20.00

❑ ❑ USA Bk9264 **Translite/Sm**, 1991. $3.00-5.00

Comments: National Distribution: USA - April 10-May 7, 1992. Distribution of Doc's Delorean Cars was restricted due to problems with the tires. A Parent's Advisory was issued stating, "Small children have been able to remove rear tires...we strongly recommend that those children who might put these toys in their mouth not be allowed to do so."

Bk9212 Bk9213

Bk9201 Bk9202 Bk9203

Bk9204

Bk9226

Bk9264

Barbie/Hot Wheels Mini-Streex III Happy Meal, 1992

Boxes:

❑ ❑ USA Ba9220 **Hm Box - Beachfront Fun**, 1992. $1.00-1.25

❑ ❑ USA Ba9221 **Hm Box - Magical World**, 1992. $1.00-1.25

❑ ❑ USA Ba9222 **Hm Box - Daredevil Racers**, 1992. $1.00-1.25

❑ ❑ USA Ba9223 **Hm Box - Star Racers**, 1992. $1.00-1.25

U-3 Premiums:

❑ ❑ USA Ba9217 **U-3 Sparkle Eyes,** 1992, Pink Sparkle Dress. $3.00-4.00

❑ ❑ USA Sx9218 **U-3 Orange Arrow,** 1991, Orange/Pink/Blue Mini Streex. $1.00-2.00

Premiums: Barbie Dolls

❑ ❑ USA Ba9201 **Birthday Surprise in a Peach dress,** 1992, Peach Dress/Brn Hair. $2.50-3.50

❑ ❑ USA Ba9202 **My First Ballerina in a Blue Dress,** 1992, Blue Dress/Brn Hair. $2.50-3.50

❑ ❑ USA Ba9203 **Rappin' Rockin in a Black skirt,** 1992, Blk Skirt/Yel Hair. $2.50-3.50

❑ ❑ USA Ba9204 **Rollerblade Barbie on Pink Rollerblades,** 1992, Pink Rollerblades/Yel Hair. $2.50-3.50

❑ ❑ USA Ba9205 **Rose Bride Barbie in a White Bride's dress,** 1992, White Bride Dress. $2.50-3.50

❑ ❑ USA Ba9206 **Snap'n Play Barbie in a Turquoise skirt,** 1992, 2p Turq Skirt/Pink-Purp Dress. $2.50-3.50

❑ ❑ USA Ba9207 **Sparkle Eyes Barbie in a Pink dress,** 1992, Pink Sparkle Dress. $2.50-3.50

❑ ❑ USA Ba9208 **Sun Sensation in a Gold Swim Suit,** 1992, Gold Swim Suit/Turq Wrap. $2.50-3.50

Premiums: Cars With Launchers

❑ ❑ USA Sx9209 **Black Arrow,** 1991, Blk/Purp/Grn with Pnk Launcher. $1.00-1.50

❑ ❑ USA Sx9210 **Blade Burner,** 1991, Yel/Blu/Pnk with Light Blu Launcher. $1.00-1.50

❑ ❑ USA Sx9211 **Flame-Out,** 1991, Blu/Red/Yel with Red Launcher. $1.00-1.50

❑ ❑ USA Sx9212 **Hot Shock,** 1991, Red/Purp/Yel with Yel Launcher. $1.00-1.50

❑ ❑ USA Sx9213 **Night Shadow,** 1991, Blk/Blu/Grn/Yel/Pnk with Purp/Pinkish Launcher. $1.00-1.50

❑ ❑ USA Sx9214 **Quick-Flash,** 1991, Purp/Blu/Grn with Purp Launcher. $1.00-1.50

❑ ❑ USA Sx9215 **Racer-Tracer,** 1991, Grn/Pnk/Blu with Grn Launcher. $1.00-1.50

❑ ❑ USA Sx9216 **Turbo Flyer,** 1991, Blu/Yel/Pnk with Dark Blue Launcher. $1.00-1.50

❑ ❑ USA Ba9226 **Display/Premiums**, 1991. $35.00-50.00

❑ ❑ USA Ba9264 **Translite/Sm**, 1992. $4.00-5.00

Comments: National Distribution: USA - August 7-September 3, 1992. Note: USA Ba9207 Sparkle Eyes Barbie = USA Ba9217 (U-3), except for the packaging.

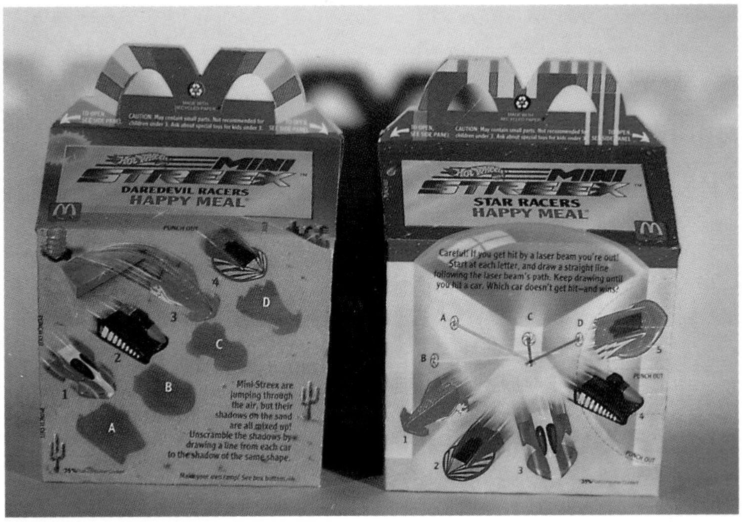

Ba9222 Ba9223

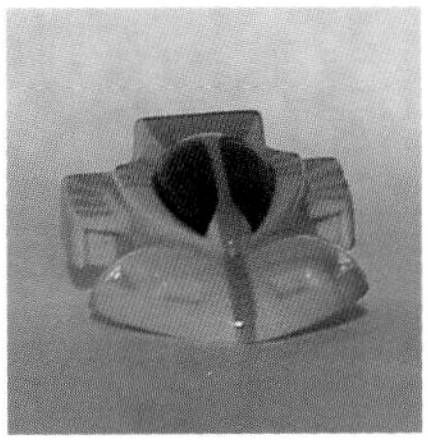

Sx9218

Ba9220 Ba9221

Ba9217 Ba9201 Ba9202 Ba9203 Ba9204

Ba9205 Ba9206 Ba9207 Ba9208

Ba9206

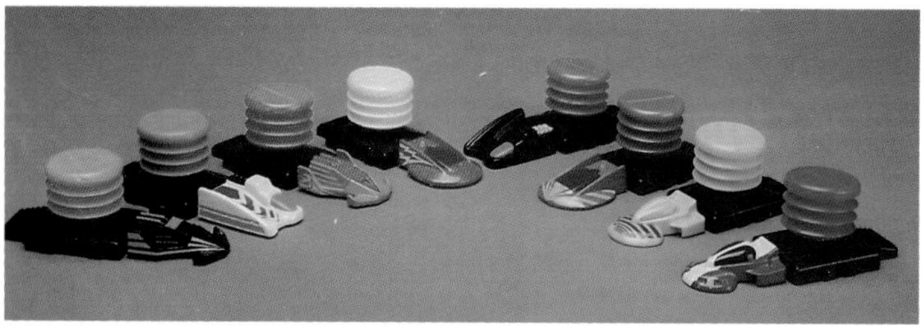

Left to right: Sx9209, Sx9210, Sx9211, Sx9212, Sx9213, Sx9214, Sx9215, Sx9216

Ba9226

Ba9264

Batman I Happy Meal, 1992

Bag:

❑ ❑ USA Bt9230 **Hm Bag - Batman Is Hero**, 1991. $1.00-1.50

Premiums:

❑ ❑ USA Bt9201 **Batman Batmissile,** 1991, Blk Car with Batman Inside/1p. $2.50-3.00

❑ ❑ USA Bt9202 **Batmobile,** 1991, Blk Batmissile/Batmobile/2p. $2.50-3.00

❑ ❑ USA Bt9203 **Catwoman Cat Coupe,** 1991, Purple Cat with Batwoman/Tail Moves/1p. $2.50-3.00

❑ ❑ USA Bt9204 **Penguin Roto-Roadster,** 1991, Yel Car with Umb Red/Wht Front/1p. $2.50-3.00

❑ ❑ USA Bt9226 **Display/Premiums**, 1992. $45.00-50.00

❑ ❑ USA Bt9264 **Translite/Sm**, 1992. $7.00-10.00

❑ ❑ USA Bt9295 **Pin,** 1992, Square/Blk/Wht Batman Returns. $4.00-5.00

❑ ❑ USA Bt9296 **Pin**, 1992, Batman's Face/McDonald's. $4.00-5.00

Comments: National Distribution: USA - June 12-July 9, 1992. A Batman Returns brown bag preceded the promotion. Promotion included ten Batman related plastic cups for drinks, plus two extra cups - special ordered.

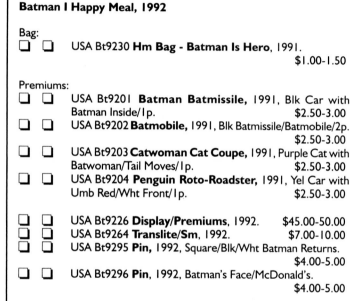

Bt9230

Bt9201 Bt9202 Bt9204

Bt9203

Behind the Scenes/Explore The Arts Happy Meal, 1992

Bag:

❑ ❑ USA Be9230 **Hm Bag, Take a Peek/Screen Play,** 1992. $1.00-1.50

Premiums:

❑ ❑ USA Be9201 **Animation Wheel,** 1992, Blk/Blu with 4 Cartoon Strips/Booklet/2p. $1.00-1.50

❑ ❑ USA Be9202 **Balance Builders,** 1992, Org/Blu/Yel/Grn/Red Stacking Figures/5p. $1.00-1.50

❑ ❑ USA Be9203 **Rub/Draw Templates,** 1992, 6 Templates/1 Turq Holder/7p. $1.00-1.50

❑ ❑ USA Be9204 **Rainbow Viewer,** 1992, Turq/Purp Rect Color Wheel/1p. $1.00-1.50

❑ ❑ USA Be9226 **Display with Premiums**, 1992. $15.00-20.00

❑ ❑ USA Be9244 **Crew Poster**, 1992. $2.00-4.00

❑ ❑ USA Be9264 **Translite/Sm**, 1992. $4.00-5.00

Comments: National Distribution: USA - September 11-October 8, 1992.

Bt9264

Be9230

Bt9295

Bt9296

Be9201 Be9202 Be9203 Be9204

Be9264

Cabbage Patch Kids/Tonka Happy Meal, 1992

Bag:
❑ ❑ USA Cp9230 **Hm Bag - Unscramble the Letters**, 1992. $1.00-1.50

U-3 Premium:
❑ ❑ USA Cp9211 **U-3 Anne Louise,** 1992, Baby Sitting/Purp Bear/Rubber. $2.00-3.00
❑ ❑ USA Tk9212 **U-3 Dump Truck,** 1992, Yel/Blu/Blk Wheels. $1.50-2.00

Left to right: Tk9212, Tk9210, Tk9206, Tk9207, Tk9208, Tk9209

Premiums: Cabbage Patch Dolls
❑ ❑ USA Cp9201 **All Dressed up - in red party dress,** 1992, Red Party Dress/Holding Gift. $1.50-2.50
❑ ❑ USA Cp9202 **Ali Marie - in purple body suit,** 1992, Tiny Dancer/Purp Body Suit/Gold Star. $1.50-2.50
❑ ❑ USA Cp9203 **Fun on Ice - in green/red dress,** 1992, Grn/Red/Wht Muff with Wht Skates. $1.50-2.50
❑ ❑ USA Cp9204 **Holiday Dreamer - in pink/blue PJs,** 1992, Pnk/Blu PJs with Grn Stocking/Bear. $1.50-2.50
❑ ❑ USA Cp9205 **Holiday Pageant - white angel,** 1992, Wht Angel/Gold Long Hair. $1.50-2.50

Premiums: Tonka Trucks
❑ ❑ USA Tk9206 **Loader,** 1992, Yel with Blk Loader. $1.50-2.50
❑ ❑ USA Tk9207 **Cement Mixer,** 1992, Org Cab/Org Mixer. $1.50-2.50
❑ ❑ USA Tk9208 **Dump Truck,** 1992, Yel Cab/Bed. $1.50-2.50
❑ ❑ USA Tk9209 **Fire Truck,** 1992, Red Truck/Wht Ladder. $1.50-2.50
❑ ❑ USA Tk9210 **Backhoe,** 1992, Blu with Blk Hoe. $1.50-2.50
❑ ❑ USA Cp9226 **Display/Premium**, 1992. $35.00-50.00
❑ ❑ USA Cp9264 **Translite/Sm**, 1992. $4.00-5.00

Comments: National Distribution: USA - November 27-December 31, 1992.

Cp9226

Cp9264

Cp9230

Cp9211

Left to right: Cp9201, Cp9202, Cp9203, Cp9204, Cp9205

Crayon Sketch Happy Meal, 1992

Bag:
❑ ❑ USA Cs9230 **Hm Bag - Crayon Sketch/ Place Mailbox**, 1992. $1.00-1.50

Comments: National Distribution: USA - January 1992 during clean-up week. Generic toys were given.

Cs9230

Crayon Squeeze Bottle Happy Meal, 1992

Bag:

❑ ❑ USA Cr9230 **Hm Bag - Kay Bee America's Store/Finish with $5 off Coupon**, 1991. $1.00-1.50

Premiums: Drink Bottles

❑ ❑ USA Cr9201 **Blue Squeeze Drink Bottle,** 1992, 4p/Blu Cup/Lid/Clear Straw/3 Crayons/Yel Box. $4.00-5.00

❑ ❑ USA Cr9202 **Green Squeeze Drink Bottle,** 1992, 4p/Grn Cup/Lid/Clear Straw/3 Crayons/Yel Box. $4.00-5.00

❑ ❑ USA Cr9203 **Red Squeeze Drink Bottle,** 1992, 4p/Red Cup/Lid/Clear Straw/3 Crayons/Yel Box. $4.00-5.00

❑ ❑ USA Cr9204 **Yellow Squeeze Drink Bottle,** 1992, 4p/Yel Cup/Lid/Clear Straw/3 Crayons/Yel Box. $4.00-5.00

❑ ❑ USA Cr9264 **Translite/Sm**, 1992. $8.00-10.00

❑ ❑ USA Cr9265 **Translite/Lg**, 1992. $10.00-15.00

Comments: Regional Distribution: USA - January 31-March 5, 1992 in Albany, New York and Connecticut. Each Happy Meal came with a $5 off yellow coupon from Kay Bee Toy Store. Cups are crayon shaped.

Cr9230

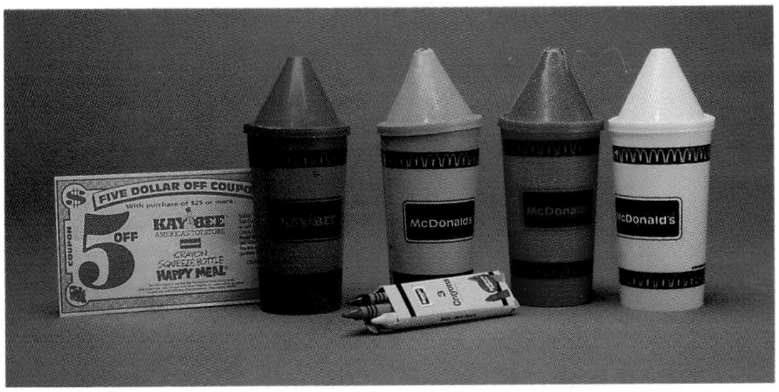

Left to right: Cr920,1 Cr9202, Cr9203, Cr9204

Cr9265

Fitness Fun/Michael Jordan Happy Meal, 1992

Bag:

❑ ❑ USA Mj9230 **Hm Bag - MJ Fitness Fun**, 1991. $1.00-1.50

Premiums: Sports Equipment

❑ ❑ USA Mj9201 **Baseball,** 1991, Wht with MJ Logo. $3.00-4.00

❑ ❑ USA Mj9202 **Basketball,** Nd, Org with MJ Logo. $3.00-4.00

❑ ❑ USA Mj9203 **Flying Disc,** 1991, Turq with MJ Logo. $3.00-4.00

❑ ❑ USA Mj9204 **Football,** 1991, Red/Yel/Turq/Grn with MJ Logo. $3.00-4.00

❑ ❑ USA Mj9205 **Jump Rope,** Nd, Grn with Purp Handle. $3.00-4.00

❑ ❑ USA Mj9206 **Soccer Ball,** 1991, Inflatable Blk/Wht Soccer Ball. $3.00-4.00

❑ ❑ USA Mj9207 **Stop Watch,** 1991, Blk/Grn Stop Watch with MJ. $3.00-4.00

❑ ❑ USA Mj9208 **Squeeze Bottle,** 1991, 3p/Blue Bottle/Purp Lid/Org Straw. $3.00-4.00

❑ ❑ USA Mj9226 **Display/Premiums**, 1992. $25.00-35.00

❑ ❑ USA Mj9264 **Translite/Sm**, 1991. $7.00-10.00

Comments: National Distribution: USA - July 10-August 6, 1992. Each Happy Meal premium came with a mini activity booklet with Michael Jordan's photo.

Mj9230

Mj9201 Mj9202 Mj9203 Mj9204

Mj9205 Mj9206 Mj9207 Mj9208

Mj9226

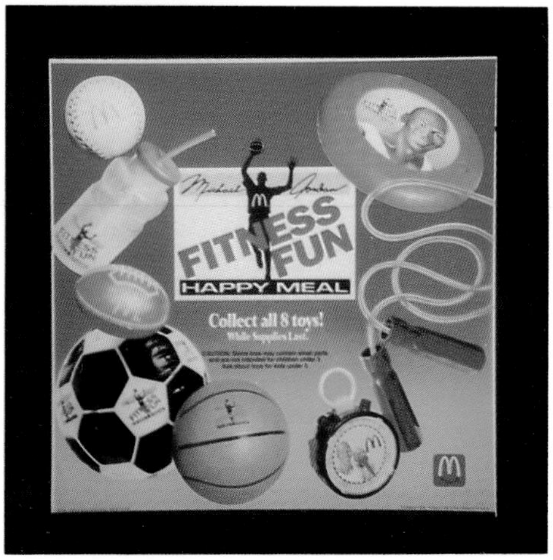

Mj9264

Halloween '92 Happy Meal, 1992

Premiums: Halloween Pails with Cookie Cutter Lids

❑ ❑ USA Ha9201 **Pail: Ghost,** 1986, 3p Wht with Cookie Cutter Lid/Blk Handle. $1.00-1.25

❑ ❑ USA Ha9202 **Pail: Pumpkin,** 1986, 3p Org Cookie Cutter Lid/Blk Handle. $1.00-1.25

❑ ❑ USA Ha9203 **Pail: Witch,** 1986, 3p Grn Cookie Cutter Insert with Blk Handle. $1.00-1.25

❑ ❑ USA Ha9226 **Display**/Paper Background with Purple Box, 1992. $2.00-3.00

❑ ❑ USA Ha9264 **Translite/Sm**, 1992. $4.00-5.00

Comments: National Distribution: USA - October 9-29, 1992.

Ha9201 Ha9202 Ha9203

Ha9226

Ha9264

Mystery of the Lost Arches Happy Meal, 1992

Bag:
❑ ❑ USA My9230 **Hm Bag - Ronald/Pyramids**, 1991. $.25-.50

U-3 Premium:
❑ ❑ USA My9205 **U-3 Magic Lens Camera,** 1991, Wht "Search Team" Decal. $4.00-5.00

Premiums:
❑ ❑ USA My9201 **Magic Lens Camera,** 1991, Silver "Search Team" Decal. $2.00-2.25
❑ ❑ USA My9202 **Micro-Cassette/Magnifier,** 1991, Grn with Slide out Magnifier. $1.00-1.25
❑ ❑ USA My9203 **Phone/Periscope,** 1991, Org Phone. $1.00-1.25
❑ ❑ USA My9204 **Flashlight/Telescope,** 1991, **Red/Blue.** $1.00-1.25
❑ ❑ USA My9206 **Flashlight/Telescope,** 1991, **Red/Yellow.** $1.00-1.25

❑ ❑ USA My9255 **Trayliner,** 1991. $.50-1.00
❑ ❑ USA My9264 **Translite/Sm**, 1991. $3.00-5.00
❑ ❑ USA My9265 **Translite/Lg**, 1991. $5.00-8.00

Comments: National Distribution: USA - January 3-February 2, 1992. The U-3 and Magic Lens camera were recalled during the national promotion due to finger entrapment. The majority of premiums were given out prior to the recall.

Nature's Watch Happy Meal, 1992

Bag:
❑ ❑ USA Na9230 **Hm Bag - Bark like a Tree!/Ron Is on a Nature Hunt,** 1991. $.50-1.00

U-3 Premium:
❑ ❑ USA Na9205 **U-3 Double Shovel-Rake,** 1991, 2p Red Shovel/1p Purp Rake. $1.00-1.50

Premiums:
❑ ❑ USA Na9201 **Bird Feeder,** 1991, 3p Org Lid/Clear Cont/Yel Bot. $1.00-1.25
❑ ❑ USA Na9202 **Double Shovel-Rake,** 1991, 2p Red Shovel/1p Purp Rake. $1.00-1.25
❑ ❑ USA Na9203 **Greenhouse,** 1991, 2p Clear Dome Top/Grn Bot with Pkg Marigold Seeds. $1.00-1.25
❑ ❑ USA Na9204 **Sprinkler,** 1991, 1p Grn Sprinkler Can with Yel Nozzle. $1.00-1.25

❑ ❑ USA Na9226 **Display/Premiums**, 1992. $5.00-10.00
❑ ❑ USA Na9264 **Translite/Sm**, 1991. $3.00-5.00
❑ ❑ USA Na9295 **Pin**, 1992, Rectangle/Turq McDonald's Nature's Watch. $3.00-4.00

Comments: National Distribution: May 8-June 4, 1992. Happy Meal bag came with attached "Toys R Us" coupons. Bird Feeders (USA Na9201) came packaged with and without two Curad Happy Strip Bandaids. USA Na9202 = USA Na9205, loose out of package.

My9230

My9265

Na9230

Left to right: My9201, My9203, My9202, My9205, My9206, My9204

Left to right: Na9201 Na9202 Na9203 Na9204

Na9226

Na9264

Po9230

Po9201

Po9208

Po9206

Po9207

Po9204

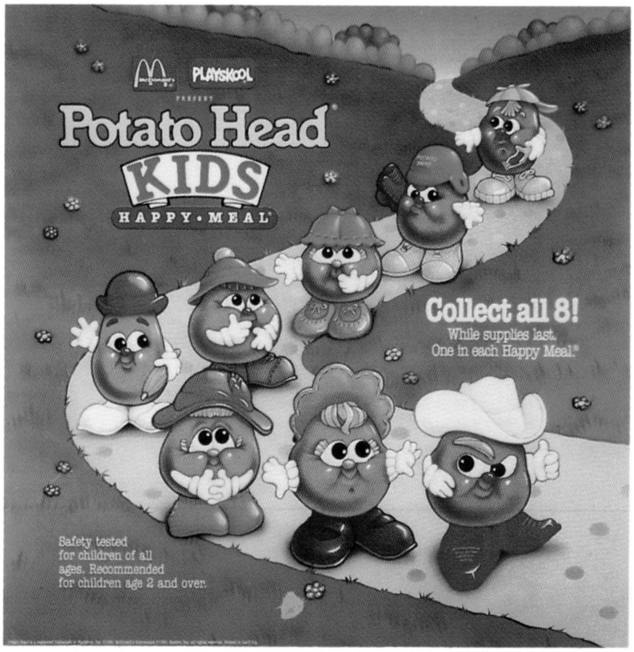

Po9265

Potato Head Kids II Happy Meal, 1992

Bag:

❑ ❑ USA Po9230 **Hm Bag - Eight Potato Head Kids,** 1991. $1.00-1.50

Premiums: Potato Head Kids

❑ ❑ USA Po9201 **Dimples,** 1986, Blu/Yel Hat with Purp Shoes/3p. $4.00-5.00

❑ ❑ USA Po9202 **Spike,** 1986, Slingshot PH with Grn Hat with Yel Shoes/3p. $4.00-5.00

❑ ❑ USA Po9203 **Potato Dumpling,** 1986, Blu Hat with Pnk Shoes/3p. $4.00-5.00

❑ ❑ USA Po9204 **Slugger,** 1986, Baseball Glove PH with PH Skins Blu Hat with Yel Shoes/3p. $4.00-5.50

❑ ❑ USA Po9205 **Slick,** 1986, Holding Umbrella PH with Pinkish Derby Hat with Wht Shoes/3p. $4.00-5.50

❑ ❑ USA Po9206 **Tulip,** 1986, Pnk Hat with Blu Shoes/3p. $4.00-5.00

❑ ❑ USA Po9207 **Potato Puff,** Pnk Hat with Purp Shoes/3p. $4.00-5.00

❑ ❑ USA Po9208 **Spud,** 1986, Yel Eyebrow PH with Wht Cowboy Hat with Red Cowboy Shoes/3p. $4.00-5.00

❑ ❑ USA Po9245 **Register Topper**/Holds 2 PH/Each, 1992. $12.00-15.00

❑ ❑ USA Po9264 **Translite/Sm**, 1992. $7.00-10.00

❑ ❑ USA Po9265 **Translite/Lg**, 1992. $10.00-15.00

Comments: Regional Distribution: USA - January 31-March 5, 1992 in Oklahoma, Texas, northern Florida, Delaware/New Jersey/Connecticut.

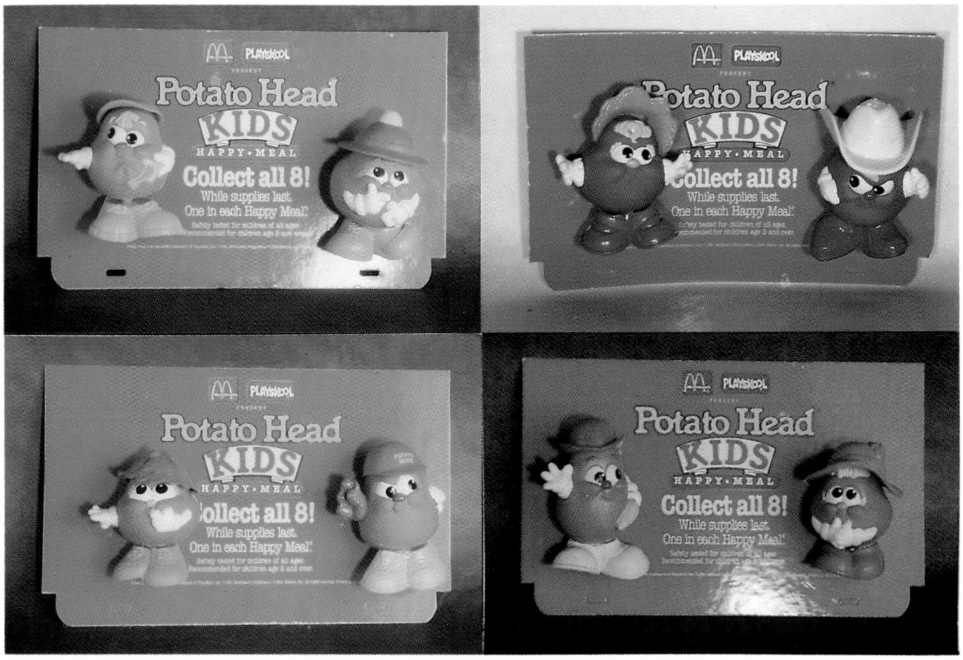

Po9245

Real Ghostbusters II Happy Meal, 1992

Bag:
- ❑ ❑ USA Re9230 **Hm Bag - Real GB Hm/Be an Amazing GB Too**, 1991. $1.00-1.25

U-3 Premium:
- ❑ ❑ USA Re9258 **U-3 Squirting Slimer Squeezer,** 1984, 1p Grn Head Slimer. $4.00-5.00

Premiums:
- ❑ ❑ USA Re9250 **Ecto Siren,** 1984, 1p Bike Siren/Wht Ecto Car with Ecto-1 Stick Sheet. $3.00- 4.00
- ❑ ❑ USA Re9253 **Egon Spinner,** 1984, 3p Grn Bike Attachment/ Blue Spinner/Yel Man. $3.00- 4.00
- ❑ ❑ USA Re9254 **Water Bottle (P.K.E.),** 1984, 2p Yel Bottle/ Blu with GB Sticker Sheet. $5.00-8.00
- ❑ ❑ USA Re9257 **Slimer Horn,** 1984, 1p Grn Slimer Attached to Blue Horn on Bike. $3.00- 4.00

- ❑ ❑ USA Re9264 **Translite/Sm**, 1992. $8.00-10.00
- ❑ ❑ USA Re9265 **Translite/Lg**, 1992. $10.00-15.00

Comments: Regional Distribution: USA - January 31-March 5, 1992 in Kansas City, Kansas. The Water Bottle was recalled prior to distribution due to quality control.

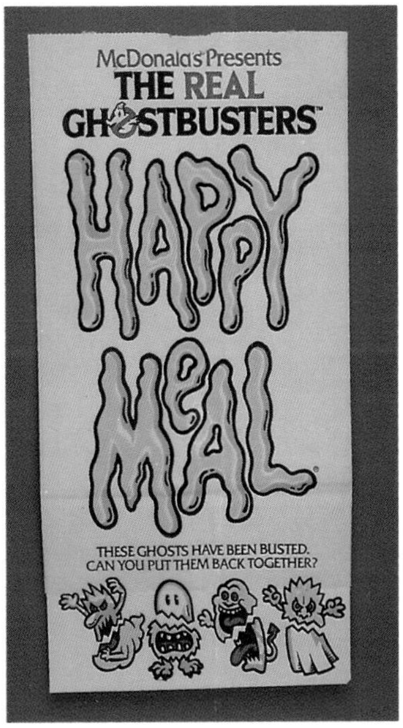

Re9230

Re9258 Re9250 Re9253 Re9254 Re9257

Tiny Toon Adventures II Happy Meal, 1992

Boxes:

❑ ❑ USA Ti9210 **Hm Box - Arctic,** 1992. $1.00-1.25

❑ ❑ USA Ti9211 **Hm Box - Cafe/Wackyland,** 1992. $1.00-1.25

❑ ❑ USA Ti9212 **Hm Box - Forest/Redwood,** 1992. $1.00-1.25

❑ ❑ USA Ti9213 **Hm Box - Jungle,** 1992. $1.00-1.25

U-3 Premium:

❑ ❑ USA Ti9209 **U-3 Sweetie,** 1992, Pink Bunny on Pavement Roller. $2.00-3.50

Premiums:

❑ ❑ USA Ti9201 **Babs Bunny with Record Player,** 1992, Pink Bunny with Tiny Toons Record Player in Bubble. $1.50-2.50

❑ ❑ USA Ti9202 **Buster Bunny in Bumper Car,** 1992, Blu Bunny in Red Bumper Car/Basketball Bubble. $1.50-2.50

❑ ❑ USA Ti9203 **Dizzy Devil in Car,** 1992, Purp Dizzy Devil in Org Bubble Car. $1.50-2.50

❑ ❑ USA Ti9204 **Elmyra in Green Car,** 1992, Girl with Yel Hat in Grn Car with Bunny in Bubble. $1.50-2.50

❑ ❑ USA Ti9205 **Gogo Dodo in Rolling Car,** 1992, Grn Gogo Dodo on Yel 3 Wheel Roller. $1.50-2.50

❑ ❑ USA Ti9206 **Montana Max in Cash Register Car,** 1992, Max in Grn Cash Register Car. $1.50-2.50

❑ ❑ USA Ti9207 **Plucky Duck in Steam Roller,** 1992, Plucky in Blu Steam Roller Car. $1.50-2.50

❑ ❑ USA Ti9208 **Sweetie on Pavement Roller,** 1992, Pink Bunny on Pavement Roller. $1.50-2.50

❑ ❑ USA Ti9226 **Display/Premiums**, 1992. $35.00-50.00

❑ ❑ USA Ti9264 **Translite/Sm**, 1992. $4.00-5.00

Comments: National Distribution: USA - October 30-November 26, 1992. Pop-up Happy Meal boxes have figurines marked "'92/1992 Tm Warner China Cw 2." USA Ti9208 = USA Ti9209, loose out of package.

Ti9210 Ti9213

Ti9212 Ti9211

Top row, left to right: Ti9202, Ti9204, Ti9217
Bottom row, left to right: Ti9201, Ti9203, Ti9215, Ti9216, Ti9218

Ti9226

Ti9264

Water Games Happy Meal, 1992

Bag:

❑ ❑ USA Wa9230 **Hm Bag - Ronald/Dot-To-Dot/How Can Ron Find All His Friends**, 1991. $1.00-1.50

U-3 Premium:

❑ ❑ USA Wa9205 **U-3 Grimace/Squirting Camera,** 1991, 1p Rubber Purp/Yel Gri. $10.00-15.00

Premiums:

❑ ❑ USA Wa9201 **Water Game: Ronald Catching French Fries,** 1991, 1p Yellow Rectangle. $4.00-5.00

❑ ❑ USA Wa9202 **Water Game: Grimace Juggling Shakes,** 1991, 1p Grn Rectangle. $4.00-5.00

❑ ❑ USA Wa9203 **Water Game: Hamburglar Stacking Burgers,** 1991, 1p Orange Rectangle. $4.00-5.00

❑ ❑ USA Wa9204 **Water Game: Birdie Sorting Eggs,** 1991, 1p Pink Rectangle 2" x 3 1/2". $4.00-5.00

❑ ❑ USA Wa9206 **Disclaimer Card,** 1991. $.50-1.00
❑ ❑ USA Wa9264 **Translite/Sm**, 1991. $7.00-10.00
❑ ❑ USA Wa9265 **Translite/Lg**, 1991. $10.00-15.00

Comments: Regional Distribution: USA - January 31-March 5, 1992 in Maryland, Hawaii, Illinois and Washington state. The U-3 Grimace with squirting camera was recalled prior to full distribution due to quality control problems. The McDonaldland Water Games came with a yellow "Parents! Please read first!" card noting "After fill-up, and with normal play, some water exposure is expected."

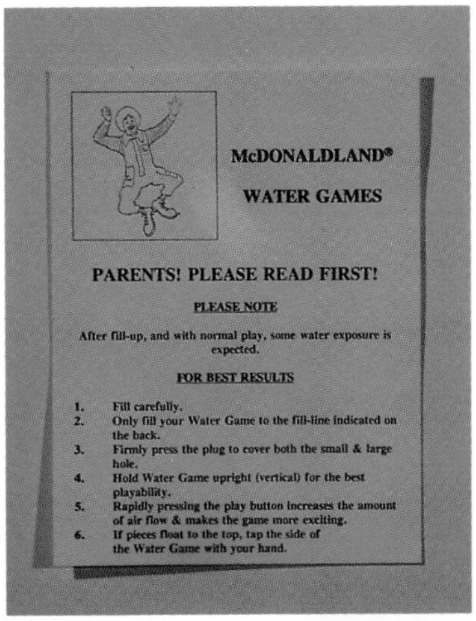
McDONALDLAND® WATER GAMES

PARENTS! PLEASE READ FIRST!

PLEASE NOTE

After fill-up, and with normal play, some water exposure is expected.

FOR BEST RESULTS

1. Fill carefully.
2. Only fill your Water Game to the fill-line indicated on the back.
3. Firmly press the plug to cover both the small & large hole.
4. Hold Water Game upright (vertical) for the best playability.
5. Rapidly pressing the play button increases the amount of air flow & makes the game more exciting.
6. If pieces float to the top, tap the side of the Water Game with your hand.

Wa9206

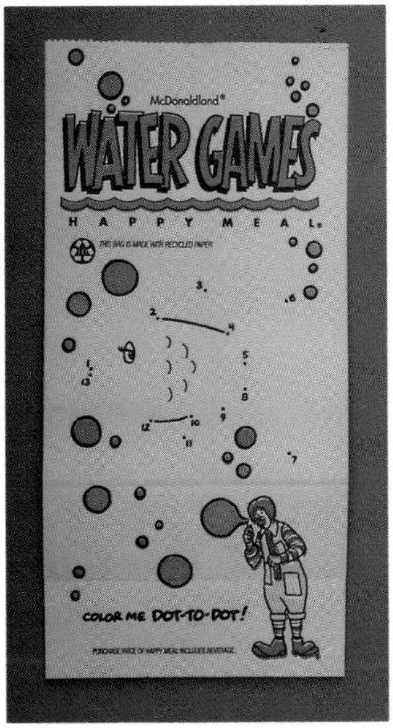

Wa9230

Wa9205

Wa9265

Wa9204 Wa9202 Wa9203 Wa9201

Wild Friends Happy Meal, 1992

Bag:
❑ ❑ USA Wi9230 **Hm Bag - 4 Wild Friends/ Gorilla/Elephant/Crock/Panda**, 1991 $1.00-1.25

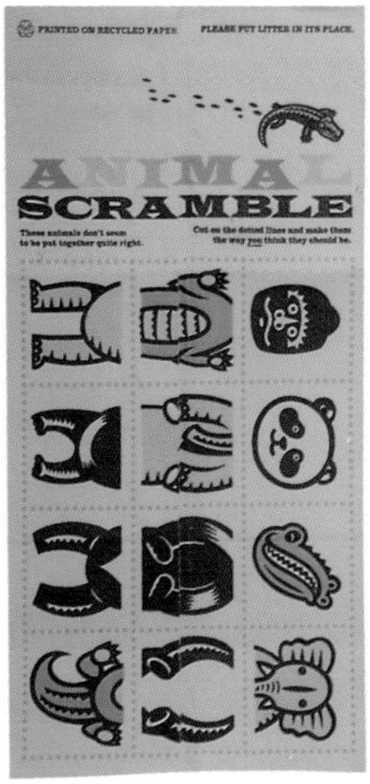

Wi9230

U-3 Premium:

❑ ❑ USA Wi9205 **U-3 Giant Panda,** Nd, 1p Blk/Wht Soft Rubber Panda with Grn Bamboo. $4.00-5.00

Premium:

❑ ❑ USA Wi9201 **Elephant on book,** 1992, Grn Book/Moving Grey Eleph. $4.00-5.00
❑ ❑ USA Wi9202 **Crocodile on book,** 1992, Pnk Book/with Grn Croc. $4.00-5.00
❑ ❑ USA Wi9203 **Gorilla on book,** 1992, Yel Book/with Moving Grey Gorilla. $4.00-5.00
❑ ❑ USA Wi9204 **Giant Panda on book,** 1992, Blu Book/with Blk/Wht Panda. $4.00-5.00

❑ ❑ USA Wi9241 **Dangler/Display**, 1992. $10.00-15.00
❑ ❑ USA Wi9264 **Translite/Sm**, 1992. $5.00-8.00
❑ ❑ USA Wi9265 **Translite/Lg**, 1992. $10.00-15.00

Comments: Regional Distribution: USA - January 31-March 5, 1992 in southern California and Indiana. The attached mini books are marked with McDonald's logo.

Yo, Yogi! Happy Meal, 1992

Bag:

❑ ❑ USA Yo9230 **Hm Bag - Yogi/Jellystone Park**, 1991. $1.00-1.25

Premiums:

❑ ❑ USA Yo9201 **Laf 1: Yo, Yogi on Wave Jumper,** 1991, Org Squad Wave Jumper. $3.00-4.00
❑ ❑ USA Yo9202 **Laf 2: Cindy Bear on Scooter,** 1991, Grn Squad Scooter. $3.00-4.00
❑ ❑ USA Yo9203 **Laf 3: Huckleberry Hound in Race Car,** 1991, Yel Race Car. $3.00-4.00
❑ ❑ USA Yo9204 **Laf 4: Boo Boo Bear on Skate Board,** 1991, Squad Skate Board. $3.00-4.00

❑ ❑ USA Yo9264 **Translite/Sm**, 1992. $5.00-8.00
❑ ❑ USA Yo9265 **Translite/Lg**, 1992. $10.00-15.00

Comments: Regional Distribution: USA - January 31-March 5, 1992 in California, northern Florida, northern Georgia and parts of Alabama.

Left to right: Wi9205, Wi920, I Wi9202, Wi9203, Wi9204

Wi9241

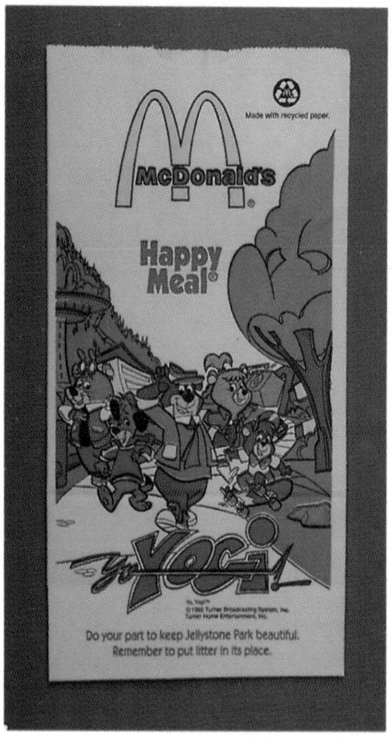

Yo9230

Yo9265

Wi9265

Yo9201 Yo9202 Yo9203 Yo9204

Young Astronauts II Happy Meal, 1992

Bag:
❑ ❑ USA As9230 **Hm Bag - From Space/Space Speak**, 1991. $1.00-1.25

U-3 Premium:
❑ ❑ USA As9205 **U-3 Ronald in Lunar Rover,** 1991, Red Rubber Rover/Yel Spacesuit Ron. $1.00-2.50

Premiums: Paper Space Vehicles
❑ ❑ USA As9201 **Command Module,** 1991, 13p/Cardboard. $1.00-1.50
❑ ❑ USA As9202 **Lunar Rover,** 1991, 13p/Cardboard. $1.00-1.50
❑ ❑ USA As9203 **Satellite Dish,** 1991, 8p/Cardboard. $1.00-1.50
❑ ❑ USA As9204 **Space Shuttle,** 1991, 10p/Cardboard. $1.00-1.50

❑ ❑ USA As9226 **Display/Premiums**, 1992. $15.00-20.00
❑ ❑ USA As9264 **Translite/Sm**, 1991. $4.00-5.00

Comments: National Distribution: USA - March 6-April 2, 1992. Sets consist of heavy printed cardboard one pieces with a black rubber connector.

As9203 As9204

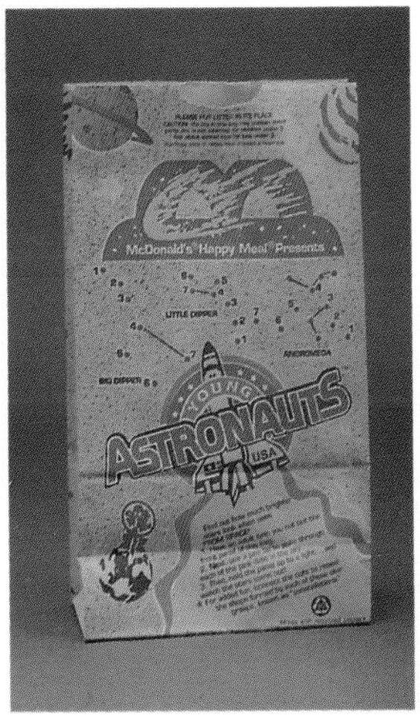

As9230

As9205

As9205

As9226

As9201 As9202

As9264

USA Generic Promotions, 1992

By January/February 1992, Fun Times Magazine resumed numbering the issues and continued them with themed issues.

❑ ❑ USA Ge9201 **FTM: 1992-Issue 1 Making Movies (Feb-Mar).** $1.00-1.50
❑ ❑ USA Ge9202 **FTM: 1992-Issue 2 Far Out Fun! (Apr-May).** $1.00-1.50
❑ ❑ USA Ge9203 **FTM: 1992-Issue 3 Super Sports (Jun-Jul).** $1.00-1.50
❑ ❑ USA Ge9204 **FTM: 1992-Issue 4 Amazing Animal Actors (Aug-Sep).** $1.00-1.50
❑ ❑ USA Ge9205 **FTM: 1992-Issue 5 Read On Write On (Oct-Nov).** $1.00-1.50
❑ ❑ USA Ge9206 **FTM: 1992-Issue 6 Cool Holiday Crafts! (Dec-Jan).** $1.00-1.50

❑ ❑ USA Ge9207 **1992 Calendar: Ronald McDonald A Celebration Of The Spirit Of Children** $2.00-3.00

Comments: Regional Distribution: USA - 1992. The world's largest McDonald's opened in Beijing, China in 1992, employing over 1,000 crew members.

The 12th National O/O Convention was held in Orlando, Florida with the theme "Together we've got what it takes" bonding the owner/operators.

1993

Barbie/Hot Wheels IV Happy Meal, 1993
Batman II, the Animated Series Happy Meal, 1993
Dino-Motion Dinosaurs Happy Meal, 1993
Field Trip Happy Meal, 1993
Food Fundamentals Happy Meal, 1993
Halloween '93 McNugget Buddies Happy Meal, 1993
Linkables Happy Meal, 1993
Looney Tunes Quack up Car Chase Happy Meal, 1993
M Squad Happy Meal, 1993
Nickelodeon Game Gadgets Happy Meal, 1993
Out for Fun Happy Meal, 1993
Snow White and the Seven Dwarfs Happy Meal, 1993
Totally Toy Holiday Happy Meal, 1993
USA Generic Promotions, 1993

• **"McWorld"**

Barbie/Hot Wheels IV Happy Meal, 1993

Bag:
❑ ❑ USA Ba9330 **Hm Bag - Barbie/Hot Wheels,** 1993. $1.00-1.25

U-3 Premium:
❑ ❑ USA Ba9317 **U-3 Tool Set,** 1991, 2p/Plastic/Blu Wrench/Yel Hammer. $2.00-3.00

Premiums: Barbie Dolls
❑ ❑ USA Ba9301 **Birthday Party - Black Barbie with Birthday Cake.** $2.00-2.50
❑ ❑ USA Ba9302 **Hollywood Hair - in a Gold Short Dress on a Blue Star Base.** $2.00-2.50
❑ ❑ USA Ba9303 **My First Ballerina - in a Purp Ballerina Dress with Brn Long Syn Hair.** $2.00-2.50
❑ ❑ USA Ba9304 **Paint 'N Dazzle - in a Pink Short Skirt/"B" Stage/Long Blonde Syn Hair.** $2.00-2.50
❑ ❑ USA Ba9305 **Romantic Bride - in a Wht Long Gown with Peach Bouquet/Long Blonde Hair.** $2.00-2.50
❑ ❑ USA Ba9306 **Secret Heart - in a Wht/Rose Long Gown/Holding Red Heart/Long Blonde Hair.** $2.00-2.50
❑ ❑ USA Ba9307 **Twinkle Lights - in a Pink/Wht Gown/Wht Purse/Long Blonde Syn Hair.** $2.00-2.50
❑ ❑ USA Ba9308 **Western Stampin' - in a Blue/Silver Western Outfit/Cow Girl Hat.** $2.00-2.50

Premiums: Hot Wheel Cars
❑ ❑ USA Hw9309 **McD Funny Car,** 1993, Red/Wht/"McDonald's" on Side. $1.00-1.50
❑ ❑ USA Hw9310 **Quaker State Racer #62,** 1993, Grn Quaker State #62. $1.00-1.50
❑ ❑ USA Hw9311 **McD Thunderbird #27,** 1993, Red Thunderbird #27 with "M" Logo on Hood. $1.00-1.50
❑ ❑ USA Hw9312 **Hot Wheels Funny Car,** 1993, Wht/Red/Yel "Hot Wheels" on Side Funny Car. $1.00-1.50
❑ ❑ USA Hw9313 **McD Dragster,** 1993, Red Dragster with "McD" Logo on Side/Hood. $1.00-1.50
❑ ❑ USA Hw9314 **Hot Wheels Camaro #1,** 1993, Blu Camaro with "Hot Wheels 1" on Side. $1.00-1.50
❑ ❑ USA Hw9315 **Duracell Racer #88,** 1993, Yel with "Duracell" on Side and Hood. $1.00-1.50
❑ ❑ USA Hw9316 **Hot Wheels Dragster,** 1993, Blk/Yel Dragster with "Hot Wheels" on Side. $1.00-1.50

❑ ❑ USA Ba9326 **Display with Premiums,** 1993. $50.00-75.00
❑ ❑ USA Ba9364 **Translite/Sm,** 1993. $5.00-10.00

Comments: National Distribution: USA - August 6-September 2, 1993. USA Ba9205 "Rose Bride Barbie" from 1992 promotion (No U-3 markings on the MIP package) was substituted for the U-3 girl premium. The U-3 boy premium was the Hot Wheels wrench and hammer set (U-3 zebra-striped bag).

Ba9330

Ba9326

Ba9364

Top row, left to right: Ba9301, Ba9302, Ba9303, Ba9304
Bottom row, left to right: Ba9305, Ba9306, Ba9307, Ba9308

Ba9317

Top row: Hw9311, Hw9314
Center row: Hw9310, Hw9313, Hw9315
Bottom row: Hw9309, Hw9312, Hw9316

Batman II, the Animated Series Happy Meal, 1993

Boxes:

❑ ❑ USA Bt9310 **Hm Box - Crazy Car - Nival**, 1993. $1.00-1.25

❑ ❑ USA Bt9311 **Hm Box - How Does Your Gotham City Grow?**, 1993. $1.00-1.25

❑ ❑ USA Bt9312 **Hm Box - The Great Catnapping Caper**, 1993. $1.00-1.25

❑ ❑ USA Bt9313 **Hm Box - Two Face/Riddler/Poison Ivy**, 1993. $1.00-1.25

U-3 Premium:

❑ ❑ USA Bt9309 **U-3 Batman,** 1993, Blk Batman with Attached Cape. $3.00-5.00

Premiums:

❑ ❑ USA Bt9301 **Joker,** 1993, Purp Car/Yel Wheels with Joker's Head as Hood Ornament. $2.00-3.50

❑ ❑ USA Bt9302 **Poison Ivy,** 1993, Red Headed Woman/Grn Car with Pnk Flower. $2.00-3.50

❑ ❑ USA Bt9303 **Robin,** 1993, Robin in Red Motorcycle/Lg R on Front. $2.00-3.50

❑ ❑ USA Bt9304 **Two Face,** 1993, Wht/Blk Two Face/Wht Flip Car with Red Wheels. $2.00-3.50

❑ ❑ USA Bt9305 **Batgirl,** 1993, Gry Batgirl with Blu Cape/2p. $2.00-3.50

❑ ❑ USA Bt9306 **Batman,** 1993, Gry/Blk Batman with Blk Removable Cape/2p. $2.00-3.50

❑ ❑ USA Bt9307 **Catwoman/Leopard,** 1993, Gry/Blk Catwoman with Yel Leopard/2p. $2.00-3.50

❑ ❑ USA Bt9308 **Riddler,** 1993, Grn Jacket/Gry Tie/Purp Mask/Gloves. $2.00-3.50

❑ ❑ USA Bt9326 **Display/Premiums**, 1993. $45.00-75.00

❑ ❑ USA Bt9364 **Translite/Sm**, 1993. $5.00-8.00

Comments: National Distribution: USA - November 5-25, 1993. The cars are marked "1993 Dc China." Note: no McDonald's markings.

Bt9310 Bt9311

From left: Bt9309, Bt9301, Bt9302, Bt9303, Bt9304, Bt9305, Bt9306, Bt9307, Bt9308

Bt9309

Bt9326

Dino-Motion Dinosaurs Happy Meal, 1993

Boxes:

❑ ❑ USA Di9310 **Hm Box - A Tree-Mendous Lunch**, 1992. $1.00-1.25

❑ ❑ USA Di9311 **Hm Box - Baby Food**, 1992. $1.00-1.25

❑ ❑ USA Di9312 **Hm Box - Bob-Labrea High School,** 1992. $1.00-1.25

❑ ❑ USA Di9313 **Hm Box - Cave Sweet Cave**, 1992. $1.00-1.25

U-3 Premium:

❑ ❑ USA Di9307 **U-3 Baby Sinclair,** 1992, 1p Rubber Yel Baby in Eggshell. $2.00-3.00

Premiums:

❑ ❑ USA Di9301 **Baby Sinclair,** 1992, 1p Yel Baby Dino Holding Pot. $1.00-1.50

❑ ❑ USA Di9302 **Charlene Sinclair,** 1992, 1p Grn Mother with Phone. $1.00-1.50

❑ ❑ USA Di9303 **Earl Sinclair,** 1992, 1p Blu/Grn Pop with Lunch Box. $1.00-1.50

❑ ❑ USA Di9304 **Fran Sinclair,** 1992, 2p Pnk/Grn Holding Spoon. $1.00-1.50

❑ ❑ USA Di9305 **Grandma Ethyl,** 1992, 1p Pnk/Purp in Chair. $1.00-1.50

❑ ❑ USA Di9306 **Robbie Sinclair,** 1992, 1p Red/Grn with Guitar. $1.00-1.50

❑ ❑ USA Di9326 **Display/Premiums**, 1992. $10.00-15.00

❑ ❑ USA Di9364 **Translite/Sm**, 1992. $3.00-5.00

Comments: National Distribution: USA - February 5-March 4, 1993.

Di9313 Di9310

Di9311 Di9312

Di9307

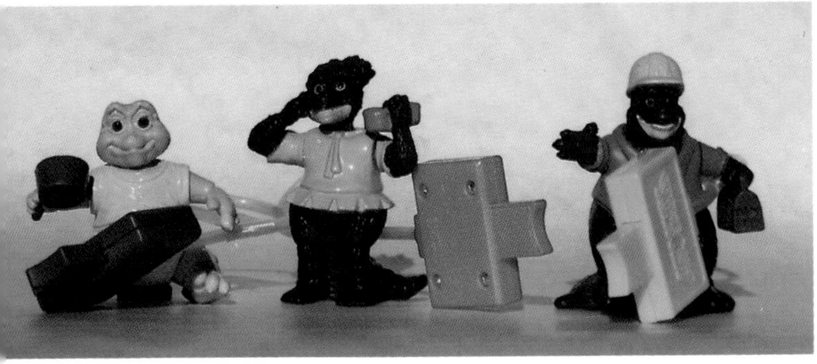
Di9301 Di9302 Di9303

Di9304 Di9305 Di9306

Di9326

Di9364

Field Trip Happy Meal, 1993

Bag:
❑ ❑ USA Fi9330 **Hm Bag - What Do Leaves Say...,** 1993. $1.00-1.25

U-3 Premium: Nature Viewer
❑ ❑ USA Fi9305 **U-3 Nature Viewer,** 1993. $3.00-5.00

Premiums:
❑ ❑ USA Fi9301 **Nature Viewer,** 1993, Magnifier Bottle/2p. $1.00-1.25
❑ ❑ USA Fi9302 **Leaf Printer,** 1993, Yellow Leaf Holder with red crayon/2p. $1.00-1.25
❑ ❑ USA Fi9303 **Kaleidoscope,** 1993, Blue viewer. $1.00-1.25
❑ ❑ USA Fi9304 **Vinyl Bag,** 1993, Explorer Bag in Wht/Grn Plastic. $1.00-1.25

❑ ❑ USA Fi9326 **Display/Premiums**, 1993. $5.00-10.00
❑ ❑ USA Fi9364 **Translite/Sm**, 1993. $3.00-4.00

Comments: National Distribution: USA - September 10-October 7, 1993. U-3 and Fi9301 are the same, except for the packaging.

Fi9330

Fi9305

Fi9301 Fi9302 Fi9303 Fi9304

Fi9326

Fi9364

Fo9326

Fo9364

Food Fundamentals Happy Meal, 1993

Bag:
❑ ❑ USA Fo9330 **Hm Bag - Rhyme Hungry!/Platter Chatter**, 1992. $1.00-1.25

U-3 Premium:
❑ ❑ USA Fo9305 **U-3 Dunkan,** 1993, 1p Rubber Yel Ear of Corn with Red Basketball. $2.00-3.00

Premiums:
❑ ❑ USA Fo9301 **Milly - Wht Milk Carton with Milk Carton Shaped Note Pad/2p.** $1.00-1.50
❑ ❑ USA Fo9302 **Otis - Brn/Blu Sandwich with Helmet with Sandwich Note Pad/2p.** $1.00-1.50
❑ ❑ USA Fo9303 **Ruby - Red Apple with Apple Shaped Note Pad/2p.** $1.00-1.50
❑ ❑ USA Fo9304 **Slugger - Brn/Grn Steak with Steak Shaped Note Pad/2p.** $1.00-1.50

❑ ❑ USA Fo9326 **Display/Premiums**, 1992. $5.00-10.00
❑ ❑ USA Fo9364 **Translite/Sm**, 1992. $3.00-4.00

Comments: National Distribution: USA - March 5-April 8, 1993.

Halloween '93 McNugget Buddies Happy Meal, 1993

Boxes:
❑ ❑ USA Ha9310 **Hm Box - Bobbin for ...What?/Pumpkin**, 1993. $1.00-1.25
❑ ❑ USA Ha9311 **Hm Box - Mummie McNugget/Skeleton**, 1993. $1.00-1.25
❑ ❑ USA Ha9312 **Hm Box - Vampire Hotel/Bat**, 1993. $1.00-1.25

U-3 Premium:
❑ ❑ USA Ha9307 **U-3 McBoo McNugget,** 1992, Wht Ghost/2p. $4.00-5.00

Premiums:
❑ ❑ USA Ha9301 **McBoo McNugget,** 1992, Wht Ghost/2p. $3.00-3.50
❑ ❑ USA Ha9302 **Monster McNugget,** 1992, Grn Hat/Purp Pants/Grn Hands/3p. $3.00-3.50
❑ ❑ USA Ha9303 **Mummy McNugget,** 1992, Wht Hat/Spider/Wht Pants/3p. $3.00-3.50

Fo9330

Fo9305 Fo9301 Fo9302 Fo9303 Fo9304

❑ ❑ USA Ha9304 **McNuggla,** 1992, Blk Hat/Bat/Blk Cape/3p. $3.00-3.50
❑ ❑ USA Ha9305 **Pumpkin McNugget,** 1992, Org Pump Hat/Pump Base/3p. $3.00-3.50
❑ ❑ USA Ha9306 **Witchie McNugget,** 1992, Blk Witch Hat/Purp Cape/Broom/3p. $3.00-3.50

❑ ❑ USA Ha9313 **Nickelodeon Magazine**, 1993. $.25-.50
❑ ❑ USA Ha9326 **Display/Premiums**, 1993. $40.00-50.00
❑ ❑ USA Ha9364 **Translite/Sm**, 1993. $4.00-7.00

Comments: National Distribution: USA - October 8-29, 1993. The Nickelodeon Halloween Magazine was distributed with the Happy Meal. USA Ha9301 = Ha9307, loose out of package.

Ha9304 Ha9306 Ha9301

Ha9302 Ha9305 Ha9303

Ha9310 Ha9311 Ha9312

Ha9307

Ha9364

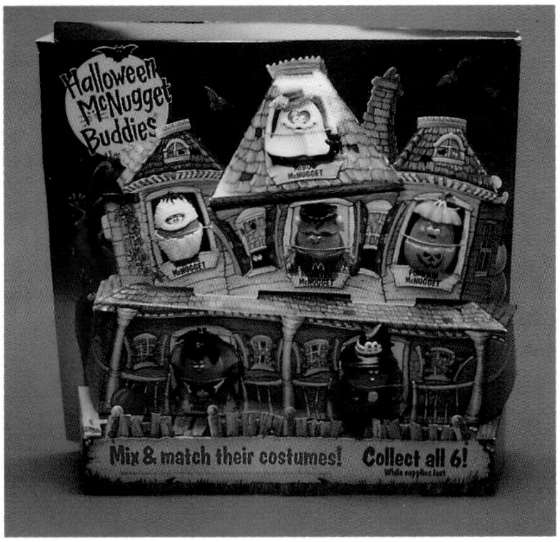

Ha9326

Linkables Happy Meal, 1993

Premiums:

❑ ❑ USA Li9301 **Birdie on a Tricycle**, 1990, 2p Blu/Pnk/Yel, 1990. $3.00-4.00
❑ ❑ USA Li9302 **Grimace in a Wagon**, 1990, 2p Red Wagon, 1990. $3.00-4.00
❑ ❑ USA Li9303 **Hamburglar in an Airplane**, 1990, 2p Grn/Yel. $3.00-4.00
❑ ❑ USA Li9304 **Ronald in a Soap-Box Racer**, 1990, 2p Yel/Red. $3.00-4.00

Li9301 Li9302 Li9303 Li9304

Comments: Limited Regional Distribution: USA - August/September 1993 during clean-up week in Vermont and parts of New England. Released in 1993 with package dated 1990. No specific Happy Meal boxes were given with these premiums.

Lo9310

Lo9326

Lo9312 Lo9313

Lo9364

Lo9301 Lo9302 Lo9303 Lo9304

Left: Lo9301
Right: Lo9307

Looney Tunes Quack up Car Chase Happy Meal, 1993

Boxes:

❑ ❑ USA Lo9310 **Hm Box - Kooky Color World/Purp,** 1992. $1.00-1.25

❑ ❑ USA Lo9311 **Hm Box - Mixed-Up World/Blu**, 1992. $1.00-1.25

❑ ❑ USA Lo9312 **Hm Box - Underwater World/Grn**, 1992. $1.00-1.25

❑ ❑ USA Lo9313 **Hm Box - Upside-Down Space World/Red**, 1992. $1.00-1.25

U-3 Premiums:

❑ ❑ USA Lo9305 **U-3 Swingin' Sedan - Bugs Bunny in Red Car**, 1992, Rubber. $3.00-4.00

❑ ❑ USA Lo9306 **U-3 Swingin' Sedan - Bugs Bunny in Orange Car**, 1992, Rubber. $4.00-5.00

Premiums:

☐ ☐ USA Lo9301 **Bugs Super Stretch Limo,** 1992, **Red Car Stretches**/Sports Car. $2.00-2.50

☐ ☐ USA Lo9307 **Bugs Super Stretch Limo,** 1992, **Org Car Stretches**/Sports Car. $2.50-3.50

☐ ☐ USA Lo9302 **Daffy Splittin Sports,** 1992, **Yel Car Splits Open.** $2.00-2.50

☐ ☐ USA Lo9303 **Porky Ghost Catcher,** 1992, **Grn Car Ghost Pops Out.** $2.00-2.50

☐ ☐ USA Lo9304 **Taz Tornado Tracker,** 1992, **Turq Car Taz Spins.** $2.00-2.50

☐ ☐ USA Lo9326 **Display/Premiums**, 1992. $35.00-50.00

☐ ☐ USA Lo9364 **Translite/Sm**, 1992. $5.00-8.00

Comments: National Distribution: USA - April 9-May 6, 1993. The orange U-3 and orange stretch limo were distributed in the southeast.

Ms9364

Ms9330

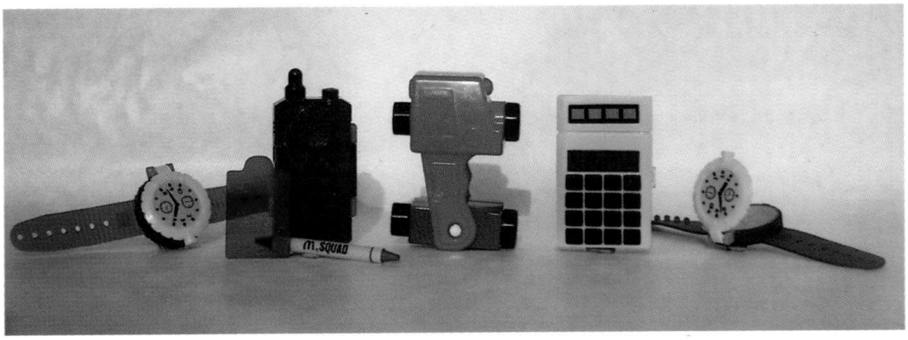

Ms9305 Ms9301 Ms9302 Ms9303 Ms9304

Ms9326

M Squad Happy Meal, 1993

Bag:

☐ ☐ USA Ms9330 **Hm Bag - Top Secret,** 1992. $1.00-1.25

U-3 Premium:

☐ ☐ USA Ms9305 **U-3 Spy-Tracker Watch,** 1992, Watch Becomes a Compass. $2.00-3.00

Premiums:

☐ ☐ USA Ms9301 **Spy-Coder,** 1992, Walkie-Talkie with Blu/Red Crayon with Decoder/3p. $2.00-2.50

☐ ☐ USA Ms9302 **Spy-Noculars,** 1992, Red/Blu Video Cam That Turns into Binoculars/1p. $2.00-2.50

☐ ☐ USA Ms9303 **Spy-Stamper Pad,** 1992, Stamper with Ink Pad Turns into a Calculator/2p. $2.00 -2.50

☐ ☐ USA Ms9304 **Spy-Tracker Watch,** 1992, Watch Becomes a Compass/Opens/1p. $2.00-2.50

☐ ☐ USA Ms9326 **Display with Premiums**, 1992. $5.00-10.00

☐ ☐ USA Ms9364 **Translite/Sm**, 1992. $3.00-5.00

Comments: National Distribution: USA - January 8-February 4, 1993.

Nickelodeon Game Gadgets Happy Meal, 1993

Bag:
❑ ❑ USA Ni9330 **Hm Bag - Nickelodeon Game Gadgets**, 1991. $1.00-1.25

U-3 Premium:
❑ ❑ USA Ni9305 **U-3 Blimp,** 1992, Red Rubber Blimp. $2.00-3.00

Premiums:
❑ ❑ USA Ni9301 **Applause Paws,** 1992, Yel Clapping Hands/Blu Base. $1.00-1.25
❑ ❑ USA Ni9302 **Blimp Game,** 1992, Grn Blimp with Whistles/Spins. $1.00-1.25
❑ ❑ USA Ni9303 **Gotcha Gusher,** 1992, Fly Spray Can Squirter. $1.00-1.25
❑ ❑ USA Ni9304 **Loud-Mouth Mike,** 1992, Pnk/Grn Microphone. $1.00-1.25

❑ ❑ USA Ni9326 **Display/Premiums**, 1992. $5.00-10.00
❑ ❑ USA Ni9364 **Translite/Sm**, 1992. $3.00-5.00

Comments: National Distribution: USA - June 11-July 8, 1993.

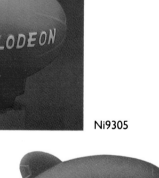

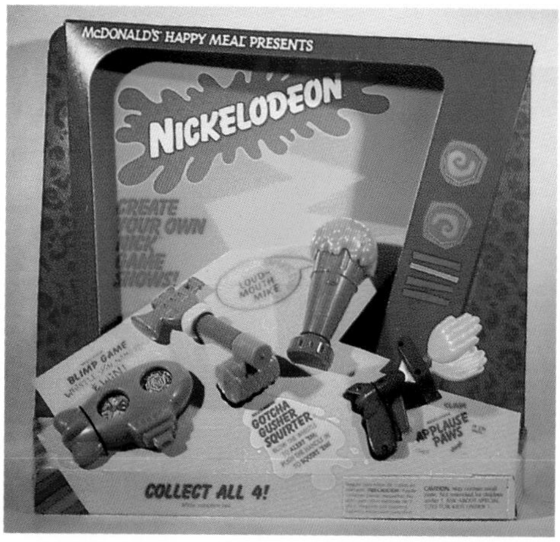

Ni9326

Ni9364

Ni9305

Ni9301 Ni9302 Ni9303 Ni9304

Ni9330

Out for Fun Happy Meal, 1993

Bag:

❑ ❑ USA Ou9330 **Hm Bag - Out for Fun**, 1992. $1.00-1.25

Premiums:

❑ ❑ USA Ou9301 **Balloon Ball,** 1992, Ronald/Blu Beach Ball/ Blow up Ball Inside. $1.00-1.25

❑ ❑ USA Ou9302 **Bubble Shoe Wand,** 1992 Red/Yel/2p. $1.00-1.50

❑ ❑ USA Ou9303 **Sand Pail,** 1992, Ron/Friends on Beach/Yel Handle/Flat Bottom. $1.00-1.25

❑ ❑ USA Ou9305 **Sand Castle Pail,** 1992, Ron/Friends on Beach/Yel Handle/Castle Mold Bottom. $1.00-1.25

❑ ❑ USA Ou9304 **Sunglasses,** 1992, Blu/Grn/Pnk. $1.00-1.25

❑ ❑ USA Ou9326 **Display/Premiums**, 1992. $5.00-10.00

❑ ❑ USA Ou9364 **Translite/Sm**, 1992. $3.00-5.00

Comments: National Distribution: USA - May 7-June 10, 1993. Sand Pail, USA Ou9303, was also the U-3 Premium (no packaging). Sunglasses, USA Ou9304, were widely distributed during clean-up week - 1993. Both types of sand pails were distributed in various markets across the USA. There appeared to be an equal distribution of both types with the castle mold sand pail showing up in USA toy stores and dollar stores selling for $1.00 during 1994/95.

Ou9326

Ou9364

Ou9330

Ou9301 Ou9302 Ou9303 Ou9304

Snow White and the Seven Dwarfs Happy Meal, 1993

Boxes:

❑ ❑ USA Sn9320 **Hm Box - Seven Dwarfs in the Diamond Mine**, 1992. $1.00-1.50

❑ ❑ USA Sn9321 **Hm Box - Seven Dwarfs at Cottage**, 1992. $1.00-1.50

❑ ❑ USA Sn9322 **Hm Box - Snow White with Bashful at Castle**, 1992. $1.00-1.50

❑ ❑ USA Sn9323 **Hm Box - Snow White with Prince with Dwarfs,** 1992. $1.00-1.50

U-3 Premium:

❑ ❑ USA Sn9309 **U-3 Dopey/Sneezy Spin,** 1992, in Blu Coat on a Purp Rug. $2.00-3.00

Premiums:

❑ ❑ USA Sn9301 **Bashful,** 1992, peeks from behind his diamonds. $2.50-3.50

❑ ❑ USA Sn9302 **Doc,** 1992, with Diamond Cart. Diamond spins when cart rolls. $2.50-3.50

❑ ❑ USA Sn9303 **Dopey/Sneezy Spin,** 1992, in Blu Coat on a Purp Rug. $2.50-3.50

❑ ❑ USA Sn9304 **Happy and Grumpy,** 1992, on Railroad Push Car. $3.00-5.00

❑ ❑ USA Sn9305 **Prince with Horse without Green Base,** 1992, with Red Cape with Wht Horse **without Grn Base.** $2.50-3.50

❑ ❑ USA Sn9310 **Prince with Horse with Green Base,** 1992, with Red Cape with Wht Horse with **Grn Base.** $5.00-6.00

❑ ❑ USA Sn9306 **Queen-Witch,** 1992, with 2p Blk Dress/Flips to Form Witch/Queen. $2.50-3.50

❑ ❑ USA Sn9307 **Sleepy,** 1992, 1p, Wht Beard with Purp Sweater. Eyes open and close. $2.50-3.50

❑ ❑ USA Sn9308 **Snow White with Wishing Well,** 1992, Yel Skirt with Grn Wishing Well. $2.50-3.50

❑ ❑ USA Sn9326 **Display/Premiums**, 1992. $50.00-75.00

❑ ❑ USA Sn9365 **Translite/Sm**, 1992. $10.00-15.00

Comments: National Distribution: USA - July 9-August 5, 1993. The Prince came in two versions: with and without the green base MIP. USA Sn9303 = USA Sn9309, loose out of package.

Sn9323

Sn9321

Sn9309 Sn9301 Sn9302 Sn9303 Sn9304

Left to right: Sn9305, Sn9310, Sn9306, Sn9307, Sn9308

Sn9322

Sn9320

Sn9326

Sn9364

Totally Toy Holiday Happy Meal, 1993

Bag:

❑ ❑ USA To9330 **Hm Bag - Kids! Let's Wrap!,** 1993. $1.00-1.25

U-3 Premiums:

❑ ❑ USA To9313 **U-3 Key Force Car with grey windshield,** 1993, Red Car with **Grey Windshield**/Tires/Purp Key. $2.00-2.50

❑ ❑ USA To9314 **U-3 Magic Nursery Doll/Boy,** 1993, Blu PJs/Candy Cane Cloth Body/Plast Face. $3.00-4.00

❑ ❑ USA To9315 **U-3 Magic Nursery Doll/Girl,** 1993, Pnk PJs/Holly Cloth Body with Hard Plast Face. $3.00-4.00

Premiums:

❑ ❑ USA To9301 **Holiday Barbie - Snow Dome,** 1993, Grn Dome/Red Red Dressed Barbie/1p/Recalled. $35.00-50.00

❑ ❑ USA To9302 **Lil Miss Candi Stripes,** 1993, Wht Doll/Grn Tutu/Snap on Red/Wht Dress/2p. $1.00-1.50

❑ ❑ USA To9303 **Magic Nursery Doll/Boy,** 1993, Blu PJs/Holly Cloth Body Doll/Plast Face. $1.00-1.50

❑ ❑ USA To9304 **Magic Nursery Doll/Girl,** 1993, Pnk PJs/Candy Cane Cloth Body/Plast Face. $1.00-1.50

❑ ❑ USA To9305 **Polly Pocket,** 1993, Green/Red Hinged Case with Yel Fig. $1.00-1.50

❑ ❑ USA To9306 **Sally Secrets (Black),** 1993, Blk Doll/Brn Hair/Punch Outs Shapes/Stickers. $2.00-2.50

❑ ❑ USA To9307 **Sally Secrets (White),** 1993, Wht Doll/Bld Hair/Punch out Shapes/Stickers. $1.00-1.50

❑ ❑ USA To9308 **Attack Pack Vehicle,** 1993, Hw Blu Shark/Car/Hook Truck/Lg Blk Whls. $1.00-1.50

❑ ❑ USA To9309 **Key Force Car with black windshield,** 1993, Hw Red Car with **Black Windshield**/Blk Tires/Grey Key on Roof. $1.00-1.50

❑ ❑ USA To9310 **Key Force Truck,** 1993, Hw Blk/Yel Truck with Purp Key on Rear Door/Marked Hot Wheels. $1.00-1.50

❑ ❑ USA To9311 **Mighty Max,** 1993, Hw Wht Skull Face with Yel Fig on Inside/Open Close Lid/Marked McD. $1.00-1.50

❑ ❑ USA To9312 **Tattoo Machine Car,** 1993, Hw Grn Car/Crocodile Sticker Sheet. $1.00-1.50

❑ ❑ USA To9326 **Display/Premiums with Holiday Dome Barbie**, 1993. $50.00-75.00

❑ ❑ USA To9327 **Display/ Premiums without Dome Barbie**, 1993. $15.00-25.00

❑ ❑ USA To9343 **Crew Reference Sheet**, 1993, Blk/Wht Pic. $1.00-1.50

❑ ❑ USA To9364 **Translite/Sm**, 1993. $5.00-8.00

Comments: National Distribution: USA - December 10, 1993-January 6, 1994. Holiday Barbie Dome was recalled due to leakage. Holiday Barbie Green Dome was present on the displays in the stores, prior to recall. USA To9308-12 Are Hot Wheels (Hw) cars.

To9330

To9301

Left to right: To9301, To9302, To9303, To9304, To9305

To9306 To9307 To9308 To9309

To9310 To9311 To9312

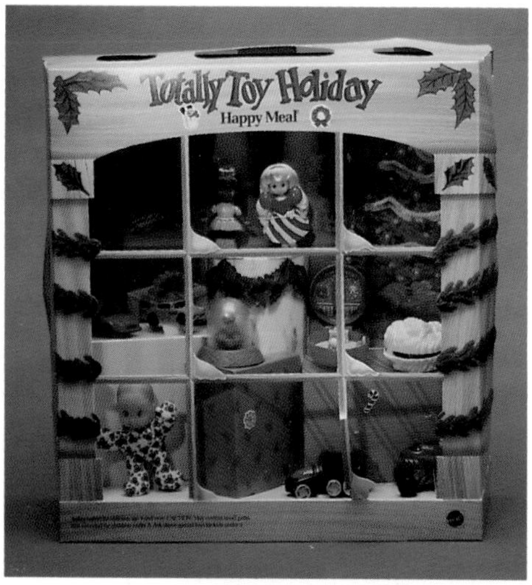

To9326

To9364

USA Generic Promotions, 1993

In 1993, along with the six issues, Fun Times Magazine issued a 1994 Calendar.

❑ ❑ USA Ge9301 **FTM: 1993-Issue 1 Earth ! What A Planet!** $.50-1.00
❑ ❑ USA Ge9302 **FTM: 1993-Issue 2 Mega Bytes Of Fun!** $.50-1.00
❑ ❑ USA Ge9303 **FTM: 1993-Issue 3 Showtime Is Funtime!** $.50-1.00
❑ ❑ USA Ge9304 **FTM: 1993-Issue 4 Wild Wheels.** $.50-1.00
❑ ❑ USA Ge9305 **FTM: 1993-Issue 5 Science Rules.** $.50-1.00
❑ ❑ USA Ge9306 **FTM: 1993-Issue 6 All Wrapped Up.** $.50-1.00
❑ ❑ USA Ge9307 **FTM: 1993-Super Action Calendar for 1994.** $.50-1.00

❑ ❑ USA Ge9308 **1993 Calendar: Ronald McDonald A Celebration Of The Spirit Of Children.** $2.00-3.00
❑ ❑ USA Ge9309 **1993 Calendar: Ronald McDonald Coloring Calendar "When I Grow Up."** $2.00-3.00

❑ ❑ USA Ge9310 **Plate: Birdie Riding Merry-Go-Round Horse.** $3.00-5.00
❑ ❑ USA Ge9311 **Plate: Grimace/Hamburglar/Ronald Riding Ferris Wheel.** $3.00-5.00
❑ ❑ USA Ge9312 **Plate: Grimace/Ronald with Fun House Mirror.** $3.00-5.00
❑ ❑ USA Ge9313 **Plate: Grimace/Hamb/Ron Riding Roller Coaster.** $3.00-5.00

Comments: Regional Distribution: USA - 1993. McWorld advertising emphasizes the global relationship between McDonald's and the earth.

Ge9310

Ge9311

Ge9312

Ge9313

Animaniacs I Happy Meal, 1994

Boxes:
❑ ❑ USA An9410 **Hm Box - Dot/EZ with R Mouths,** 1993. $1.00-1.25
❑ ❑ USA An9411 **Hm Box - Good Skate Good Feathers,** 1993. $1.00-1.25
❑ ❑ USA An9412 **Hm Box - Trio Bicycle**, 1993. $1.00-1.25
❑ ❑ USA An9413 **Hm Box - Pinky,** 1993. $1.00-1.25

U-3 Premium:
❑ ❑ USA An9409 **U-3 Bicycle Built for Trio,** 1993, Purp Bike with 3 Red Whls/3 Chars Riding. $2.00-3.00

Premiums:
❑ ❑ USA An9401 **Bicycle Built for Trio,** 1993, Purp Bike with 3 Red Whls/3 Chars Riding. $1.00-1.50
❑ ❑ USA An9402 **Dot's Ice Cream Machine,** 1993, Ice Cream Truck with 3 Pnk Wheels/Dot Riding. $1.00-1.50
❑ ❑ USA An9403 **Goodskate Goodfeathers,** 1993, Yel Skateboard/Blu Wheels/3 Birdlike Chars Riding. $1.00-1.50
❑ ❑ USA An9404 **Mindy/Buttons' Wild Ride,** 1993, Turq Auto/Boy and Animal Riding. $1.00-1.50
❑ ❑ USA An9405 **Pinky and the Brain Mobile,** 1993, Org Tricycle with Char Riding in Front Wheel. $1.00-1.50
❑ ❑ USA An9406 **Slappy/Skippy's Chopper,** 1993, Pnk/Grn Cycle with Side Car/2 Chars Riding. $1.00-1.50
❑ ❑ USA An9407 **Upside-Down Wakko,** 1993, Grn Tricycle/Purp Wheels with Char Riding up Side Down. $1.00-1.50
❑ ❑ USA An9408 **Yakko Ridin' Ralph,** 1993, Char Riding Ralph as a Tricycle. $1.00-1.50

❑ ❑ USA An9426 **Display with Premiums,** 1993. $25.00-40.00
❑ ❑ USA An9464 **Translite/Sm**, 1993. $4.00-7.00

Comments: National Distribution: USA - May 6-June 2, 1994. Premium markings "1993 Warner Bros." The U-3 is the same as USA An9401, loose out of package.

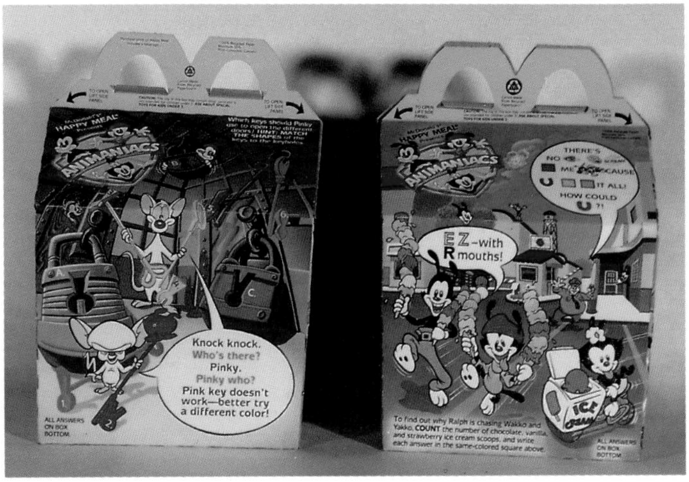

An9413 An9410

1994

Animaniacs I Happy Meal, 1994
Barbie/Hot Wheels V Happy Meal, 1994
Bobby's World Happy Meal, 1994
Cabbage Patch Kids II/Tonka II Happy Meal, 1994
Earth Days Happy Meal, 1994
Flintstones Happy Meal, 1994
Halloween '94 Happy Meal, 1994
Magic School Bus Happy Meal, 1994
Makin' Movies Happy Meal, 1994
Mickey & Friends/Epcot Center '94 Adventure HM, 1994
Ronald Celebrates Happy Birthday Happy Meal, 1994
Sonic 3 the Hedgehog Happy Meal, 1994
USA Generic Promotions, 1994

- **"Fifteenth Birthday" of the Happy Meal**
- **McDonald's Collectors Club tops one thousand members**
- **1st Worldwide O/O Convention held**
- **"Great Expectations" - O/O advertising theme**

An9412 An9411

An9401 An9402 An9403 An9404

An9405 An9406 An9407 An9408

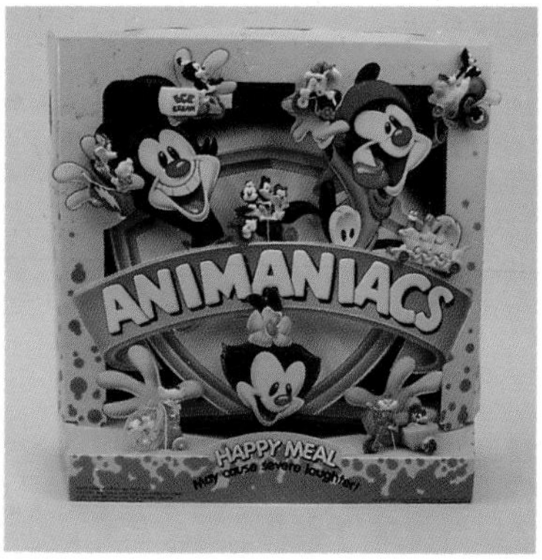

An9426

An9464

Barbie/Hot Wheels V Happy Meal, 1994

Bags:

❑ ❑ USA Ba9430 **Hm Bag - Barbie and Friends/World of Hot Wheels,** 1994. $.50-1.00

❑ ❑ USA Ba9431 **Hm Bag - Treasure Hunt/ Barbie and Hot Wheels,** 1994. $2.00-3.00

❑ ❑ USA Ba9432 **Hm Test Market Bag - Win one of 100 Bikes,** 1994. $10.00-15.00

U-3 Premiums:

❑ ❑ USA Ba9417 **U-3 Barbie Ball,** 1994, Lilac Ball with Barbie Picture. $2.00-3.00

❑ ❑ USA Sx9418 **U-3 Fast Forward,** 1991, Grn/Purple Mini-Streex Car with Wheels. $2.00-3.00

Premiums: Barbie, Ken and Skipper Dolls

❑ ❑ USA Ba9401 **#1 Bicyclin Barbie,** 1994, Grn/Pnk Barbie on Pnk Bike. $2.00-2.50

❑ ❑ USA Ba9402 **#2 Jewel/Glitter Shani,** 1994, Black Barbie with Org Dress. $2.00-2.50

❑ ❑ USA Ba9403 **#3 Camp Barbie,** 1994, Pnk Jacket/Blonde Hair/Blu Shorts/Grn Base. $2.00-2.50

❑ ❑ USA Ba9404 **#4 Camp Teresa,** 1994, Blu Shirt/Yel Sunglasses/Brn Hair/Yel Pants. $2.00-2.50

❑ ❑ USA Ba9419 **#4 Camp Teresa,** 1994, Blu Shirt/Blu Sunglasses/**Blu Fishing Patch on Yel Pants.** $3.00-5.00

❑ ❑ USA Ba9405 **#5 Locket Surprise Barbie,** 1994, **Wht Barbie**/Pnk Party Dress/Blonde Hair/Pnk Heels. $2.00-2.50

❑ ❑ USA Ba9420 **#5 Locket Surprise Barbie,** 1994, **Blk Barbie**/Pnk Party Dress/Blk Hair/ Pnk Heels. $4.00-5.00

❑ ❑ USA Ba9406 **#6 Locket Surprise Ken,** 1994, **Wht Ken** with Gold Jacket/Turq Slacks. $2.00-2.50

❑ ❑ USA Ba9421 **#6 Locket Surprise Ken,** 1994, **Blk Ken** with Gold Jacket/Turq Slacks. $4.00-5.00

❑ ❑ USA Ba9407 **#7 Jewel/Glitter Bride,** 1994, Wht Long Dress/Blonde Hair/Pnk Flowers. $2.00-2.50

❑ ❑ USA Ba9408 **#8 Bridesmaid Skipper,** 1994, Lilac Dress/Blonde Hair. $2.00-2.50

Premiums: Hot Wheel Cars

❑ ❑ USA Hw9409 **#9 Bold Eagle,** 1994, Yel/ Silver Hot Rod. $2.00-2.50

❑ ❑ USA Hw9410 **#10 Black Cat,** 1994, Black Hot Rod. $2.00-2.50

❑ ❑ USA Hw9411 **#11 Flame Rider,** 1994, Blk/Red Hot Rod with McD Logo. $2.00-2.50

❑ ❑ USA Hw9412 **#12 Gas Hog,** 1994, Red Convertible. $2.00-2.50

❑ ❑ USA Hw9413 **#13 Turbine 4-2,** 1994, Blu Turbine/Jet Car. $2.00-2.50

- ❑ ❑ USA Hw9414 **#14 2-Cool,** 1994, Purp/Sil Sports Car. $2.00-2.50
- ❑ ❑ USA Hw9415 **#15 Street Shocker,** 1994, Grn Sports Car. $2.00-2.50
- ❑ ❑ USA Hw9416 **#16 X21J Cruiser,** 1994, Blu/Sil Formula 1 Car. $2.00-2.50

- ❑ ❑ USA Ba9426 **Display/Premiums**, 1994. $40.00-50.00
- ❑ ❑ USA Ba9427 **Color Card with 16 toys pictured.** $1.00-2.00
- ❑ ❑ USA Ba9464 **Translite/Sm**, 1994. $4.00-5.00

Comments: National Distribution: USA - August 5-September 8, 1994. Baton Rouge, Louisiana tested the "Treasure Hunt Happy Meal Bag." Test market bag says, "Treasure Hunt starring Barbie and Hot Wheels — win one of 100 bikes or thousands of cash prizes..cut out this game piece. Bring it to wherever Barbie and Hot Wheels are sold. Look for the Treasure Chest display in the Barbie & Hot Wheels aisles. Place game piece behind red screen to see if you've won a prize."

Ba9401 Ba9403 Ba9402

Ba9430

Ba9432

Ba9419 Ba9404

Left to right: Ba9405, Ba9406, Ba9420, Ba9421

Ba9417

Ba9407 Ba9408

The following photos are close-ups of the Color Card.

Ba9403

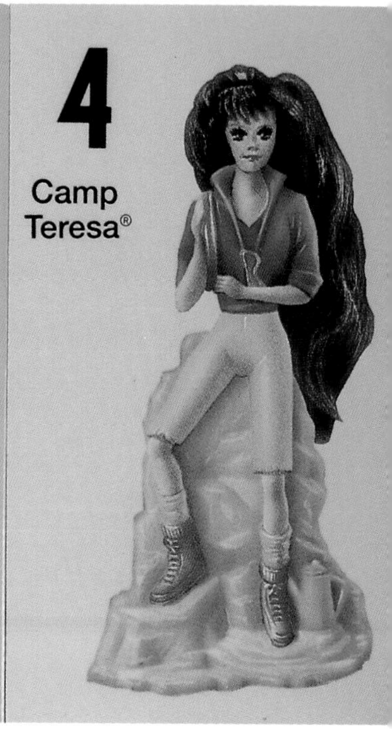

Ba9404

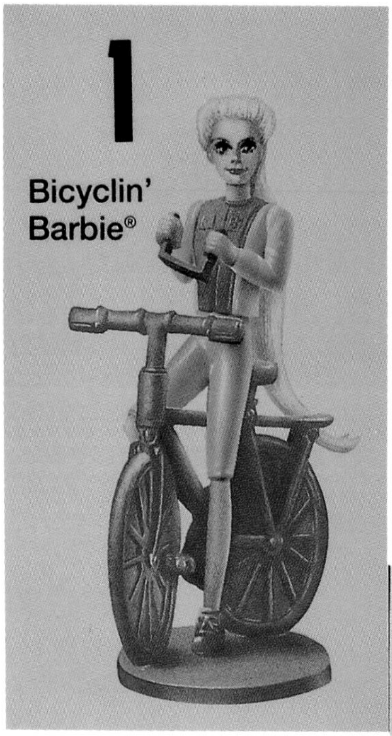

Ba9401

Ba9405

Ba9406

Ba9402

Ba9407

Ba9408

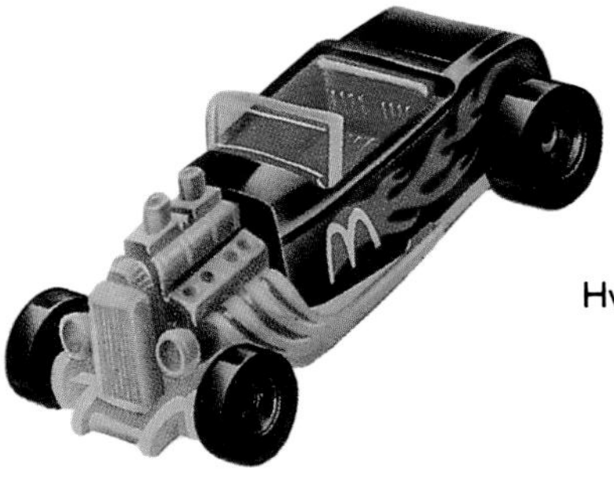

Hw9411

Hw9412

Hw9409

Hw9413

Hw9410

Hw9414

Hw9415

Hw9416

Bobby's World Happy Meal, 1994

Boxes:

❑ ❑ USA Bo9410 **Hm Box - Cheap Skates/Bobby Skating**, 1993. $1.00-1.25

❑ ❑ USA Bo9411 **Hm Box - Drag/Bobby in Wagon**, 1993. $1.00-1.25

❑ ❑ USA Bo9412 **Hm Box - Plan(et)/Bobby on Big Wheels,** 1993. $1.00-1.25

❑ ❑ USA Bo9413 **Hm Box - Wave/Bobby in Pool,** 1993. $1.00-1.25

U-3 Premium:

❑ ❑ USA Bo9405 **U-3 Bobby/Inner Tube,** 1993, Bobby in Inner Tube/Rubber. $2.00-3.00

Premiums:

❑ ❑ USA Bo9401 **3-Wheeler/Spaceship,** 1993, Yel 3-Wheeler/Red Spaceship/3p. $1.00-1.50

❑ ❑ USA Bo9402 **Innertube/Submarine,** 1993, Grn Innertube/Org Submarine/3p. $1.00-1.50

❑ ❑ USA Bo9403 **Skates/Roller Coaster,** 1993, Blu Skates/Grn Roller Coaster/3p. $1.00-1.50

❑ ❑ USA Bo9404 **Wagon/Race Car,** 1993, Red Wagon/Blu Race Car/3p. $1.00-1.50

❑ ❑ USA Bo9426 **Display with Premiums**, 1993. $5.00-15.00

❑ ❑ USA Bo9464 **Translite/Sm**, 1993. $3.00-5.00

Comments: National Distribution: USA - March 4-31, 1994.

Ba9427

Bo9410 Bo9413

Ba9464

Bo9411 Bo9412

Bo9405

Bo9426

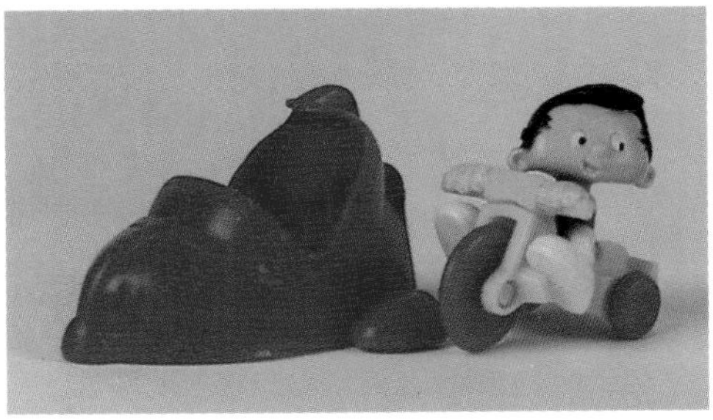

Bo9401

Bo9464

Bo9402

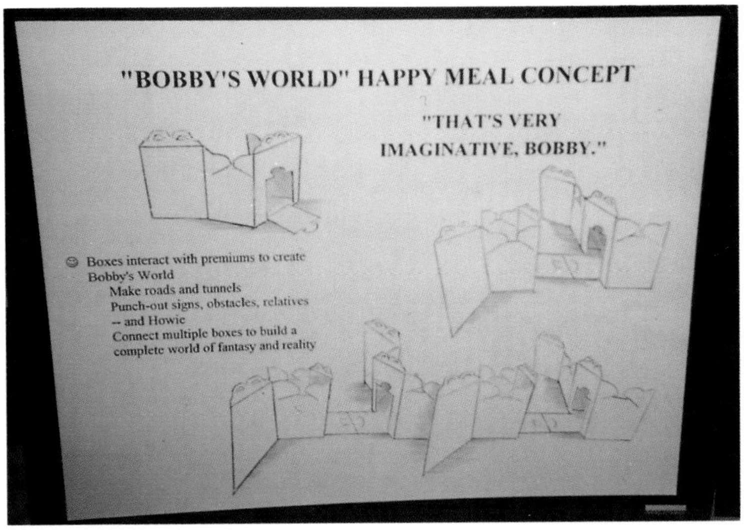

Bo9403

Bo9404

Cabbage Patch Kids III/Tonka II Happy Meal, 1994

Bag:

❑ ❑ USA Cp9430 **Hm Bag - Cabbage Patch Kids/Tonka,** 1994. $.50-1.00

U-3 Premiums:

❑ ❑ USA Cp9409 **U-3 SaraJane,** 1994, CPK Doll/Rubber. $2.00-3.00

❑ ❑ USA Tk9410 **U-3 Dump Truck,** 1994, Yel/Blu Rubber. $2.00-3.00

Premiums: Cabbage Patch Kids

❑ ❑ USA Cp9401 **Wk 1 Mimi Kristina,** 1994, Angel/Gold Horn. $1.00-2.50

❑ ❑ USA Cp9402 **Wk 2 Kimberly Katherine,** 1994, Santa's Helper/Wht Apron. $1.00-2.50

❑ ❑ USA Cp9403 **Wk 3 Abigail Lynn,** 1994, Toy Soldier/Blu Top Hat/Candy Cane/Blk Doll. $1.00-2.50

❑ ❑ USA Cp9404 **Wk 4 Michelle Elyse,** 1994, Snow Fairy/Wht Dress/Snowflake/Wht Doll. $1.00-2.50

Premiums: Tonka Trucks

❑ ❑ USA Tk9405 **Wk 1 Loader,** 1994, Org with Blk Lift. $1.00-2.50

❑ ❑ USA Tk9406 **Wk 2 Crane,** 1994, Grn with Blk Hook. $1.00-2.50

❑ ❑ USA Tk9407 **Wk 3 Grader,** 1994, Yel with Yel Blade. $1.00-2.50

❑ ❑ USA Tk9408 **Wk 4 Bulldozer,** 1994, Yel with Blk Blade. $1.00-2.50

❑ ❑ USA Cp9426 **Display with Premiums,** 1994. $20.00-25.00

❑ ❑ USA Cp9464 **Translite/Sm,** 1994. $4.00-5.00

Comments: National Distribution: USA - December 2-29, 1994.

Cp9401 Cp9402 Cp9403 Cp9404

Tk9405 Tk9406 Tk9407 Tk9408

Cp9426

Cp9430

Cp9464

Tk9410 Cp9409

Earth Days Happy Meal, 1994

Bag:
❑ ❑ USA Ea9430 **Hm Bag - Earth Days**, 1993. $.25-.50

U-3 Premium:
❑ ❑ USA Ea9405 **U-3 Tool Carrier,** 1993, Blu with Red Shovel with Yel Strap. $.50-1.00

Premiums:
❑ ❑ USA Ea9401 **Binoculars,** 1993, 1p Hinge Open Earth Shaped/Grn. $1.00-1.25
❑ ❑ USA Ea9402 **Birdfeeder,** 1993, Bird House Shaped Birdfeeder. $1.00-1.25
❑ ❑ USA Ea9403 **Terrarium/Globe,** 1993, Clear Cylinder Top with Bottom. $1.00-1.25
❑ ❑ USA Ea9404 **Tool Carrier,** 1993, Blu with Red Shovel with Yel Strap/3p. $.50-1.00

❑ ❑ USA Ea9426 **Display/Premiums**, 1993. $5.00-10.00
❑ ❑ USA Ea9464 **Translite/Sm**, 1993. $3.00-4.00

Comments: National Distribution: USA - April 8-May 5, 1994.

Ea9401 Ea9402 Ea9403 Ea9404

Ea9426

Ea9430

Ea9405

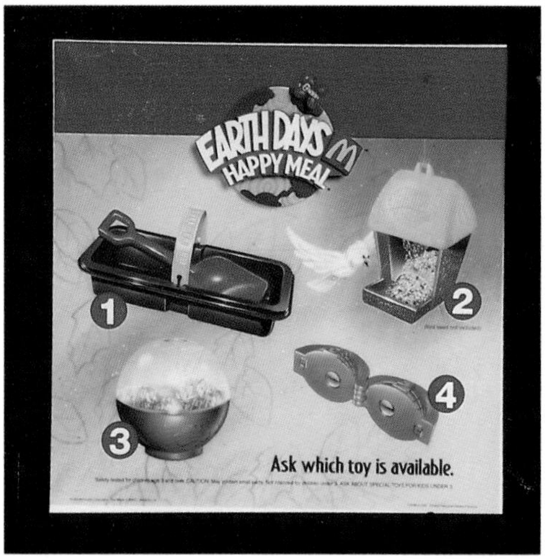

Ea9464

Flintstones Happy Meal, 1994

Bag:
- ❑ ❑ USA FI9430 **Hm Bag - Roc Donald's Drive -Thru/Look out!**, 1993. $.25-.50

U-3 Premium:
- ❑ ❑ USA FI9406 **U-3 Rocking Dino,** 1993, Purp Rubber Dino Dinosaur. $2.50-4.00

Premiums: Flintstones Characters in Buildings
- ❑ ❑ USA FI9401 **Barney/Fossil Fill-Up,** 1993, Grey Bldg/Door/Barney in Car/Sticker Sheet/3p. $.50-1.00
- ❑ ❑ USA FI9402 **Betty/Bamm Bamm/Roc D,** 1993, Yel Bldg/Door/Betty in Brn-Log Car/Sticker/3p. $.50-1.00
- ❑ ❑ USA FI9403 **Fred/Bedr Bowl-O-Rama,** 1993, Grn Bldg/Door/Fred in Red Car/Sticker/3p. $.50-1.00
- ❑ ❑ USA FI9404 **Pebbles/Dino/Toys-S-A,** 1993, Red Bldg/Door/Pebbles in Blu Cycle/Sticker/3p. $.50-1.00
- ❑ ❑ USA FI9405 **Wilma/Flintstone House,** 1993, Peach Bldg/Door/Wilma in Gry Car/Sticker/3p. $.50-1.00

- ❑ ❑ USA FI9426 **Display with Premiums**, 1993. $5.00-15.00
- ❑ ❑ USA FI9450 **Button**, 1993, I Love Roc Donald's. $2.00-3.00
- ❑ ❑ USA FI9464 **Translite/Sm**, 1993. $3.00-4.00
- ❑ ❑ USA FI9495 **Pin**, 1994, the Flintstones/Roc Donald's Summer '94. $3.00-4.00
- ❑ ❑ USA FI9496 **Pin,** 1994, Grand Poobah Meals. $2.50-3.00

Comments: National Distribution: USA - June 3-July 7, 1994.

FI9430

FI9406

Top row, left to right: FI9406, FI9405, FI9404
Bottom row, left to right: FI9402, FI9407, FI9403

FI9426

FI9450

FI9495

FI9496

Fl9464

Ha9426

Ha9464

Halloween '94 Happy Meal, 1994

Premiums: Halloween Pails With Lids

- ❑ ❑ USA Ha9401 **Ghost,** 1986, 3p Wht Ghost with Cookie Cutter Insert with Blk Handle. $.50-1.00
- ❑ ❑ USA Ha9402 **Pumpkin,** 1986, 3p Org Pumpkin with Cookie Cutter Insert with Blk Handle. $.50-1.00
- ❑ ❑ USA Ha9403 **Witch,** 1986 3p Purp Witch with Cookie Cutter Insert with Blk Handle. $.50-1.00

- ❑ ❑ USA Ha9426 **Display,** 1994. $5.00-10.00
- ❑ ❑ USA Ha9464 **Translite/Sm**, 1994. $2.00-3.00

Comments: National Distribution: USA - October 7-October 27, 1994.

Crew Reference Sheet

Ha9402 Ha9401 Ha9403

Magic School Bus Happy Meal, 1994

Bag:
❑ ❑ USA Ma9430 **Hm Bag - The Magic School Bus/Wahoo!,** 1994. $.25-.50

U-3 Premium:
❑ ❑ USA Ma9405 **U-3 Undersea Adventure Game,** 1994, Grn Bead Game Without Tab/1p. $1.00-1.50

Premiums:
❑ ❑ USA Ma9401 **Collector Card Kit,** 1994, Yel School Bus/10 Cards/Sticker Sheet. $1.00-1.25
❑ ❑ USA Ma9402 **Geo Fossil Finder,** 1994, Fossil Tracer with Pencil/4p. $1.00-1.25
❑ ❑ USA Ma9403 **Space Tracer,** 1994, Blu Tracing Protractor/Planets/1p. $1.00-1.25
❑ ❑ USA Ma9404 **Undersea Adventure Game,** 1994, Grn Bead Game with Yel Tab/1p. $1.00-1.25

❑ ❑ USA Ma9426 **Display**, 1994. $5.00-15.00
❑ ❑ USA Ma9464 **Translite/Sm**, 1994. $3.00-5.00

Comments: National Distribution: USA - September 9-October 6, 1994

Ma9426

Ma9464

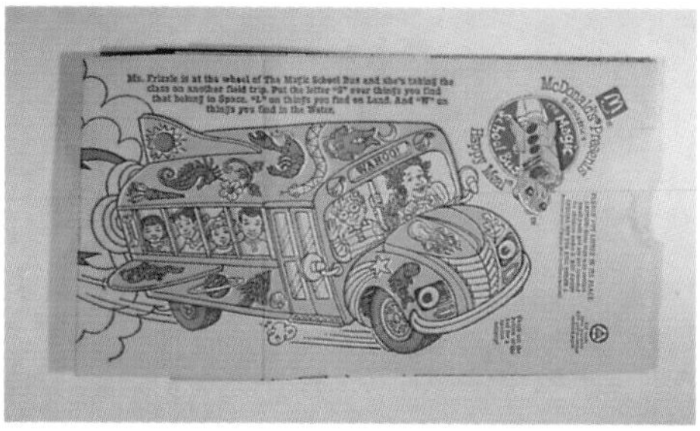
Ma9430

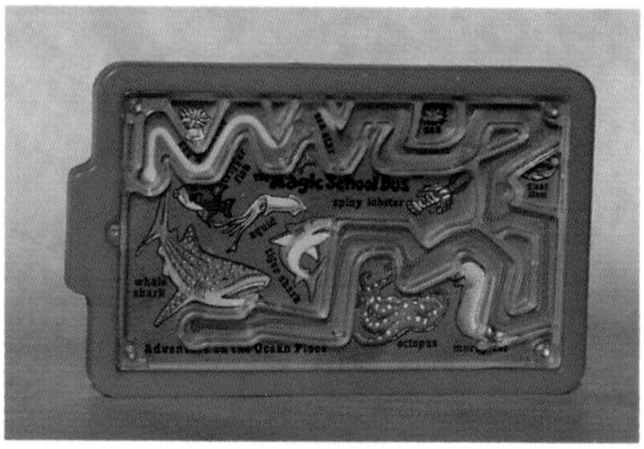
Ma9405

Top row, left to right: Ma9404, Ma9403
Bottom row, left to right: Ma9402, Ma9401

Makin' Movies Happy Meal, 1994

Boxes:
❑ ❑ USA Mm9410 **Hm Box - Making Prints,** 1993. $1.00-1.25
❑ ❑ USA Mm9411 **Hm Box - Popcorn**, 1993. $1.00-1.25
❑ ❑ USA Mm9412 **Hm Box - Scoreboard,** 1993. $1.00-1.25
❑ ❑ USA Mm9413 **Hm Box - Tickets**, 1993. $1.00-1.25

U-3 Premiums:
❑ ❑ USA Mm9405 **U-3 Sound Machine,** 1993, Purp/Turq/Blk. $1.00-1.50

Premiums:
❑ ❑ USA Mm9401 **Clapboard,** 1993, Blk Chalk Board with Chalk/2p. $1.00-1.25
❑ ❑ USA Mm9402 **Megaphone/Director's,** 1993, Red/Yel Megaphone. $1.00-1.25
❑ ❑ USA Mm9403 **Movie Camera,** 1993, Blu/Yel/Blk/Red Movie Camera. $1.00-1.25
❑ ❑ USA Mm9404 **Sound Effects Machine,** 1993, Purp/Turq/Blk Sound Machine. $1.00-1.25

❑ ❑ USA Mm9426 **Display with Premiums,** 1993. $5.00-15.00
❑ ❑ USA Mm9464 **Translite/Sm**, 1993. $3.00-4.00

Comments: National Distribution: USA - January 7-February 3, 1994.

Mm9410

Mm9401 Mm9402 Mm9403 Mm9404

Mm9411

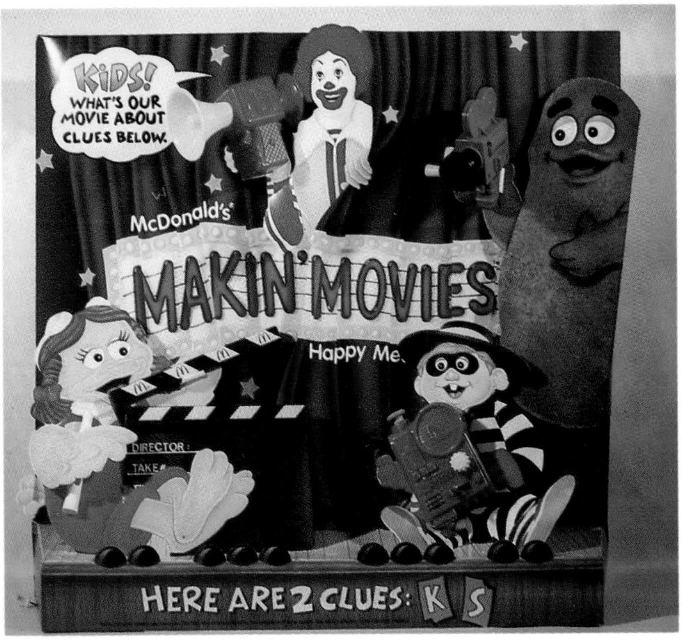

Mm9426

Mm9412

Mm9464

Mm9413

Mickey & Friends/Epcot Center '94 Adventure Happy Meal, 1994

Boxes:

❑ ❑ USA Mi9410 **Hm Box - Chip in China/Dale in Morocco,** 1994. $1.00-1.25

❑ ❑ USA Mi9411 **Hm Box - Daisy in Germany/Donald in Mexico**, 1994. $1.00-1.25

❑ ❑ USA Mi9412 **Hm Box - Mickey in USA/Minnie in Japan,** 1994. $1.00-1.25

❑ ❑ USA Mi9413 **Hm Box - Pluto in France/Goofy in Norway**, 1994. $1.00-1.25

U-3 Premium:

❑ ❑ USA Mi9409 **U-3 Mickey in USA,** 1994, Mickey with Arms Extended. $2.00-3.00

Premiums:

❑ ❑ USA Mi9401 **Chip in China,** 1994, Chip with Chinese Hat. $2.00-2.50

❑ ❑ USA Mi9402 **Daisy in Germany,** 1994, Daisy Duck. $2.00-2.50

❑ ❑ USA Mi9403 **Dale in Morocco,** 1994, Dale. $2.00-2.50

❑ ❑ USA Mi9404 **Donald in Mexico,** 1994, Donald Duck. $2.00-2.50

❑ ❑ USA Mi9405 **Goofy in Norway,** 1994, Goofy. $2.00-2.50

❑ ❑ USA Mi9406 **Mickey in USA,** 1994, Mickey with Arms Extended. $2.00-2.50

❑ ❑ USA Mi9407 **Minnie in Japan,** 1994, Minnie. $2.00-2.50

❑ ❑ USA Mi9408 **Pluto in France,** 1994, Pluto. $2.00-2.50

❑ ❑ USA Mi9426 **Display/Premiums**, 1994. $35.00-50.00

❑ ❑ USA Mi9464 **Translite/Sm**, 1994. $5.00-8.00

Comments: National Distribution: USA - July 8-August 4, 1994. USA Mi9406 = USA Mi9409, loose out of package. USA Mi9409 is packaged in U-3 striped packaging.

Left to right: Mi9402, Mi9401, Mi9404, Mi9403

Left to right: Mi9406, Mi9405, Mi9408, Mi9407

Mi9411 Mi9410 Mi9412 Mi9413

Mi9426

Mi9464

Ronald Celebrates Happy Birthday/Happy Birthday Happy Meal, 1994

Boxes:

❑ ❑ USA Fi9420 **Hm Box - Candies/Find All The**, 1994. $1.00-1.25

❑ ❑ USA Fi9421 **Hm Box - Party/Ronald Invited,** 1994. $1.00-1.25

❑ ❑ USA Fi9422 **Hm Box - Portrait/Berenstain Bears**, 1994. $1.00-1.25

❑ ❑ USA Fi9423 **Hm Box - Parade/Birthday Party**, 1994. $1.00-1.25

U-3 Premium:

❑ ❑ USA Fi9416 **U-3 Ronald McDonald,** 1994, in Red Hm Box with Hm Writing on Box. $3.00-4.00

Premiums:

❑ ❑ USA Fi9401 **Wk 1 Ronald McDonald in Red Hm Box Waving**, 1994, 1p. $2.00-3.00

❑ ❑ USA Fi9402 **Wk 1 Barbie as Pink/Purple Ballerina**, Purp Stand, 1994. $3.00-4.00

❑ ❑ USA Fi9403 **Wk 1 Hot Wheels in Orange Track,** 1994, Blu Hw Car in Org Track, 1994. $2.00-3.00

❑ ❑ USA Fi9404 **Wk 2 E.T. on Blue Stage,** with Purp Hat on Blu Stage, 1994. $2.00-3.00

❑ ❑ USA Fi9405 **Wk 2 Sonic the Hedgehog on TV,** on Pnk TV, 1994. $2.00-3.00

❑ ❑ USA Fi9406 **Wk 2 Berenstain Bears on See Saw,** on Yel See Saw, 1994. $2.00-3.00

❑ ❑ USA Fi9407 **Wk 3 Cabbage Patch Kids on Rocking Horse,** on Blu Rocking Horse, 1994. $2.00-3.00

❑ ❑ USA Fi9408 **Wk 3 Tonka Truck Carrying Red Package, 2p**, 1994. $7.00 -10.00

❑ ❑ USA Fi9409 **Wk 3 101 Dalmatians in Box,** Dogs on Blk/Wht Box, 1994. $4.00-5.00

❑ ❑ USA Fi9410 **Wk 4 Peanuts on Calliope,** in Grn Calliope, 1994. $2.00-3.00

❑ ❑ USA Fi9411 **Wk 4 Muppet Babies with White Tie on Blue Base,** Miss Piggy/Kermit with **Wht Tie**, 1994. $2.00-3.00

❑ ❑ USA Fi9417 **Wk 4 Muppet Babies with Blue Tie On Blue Base,** Miss Piggy/Kermit with **Blu Tie**, 1994. $3.00-5.00

❑ ❑ USA Fi9412 **Wk 4 Little Mermaid with Flounder,** with Flounder on Blu Base, 1994. $2.00-3.00

❑ ❑ USA Fi9413 **Wk 5 Tiny Toons on Cake,** with Pnk Cake/Wht Candle, 1994. $2.00-3.00

❑ ❑ USA Fi9414 **Wk 5 Looney Tunes/Bugs Bunny Playing Symbols, Bugs/Sylvester with Horn/Symbols**, 1994. $5.00-8.00

❑ ❑ USA Fi9415 **Wk 5 Happy Meal Guys Blowing Party Horn,** Hamb/Fries/Shake, 1994. $2.00-3.00

❑ ❑ USA Fi9425 **Toy Safety Notice,** 1994. $1.00-1.50

❑ ❑ USA Fi9426 **Display/Premiums**, 1994. $50.00-75.00

❑ ❑ USA Fi9464 **Translite/Sm**, 1994. $5.00-8.00

Comments: National Distribution: USA - October 28-December 1, 1994. Fifteenth Anniversary/Birthday of USA Happy Meal. USA Fi9402 Barbie was recalled for safety concerns; recall was at the end of distribution cycle. USA Fi9411 was distributed both ways, with white tie and with blue painted tie.

Fi9420 Fi9421

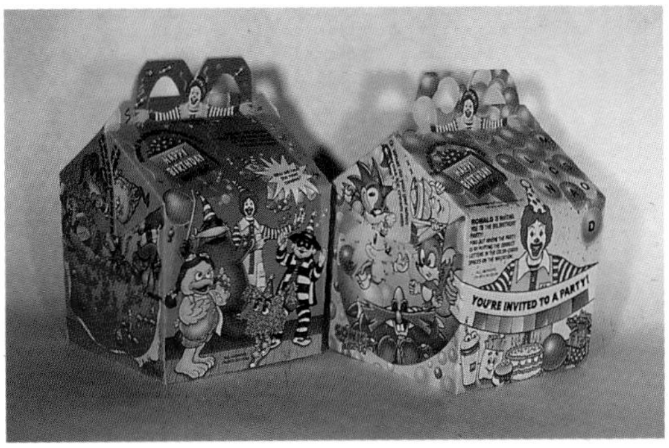

Fi9422 Fi9423

Fi9401 Fi9402 Fi9403 Fi9404 Fi9417 Fi9411

Fi9405 Fi9406 Fi9408 Fi9407

Fi9409 Fi9410 Fi9411 Fi9412

Fi9415 Fi9414 Fi9413

Top row, left to right: Fi9409, Fi9412, Fi9411, Fi9410, Fi9413, Fi9414, Fi9415
Bottom row, left to right: Fi9401, Fi9402, Fi9403, Fi9406, Fi9405, Fi9404, Fi9408, Fi9407

Fi9464

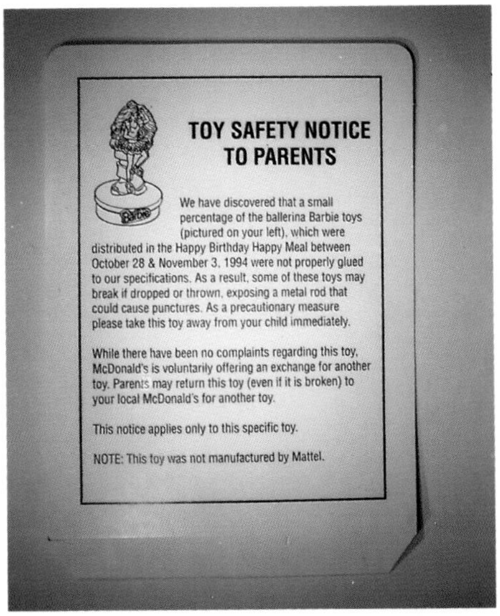

TOY SAFETY NOTICE TO PARENTS

We have discovered that a small percentage of the ballerina Barbie toys (pictured on your left), which were distributed in the Happy Birthday Happy Meal between October 28 & November 3, 1994 were not properly glued to our specifications. As a result, some of these toys may break if dropped or thrown, exposing a metal rod that could cause punctures. As a precautionary measure please take this toy away from your child immediately.

While there have been no complaints regarding this toy, McDonald's is voluntarily offering an exchange for another toy. Parents may return this toy (even if it is broken) to your local McDonald's for another toy.

This notice applies only to this specific toy.

NOTE: This toy was not manufactured by Mattel.

Fi9425

Prototype toy layout board for 15th birthday. Toys were not selected.

Fi9426

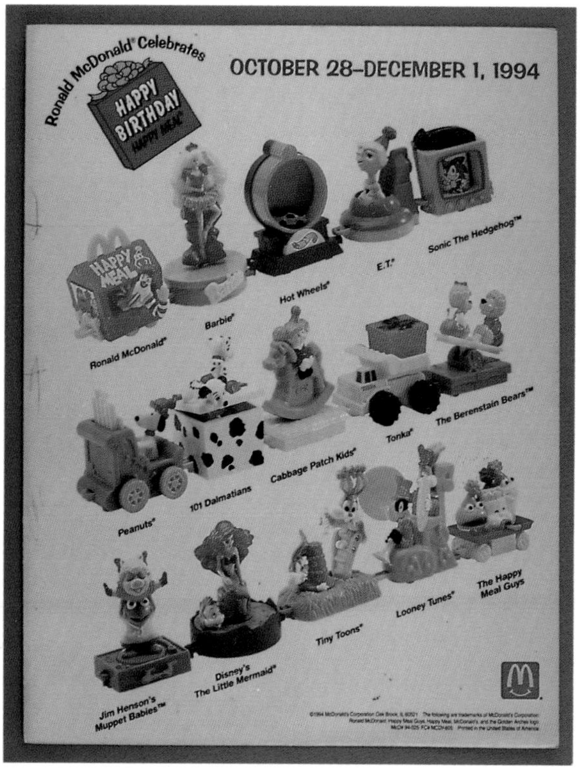

So9405

So9401 So9402 So9403 So9404

So9426

Sonic 3 the Hedgehog Happy Meal, 1994

Bag:

❑ ❑ USA So9430 **Hm Bag - Sonic 3 the Hedgehog**, 1993. $.25-.50

U-3 Premium:

❑ ❑ USA So9405 **U-3 Sonic Ball,** 1993, Yel with No McDonald's Markings/Sonic. $2.00-2.50

Premiums:

❑ ❑ USA So9401 **Dr. Ivo Robotnik,** 1993, Brn/Wht/Grey Auto/Hand Crank. $1.00-1.50

❑ ❑ USA So9402 **Knuckles,** White Cloud with Red Fig, 1993. $1.00-1.50

❑ ❑ USA So9403 **Miles/Tails/Prow,** 1993, Blu Pull String Prower/Org Whirly Spinner/2p. $1.00-1.50

❑ ❑ USA So9404 **Sonic/Hedgehog,** 1993, Blu/Org Sonic the Hedgehog/2p. $1.00-1.50

❑ ❑ USA So9426 **Display/Premiums**, 1993. $20.00-25.00

❑ ❑ USA So9464 **Translite/Sm**, 1993. $3.00-5.00

Comments: National Distribution: USA - February 4-March 3, 1994. USA So9403 Miles "Tails" Prower was recalled during the last week of promotion due to string/pull problems. The majority of premiums were given out prior to recall.

So9464

So9430

USA Generic Promotions, 1994

❑ ❑ USA Ge9410 **Hm Box - Healing Through Happiness with Sunshine/Baxter box**, 1994. $20.00-25.00

❑ ❑ USA Ge9430 **Hm Box - Healing Through Happiness with Rainbow/Medline box**, 1994. $20.00-25.00

Premiums:

❑ ❑ USA Ge9401 **Hockey Game,** 1994, Shoot and Score. $.50-1.00

❑ ❑ USA Ge9402 **Comic Book-Mystery of the Lost Treasure,** 1994, Paper. $.50-1.00

❑ ❑ USA Ge9403 **Comic Book-Mystery of the Missing Sea Horses,** 1994, Paper. $.50-1.00

❑ ❑ USA Ge9404 **License Plate,** 1994, Yel Plastic with Red Stickers. $.50-1.00

❑ ❑ USA Ge9405 **Paint Kit,** 1994, 4 1/4" x 5 1/4"/4 Pgs. $.50-1.00

❑ ❑ USA Ge9406 **Stickers - Ronald/Grimace,** 1994, Scratch 'n Sniff. $.50-1.00

❑ ❑ USA Ge9407 **Stickers - Birdie/Hamb,** 1994, Scratch 'n Sniff. $.50-1.00

❑ ❑ USA Ge9408 **Tattoo Fun,** 1994. $.50-1.00

❑ ❑ USA Ge9409 **Activity Book - Time out for Fun,** 1994, 5 1/2" x 8 1/2"/8 Pgs. $.50-1.00

❑ ❑ USA Ge9411 **Greeting Card - Friends like You,** 1994, Paper. $.50-1.00

❑ ❑ USA Ge9412 **Greeting Card - You're Totally Cool,** 1994, Paper. $.50-1.00

❑ ❑ USA Ge9413 **Decoder,** 1994, Clubhouse/Birdie. $.50-1.00

❑ ❑ USA Ge9414 **Photo Card: Ronald at Happy Meal Workshop,** 1994. $2.00-3.00

❑ ❑ USA Ge9415 **FTM: 1994-Issue 1 Be A Detective!** $.50-1.00

❑ ❑ USA Ge9416 **FTM: 1994-Issue 2 Bugs And Beasts.** $.50-1.00

❑ ❑ USA Ge9417 **FTM: 1994-Issue 3 Have A Ball!** $.50-1.00

❑ ❑ USA Ge9418 **FTM: 1994-Issue 4 Wonderful Water!** $.50-1.00

❑ ❑ USA Ge9419 **FTM: 1994-Issue 5 All Aboard/Magic School Bus.** $.50-1.00

❑ ❑ USA Ge9420 **FTM: 1994-Issue 6 Let's Party!** $.50-1.00

❑ ❑ USA Ge9421 **1994 Calendar: Ronald McDonald Coloring Calendar "1993 - 1994"** $2.00-3.00

❑ ❑ USA Ge9422 **1994 Calendar: Ronald/Friends See America the Spectacular/Coloring.** $2.00-3.00

❑ ❑ USA GE9423 **1994 Calendar: Ronald McDonald A Celebration of the Spirit of Children.** $2.00-3.00

Comments: Regional Distribution: USA - 1994 during fun treat periods. USA Ge9410 Hm Box was distributed only at the McDonald's Collectors Club Convention in Chicago, Illinois during April 1994. These are a sampling of the generic premiums given out.

Ge9410

Ge9430

Ge9401

Ge9402 Ge9403

1995

Amazing Wildlife Happy Meal, 1995
Animaniacs II Happy Meal, 1995
Barbie/Hot Wheels VI Happy Meal, 1995
Busy World of Richard Scarry Happy Meal, 1995
Disneyland 40 Years of Adventure Happy Meal, 1995
Halloween '95 Happy Meal, 1995
Muppet Workshop Happy Meal, 1995
Polly Pocket/Attack Pack Happy Meal, 1995
Power Rangers the Movie/Mighty Morphin HM, 1995
Space Rescue Happy Meal, 1995
Spider-Man Happy Meal, 1995
Totally Toys Happy Meal, 1995
Power Ranger Supplemental/Self-Liquidating Promotion, 1995
USA Generic Promotions, 1995

- **"Have You Had Your Break Today?"**
- **McDonald's 40th Year Anniversary (1955-1995)**

Am9501 Am9502 Am9504 Am9503

Am9505 Am9506 Am9508 Am9507

Amazing Wildlife Happy Meal, 1995

Boxes:

❑ ❑ USA Am9510 **Hm Box - Elephant/Koala,** 1995. $1.00-1.50

❑ ❑ USA Am9511 **Hm Box - Turtle/Camel**, 1995. $1.00-1.50

❑ ❑ USA Am9512 **Hm Box - Lion/Monkey,** 1995. $1.00-1.50

❑ ❑ USA Am9513 **Hm Box - Tiger/Polar Bear**, 1995. $1.00-1.50

Premiums:

❑ ❑ USA Am9501 **Asiatic Lion,** 1994, Beige/Tan Stuffed Lion. $1.00-1.25

❑ ❑ USA Am9502 **Chimpanzee,** 1994, Brn/Tan Stuffed Chimpanzee. $1.00-1.25

❑ ❑ USA Am9503 **African Elephant,** 1994, Gry Stuffed Elephant. $1.00-1.25

❑ ❑ USA Am9504 **Koala,** 1994, Tan/Wht Stuffed Bear. $1.00-1.25

❑ ❑ USA Am9505 **Dromedary Camel,** 1994, Brn Stuffed Camel. $1.00-1.25

❑ ❑ USA Am9506 **Galapagos Tortoise,** 1994, Grn Stuffed Tortoise. $1.00-1.25

❑ ❑ USA Am9507 **Polar Bear,** 1994, Wht Stuffed Bear. $1.00-1.25

❑ ❑ USA Am9508 **Siberian Tiger,** 1994, Gold/Blk/Wht Stuffed Tiger. $1.00-1.25

❑ ❑ USA Am9526 **Display**, 1994, with 8 Premiums. $5.00-10.00

❑ ❑ USA Am9543 **Crew Reference Sheet,** 1995, Blk/Wht Pic. $1.00-1.50

❑ ❑ USA Am9544 **Crew Poster**, 1995. $1.50-3.00

❑ ❑ USA Am9564 **Translite/Sm**, 1994. $3.00-4.00

Comments: National Distribution: USA - April 1-28, 1995. The advertising tie-in partner was the National Wildlife Federation. Promotion included promo ad for *Ranger Rick Magazine*.

Am9526

Am9564

Am9543

❑ ❑ USA An9526 **Display with Premiums,** 1995. $5.00-10.00

❑ ❑ USA An9564 **Translite/Sm**, 1995. $3.00-5.00

Comments: National Distribution: USA - November 1 - 30, 1995. Premium markings "1995 Warner Bros." The 1995 four U-3 premiums, USA An9514/15/16/17, were the same as the 1994 USA Animaniacs I Happy Meal premiums - USA An94/01/03/04/08, loose out of package. In some markets the U-3 Sonic Ball (USA/Mex/Can) was distributed in place of the U-3 Animaniacs characters. This substitution was due to a prior distribution shortage as a result of a warehouse fire in the south.

Animaniacs II Happy Meal, 1995

Boxes:

❑ ❑ USA An9510 **Hm Box - Crowd,** 1995. $.50-1.00

❑ ❑ USA An9511 **Hm Box - Adventure**, 1995. $.50-1.00

❑ ❑ USA An9512 **Hm Box - Comedy,** 1995. $.50-1.00

❑ ❑ USA An9513 **Hm Box - Scary,** 1995. $.50-1.00

U-3 Premiums: In Zebra Striped Packaging

❑ ❑ USA An9514 **U-3 Bicycle Built for Trio,** 1995, Purp Bike with 3 Red Whls/3 Chars Riding. $4.00-5.00

❑ ❑ USA An9515 **U-3 Goodskate Goodfeathers,** 1995, Yel Skateboard/Blu Whls/3 Chars Riding. $4.00-5.00

❑ ❑ USA An9516 **U-3 Mindy/Buttons' Wild Ride,** 1995, Turq Auto/Boy and Animal Riding. $4.00-5.00

❑ ❑ USA An9517 **U-3 Yakko Ridin' Ralph,** 1995, Char Riding Ralph as a Tricycle. $4.00-5.00

❑ ❑ USA So9405 **U-3 Sonic Ball,** 1993, Yel Ball with No McD Markings/Sonic. $2.00-2.50

Premiums:

❑ ❑ USA An9501 **Pinky & the Brain in Pnk Vehicle Lifting Blue Ball,** 1995, Popoid Type Extension. $ .50-1.00

❑ ❑ USA An9502 **Goodfeathers in Red Truck with Yellow Key,** 1995, Popoid Type Extension. $.50-1.00

❑ ❑ USA An9503 **Dot & Ralph in Blue/Red Vehicle,** 1995, Popoid Type Extension. $.50-1.00

❑ ❑ USA An9504 **Wakko & Yakko in Blue Launcher Vehicle,** 1995, Popoid Type Extension. $.50-1.00

❑ ❑ USA An9505 **Slappy & Skippy in Yellow Helicopter,** 1995, Popoid Type Extension. $.50-1.00

❑ ❑ USA An9506 **Mindy & Buttons in Blue Baby Carriage,** 1995, Popoid Type Extension. $ .50-1.00

❑ ❑ USA An9507 **Wakko, Yakko & Dot in Red/Yellow Rocket,** 1995, Popoid Type Extension. $ .50-1.00

❑ ❑ USA An9508 **Hip Hippos in Red Boat,** 1995, Popoid Type Extension. $ .50-1.00

An9515 An9516 An9517 An9514

An9514 An9516 An9515 An9517

Top row, left to right: An9503, An9501
Bottom row, left to right: An9505, An9507, An9504

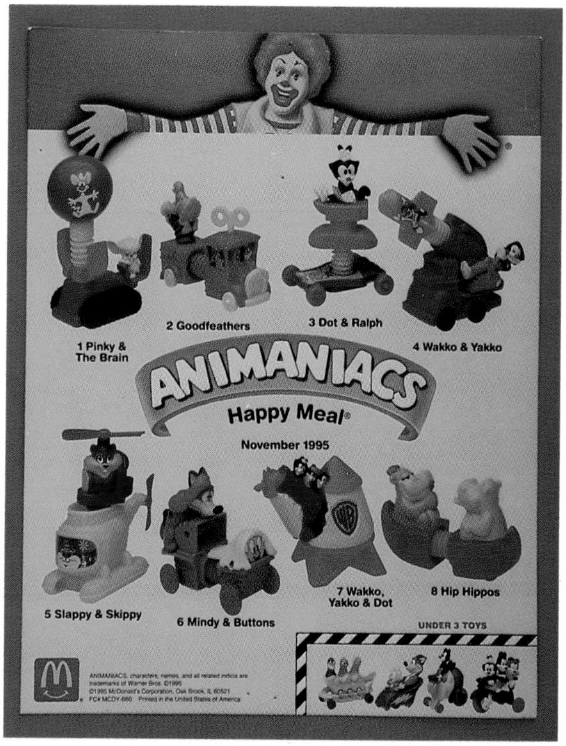

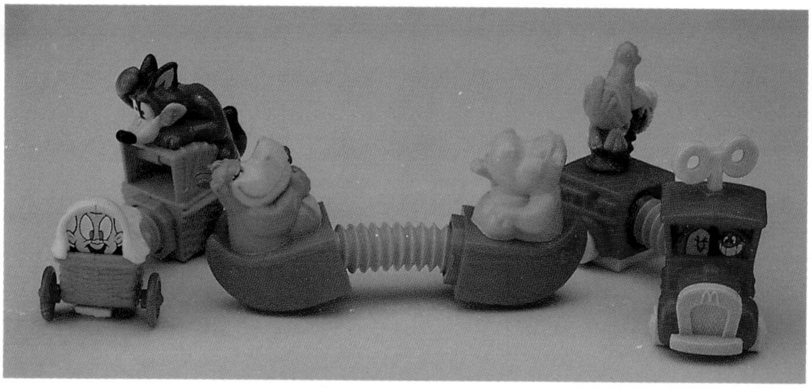

An9506 An9508 An9502

An9564

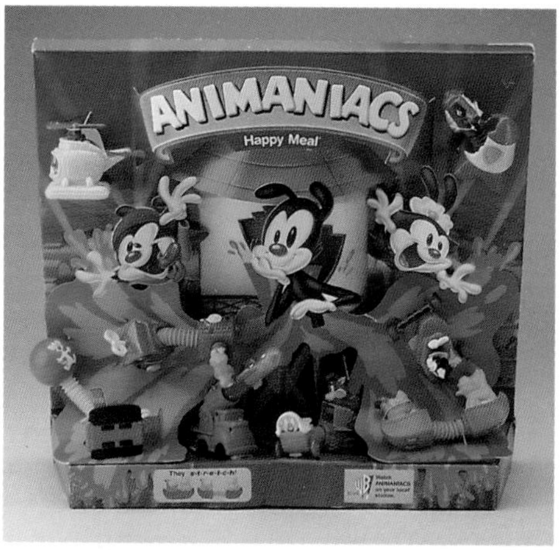

An9526

Crew Reference Sheet

Barbie/Hot Wheels VI Happy Meal, 1995

Bag:

❏ ❏ USA Ba9530 **Hm Bag - Hot Skatin' Barbie/Finish,** 1995. $.50-1.00

U-3 Premiums:

❏ ❏ USA Ba9517 **U-3 Lil Miss Candi Stripes Girl,** 1993, Wht Girl/Long Blonde Hair/Grn Dress. $2.00-2.50

❏ ❏ USA Hw9518 **U-3 Key Force Car,** 1993, Red Car with Grey Tires/Purp Key (same as USA To9313 loose). $2.00-2.50

Premiums: Barbie & Ken Dolls

❏ ❏ USA Ba9501 **#1 Hot Skatin' Barbie,** 1994, Turq/Pnk Outfit with Yel Skates. $2.00-2.50

❏ ❏ USA Ba9502 **#2 Dance Moves Barbie,** 1994, Pnk/Yel Tutu/Yel Shoes with Grn Stand/2p. $2.00-2.50

❏ ❏ USA Ba9503 **#3 Butterfly Princess Teresa,** 1994, Pnk Long Dress with Cut-Outs/Holding Yel Butterfly. $2.00-2.50

❏ ❏ USA Ba9504 **#4 Cool Country Barbie,** 1994, Purp/Pnk Cow Girl Barbie Riding Beige Horse. $2.00-2.50

❏ ❏ USA Ba9505 **#5 Lifeguard Ken-White,** 1994, Wht Ken with Yel Jet Ski/2p. $2.00-2.50

❏ ❏ USA Ba9519 **#5 Lifeguard Ken-Black,** 1994, **Blk Ken** with Yel Jet Ski/2p. $4.00-5.00

❏ ❏ USA Ba9506 **#6 Lifeguard Barbie-White,** 1994, Wht Barbie/Red-Wht-Blu Outfit Holding Blk Binoculars. $2.00-2.50

❏ ❏ USA Ba9520 **#6 Lifeguard Barbie-Black,** 1994, **Blk Barbie**/Red-Wht-Blu Outfit Holding Blk Binoculars. $4.00-5.00

❏ ❏ USA Ba9507 **#7 Blue Angel Barbie,** 1994, Lt/Dk Blu Wrap Dress/Lt Blu Butterfly Wings/Bubble Holes. $2.00-2.50

❏ ❏ USA Ba9508 **#8 Ice Skatin' Barbie,** 1994, Blk Barbie with Turq/Pnk Outfit with Pnk/Sil Skates with Lt Blue Stand/2p. $2.00-2.50

Premiums: Hot Wheels Cars

❏ ❏ USA Hw9509 **#9 Lightning Speed,** 1994, Org/Blu with Clear Dome Cover. $2.00-2.50

❏ ❏ USA Hw9510 **#10 Shock Force,** 1994, Black Hot Rod with Yel Center/Top with Sil Pipes. $2.00-2.50

❏ ❏ USA Hw9511 **#11 Twin Engine,** 1994, Grn with Purp/Silver Engines/Blu Accents. $2.00-2.50

❏ ❏ USA Hw9512 **#12 Radar Racer,** 1994, Blu/Purp with Clear Dome. $2.00-2.50

❏ ❏ USA Hw9513 **#13 Blue Bandit,** 1994, Blu with Blk/Silver Accents. $2.00-2.50

❏ ❏ USA Hw9514 **#14 Power Circuit,** 1994, Red/Yel with Clear Dome. $2.00-2.50

❏ ❏ USA Hw9515 **#15 Black Burner,** 1994, Burg Red with Sil/Blk Accents. $2.00-2.50

❏ ❏ USA Hw9516 **#16 After Blast,** 1994, Pea Grn with Clear Dome Windshield/Blk Accents. $2.00-2.50

❏ ❏ USA Ba9526 **Display/Premiums**, 1995, with 16 Premiums. $25.00-40.00

❏ ❏ USA Ba9543 **Crew Reference Sheet**, 1995, Blk/Wht Pic. $1.00-1.50

❏ ❏ USA Ba9544 **Crew Poster,** 1995. $1.50-3.00

❏ ❏ USA Ba9564 **Translite/Sm**, 1995. $3.00-5.00

Comments: National Distribution: USA - August 1-28, 1995. Many stores started distribution a week to ten days early, creating a mixed-up distribution of Barbies and Hot Wheels. U-3 (Girl) USA Ba9517 = USA To9302 without the clip-on clothes; U-3 (Boy) USA Hw9518 = USA To9313, loose out of package. USA Ba9519/20 were selectively distributed throughout the USA.

Left to right: Ba9503, Ba9501, Ba9502, Ba9507

Ba9519 Ba9505

Ba9506 Ba9501 Ba9503 Ba9520

Left to right: Ba9517, Hw9518, Ba9504

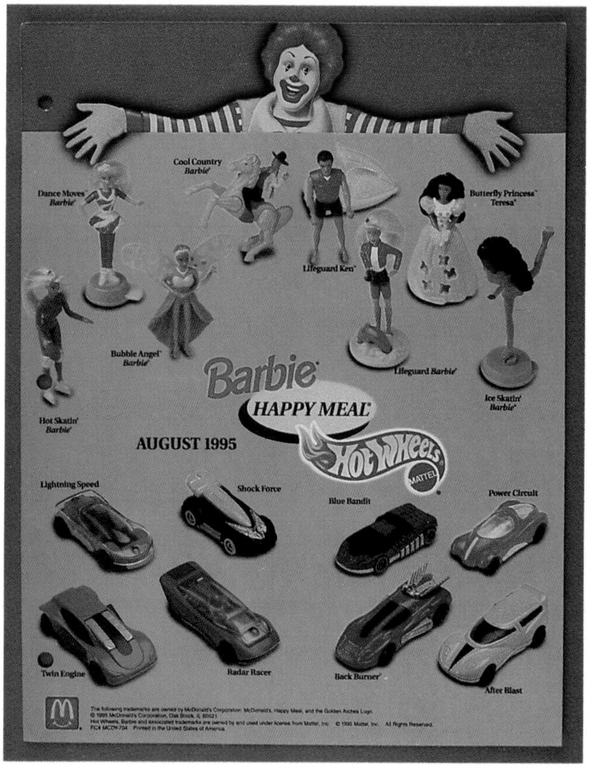

Hw9509 Hw9510 Hw9511 Hw9512

Hw9513 Hw9514 Hw9515 Hw9516

Ba9526

Ba9564

The Busy World of Richard Scarry Happy Meal, 1995

Ri9505 (on left)

Bag:

❑ ❑ USA Ri9530 **Hm Bag - Busytown Library**, 1995. $.50-1.00

U-3 Premium:

❑ ❑ USA Ri9505 **U-3 Lowly Worm,** 1995, Red Rubber Apple with Worm Driving. $1.00-1.50

Premiums:

❑ ❑ USA Ri9501 **Lowly Worm Red Apple Vehicle and Blue Post Office,** 1995, Red Plastic Apple/Blue Post Office/C Board/3p. $.50-1.00

❑ ❑ USA Ri9502 **Huckle Cat in Blue Vehicle and Yellow School,** 1995, Cat in Blu Car/Yel School/ Cardboard Photo/3p. $.50-1.00

❑ ❑ USA Ri9503 **Mr. Frumble in Green Vehicle and Red Fire Station,** 1995, in Grn Car/Red Fire Station/Cardboard/3p. $.50-1.00

❑ ❑ USA Ri9504 **Banana Gorilla in Yellow Vehicle and Green Grocery Store,** 1995, in Yel Car/Grn Grocery Store/C Board/3p. $.50-1.00

❑ ❑ USA Ri9526 **Display,** 1995, with 4 Premiums. $5.00-10.00

❑ ❑ USA Ri9543 **Crew Reference Sheet**, 1995, Blk/Wht Pic. $1.00-1.50

❑ ❑ USA Ri9544 **Crew Poster,** 1995. $1.50-3.00

❑ ❑ USA Ri9564 **Translite/Sm**, 1995. $3.00-4.00

Comments: National Distribution: USA - September 1-30, 1995.

Ri9501 Ri9502

Ri9530

Ri9503 Ri9504

Ri9526

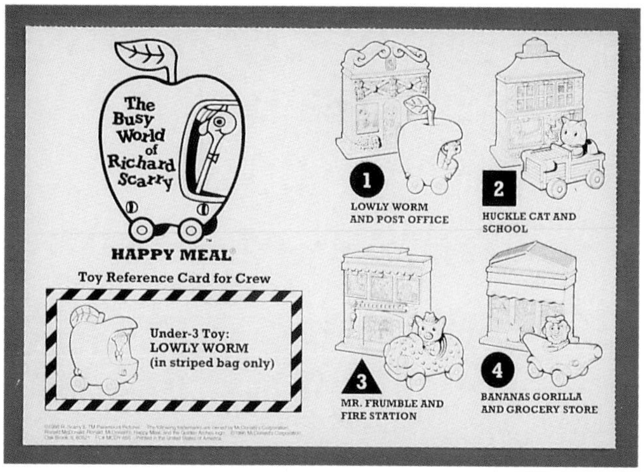

Ri9543

Ri9564

Happy Meal watch

September – The busy world of Richard Scarry

This back-to-school Happy Meal focuses on reading and literacy, with premiums based on characters from children's books by Richard Scarry. Each toy, in a series of four (one available each week), comes with a molded building, a two-sided color insert that depicts different Busytown scenes, and a push-along vehicle with a character in it. The toys include: Lowly Worm and Post Office; Huckle Cat and School; Mr. Frumble and Fire Station; and Bananas Gorilla and Grocery Store.

Disneyland 40 Years of Adventure Happy Meal, 1995

Boxes:

❑ ❑ USA Di9510 **Hm Box - Aladdin Oasis/Dancers**, 1995. $1.00-1.25

❑ ❑ USA Di9511 **Hm Box - Fantasmic/Pirates**, 1995. $1.00-1.25

❑ ❑ USA Di9512 **Hm Box - Lion King Celebration,** 1995. $1.00-1.25

❑ ❑ USA Di9513 **Hm Box - Space Mountain/Mickey Mouse**. 1995 $1.00-1.25

U-3 Premium:

❑ ❑ USA Di9509 **U-3 Winnie the Pooh/Thunder Mountain,** 1995, **in Red Train with Grn Cab/No Viewer.** $2.00-2.50

Premiums:

❑ ❑ USA Di9501 **Brer Bear on Splash Mountain in Log Boat.** $2.00-2.50

❑ ❑ USA Di9502 **Aladdin & Jasmine at Aladdin's Oasis on Elephant.** $2.00-2.50

❑ ❑ USA Di9503 **Simba in the Lion King Celebration on Rock/Mountain.** $2.00-2.50

❑ ❑ USA Di9504 **Mickey Mouse on Space Mountain in Space Car.** $2.00-2.50

❑ ❑ USA Di9505 **Roger Rabbit in Mickey's Toontown in Car.** $2.00-2.50

❑ ❑ USA Di9506 **Winnie/Pooh on Big Thunder Mountain in Red Train with Black Cab/Viewer.** $2.00-2.50
❑ ❑ USA Di9514 **Winnie/Pooh on Big Thunder Mountain in Red Train with Green Cab/Viewer.** $2.00-2.50

❑ ❑ USA Di9507 **Peter Pan in Fantasmic! in Boat.** $2.00-2.50
❑ ❑ USA Di9508 **King Louie on the Jungle Cruise in Jungle Boat.** $2.00-2.50

❑ ❑ USA Di9526 **Display**, 1995, with 8 Premiums. $25.00-35.00
❑ ❑ USA Di9543 **Crew Reference Sheet**, 1995, Blk/Wht Pic. $1.00-1.50
❑ ❑ USA Di9544 **Crew Poster**, 1995. $1.50-3.00
❑ ❑ USA Di9564 **Translite/Sm**, 1995. $5.00-7.00

Comments: National Distribution: USA - June 1-31, 1995. USA Di9509 and USA Di9506 are not the same. Premiums are copyright of the Walt Disney Company. Roger Rabbit characters are copyright of Disney-Amblin. USA Di9506 and USA Di9514 are essentially the same except for the color of the engine cab. In the USA, both colors seemed to be distributed widely.

Di9514 Di9506

Di9526

Di9509

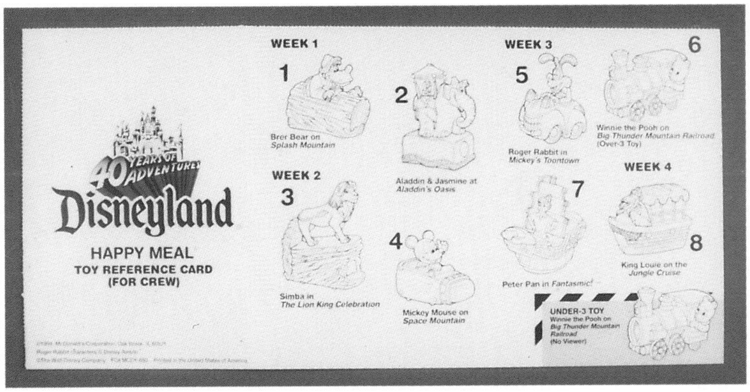

Di9543

Top row: Di9502
Bottom row, left to right: Di9503, Di9501, Di9508

Top row: Di9507
Bottom row, left to right: Di9505, Di9504, Di9509

Di9564

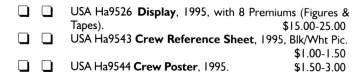

- ❑ ❑ USA Ha9526 **Display**, 1995, with 8 Premiums (Figures & Tapes). $15.00-25.00
- ❑ ❑ USA Ha9543 **Crew Reference Sheet**, 1995, Blk/Wht Pic. $1.00-1.50
- ❑ ❑ USA Ha9544 **Crew Poster**, 1995. $1.50-3.00
- ❑ ❑ USA Ha9564 **Translite/Sm**, 1995. $4.00-5.00

Comments: National Distribution: USA - October 1-31, 1995.

Halloween '95/What Am I Going to Be for Halloween? Happy Meal, 1995

Boxes:

- ❑ ❑ USA Ha9510 **Hm Box - Look Behind Me and Find Costume "Clues,"** 1995. $.50-1.00
- ❑ ❑ USA Ha9511 **Hm Box - Gang Is Carving Pumpkins for the Party!**, 1995. $.50-1.00
- ❑ ❑ USA Ha9512 **Hm Box - Ronald Is Helping Grimace with His Costume**, 1995. $.50-1.00
- ❑ ❑ USA Ha9513 **Hm Box - Ronald Is Helping Hamburglar with His Costume**, 1995. $.50-1.00

U-3 Premium:

- ❑ ❑ USA Ha9509 **U-3 Halloween Pumpkin with Pop-Up Grimace**, 1995, Orange Pumpkin/Lid Rises. $2.00-3.00

Premiums: Tapes

- ❑ ❑ USA Ha9501 **Tape: Ronald Makes it Magic Cassette**, 1995, 10 Minute Cassette. $1.00-1.50
- ❑ ❑ USA Ha9502 **Tape: Travel Tunes Cassette**, 1995, 10 Minute Cassette. $1.00-1.50
- ❑ ❑ USA Ha9503 **Tape: Silly Sing-Along Cassette**, 1995, 10 Minute Cassette. $1.00-1.50
- ❑ ❑ USA Ha9504 **Tape: Scary Sound Effects Cassette**, 1995, 10 Minute Cassette. $1.00-1.50

Premiums: Character Figurines with Costumes

- ❑ ❑ USA Ha9505 **Hamburglar with Witch costume**, 1995, Hamb Figurine with Blk Witch Snap-On/3p. $2.00-2.50
- ❑ ❑ USA Ha9506 **Grimace with Ghost costume**, 1995, Grimace with Wht Ghost Snap-On/3p. $2.00-2.50
- ❑ ❑ USA Ha9507 **Ronald with Frankenstein costume**, 1995, Ronald with Grn Frankenstein Snap-On/3p. $2.00-2.50
- ❑ ❑ USA Ha9508 **Birdie with Pumpkin costume**, 1995, Birdie with Org Pumpkin Snap-On/3p. $2.00-2.50

Ha9510

Ha9513

Ha9512

Ha9511

Ha9509

Ha9526

Left to right: Ha9501, Ha9503, Ha9502, Ha9504

Ha9543

Ha9505

Ha9507

Ha9508

Ha9506

Original storyboard drawing by Rich Seidelman.

Ha9564

Muppet Workshop Happy Meal, 1995

Boxes:
❑ ❑ USA Mu9510 **Hm Box - Bird Puppet**, 1995. $1.00-1.25
❑ ❑ USA Mu9511 **Hm Box - Dog Puppet**, 1995. $1.00-1.25
❑ ❑ USA Mu9512 **Hm Box - Monster Puppet,** 1995. $1.00-1.25
❑ ❑ USA Mu9513 **Hm Box - What-Not Puppet,** 1995. $1.00-1.25

U-3 Premium:
❑ ❑ USA Mu9505 **U-3 What-Not Muppet,** 1995, Yel Monster/Purp Cowboy Hat/Red Guitar/4p. $.50-1.00

Premiums:
❑ ❑ USA Mu9501 **Wk 1 Bird Muppet,** 1995, Turq Bird/Red Hat/Purp Bow/4p. $.50-1.00
❑ ❑ USA Mu9502 **Wk 2 Dog Muppet,** 1995, Pnk Dog/Org Bird Hat/Grn Camera/4p. $.50-1.00
❑ ❑ USA Mu9503 **Wk 3 Monster Muppet,** 1995, Grn Monster/Org Hat/Blu Bear/4p. $.50-1.00
❑ ❑ USA Mu9504 **Wk 4 What-Not Muppet,** 1995, Yel Monster/Purp Cowboy Hat/Red Guitar/4p. $.50-1.00

❑ ❑ USA Mu9526 **Display**, 1995, with 4 Premiums. $5.00-10.00
❑ ❑ USA Mu9543 **Crew Reference Sheet,** 1995, Blk/Wht Pic. $1.00-1.50
❑ ❑ USA Mu9544 **Crew Poster**, 1995. $1.50-3.00
❑ ❑ USA Mu9564 **Translite/Sm**, 1995. $3.00-4.00

Comments: National Distribution: USA - January 6-February 2, 1995.

Top row, left to right: Mu9510, Mu9512
Bottom row, left to right: Mu9511, Mu9513

Mu9501 Mu9502 Mu9503 Mu9504

Mu9526

Mu9564

Polly Pocket/Attack Pack Happy Meal, 1995

Bag:
❑ ❑ USA Po9530 **Hm Bag - Polly Pocket/Attack Pack**, 1995. $.25-.50

U-3 Premiums:
❑ ❑ USA Po9509 **U-3 Watch,** 1995, Yel Case/Turq Dial, same as Po9503. $2.00-2.50
❑ ❑ USA Hw9510 **U-3 Truck,** 1995, Gry/Blk/Red Truck, same as Hw9505. $2.00-2.50

Premiums: Jewelry
❑ ❑ USA Po9501 **Ring,** 1995, Pnk/Yel/Grn Polly Pocket on Flower Petal. $.50-1.00
❑ ❑ USA Po9502 **Locket,** 1995, Pnk Heart Locket with Pnk Cord. $.50-1.00
❑ ❑ USA Po9503 **Watch,** 1995, Yel Case/Turq Dial. $.50-1.00
❑ ❑ USA Po9504 **Bracelet,** 1995, Pnk/Turq Butterfly Case/Yel Strap. $.50-1.00

Premiums: Vehicles
❑ ❑ USA Hw9505 **Truck,** 1995, Gry/Blk/Red Truck. $.50-1.00
❑ ❑ USA Hw9506 **Battle Bird,** 1995, Grn/Wht Airplane/Bird. $.50-1.00
❑ ❑ USA Hw9507 **Lunar Invader,** 1995, Yel/Gry Lunar Module. $.50-1.00
❑ ❑ USA Hw9508 **Sea Creature,** 1995, Turq/Wht Sea Creature. $.50-1.00

❑ ❑ USA Po9526 **Display**, 1995, with 8 Premiums. $5.00-15.00
❑ ❑ USA Po9543 **Crew Reference Sheet**, 1995, Blk/Wht Pic $1.00-1.50
❑ ❑ USA Po9544 **Crew Poster** 1995. $1.50-3.00
❑ ❑ USA Po9564 **Translite/Sm**, 1995. $3.00-5.00

Comments: National Distribution: USA - February 3-March 2, 1995. USA Hw9505 = USA Hw9510, loose out of package.

Po9530

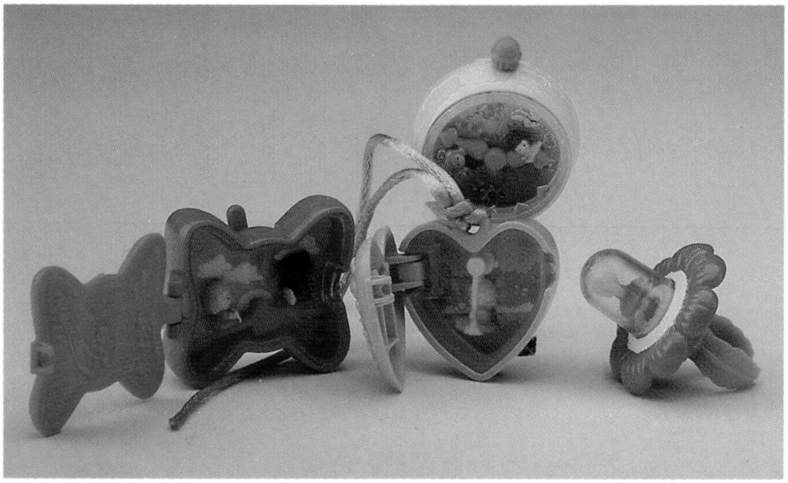

Top row: Po9503
Bottom row, left to right: Po9504, Po9502, Po9501

Top row: Hw9506
Bottom row, left to right: Hw9505, Hw9507, Hw9508

Po9526

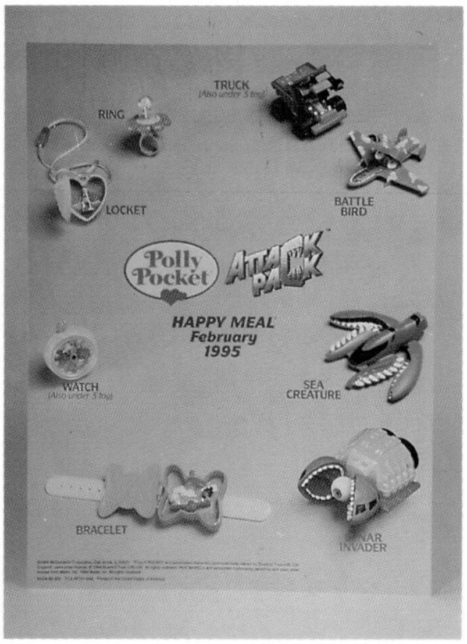

Po9543

Po9564

Power Rangers the Movie/Mighty Morphin Happy Meal, 1995

Bag:

❑ ❑ USA Pr9530 **Hm Bag - Power Rangers/ Our Story,** 1995. $.25-.50

U-3 Premium:

❑ ❑ USA Pr9505 **U-3 Power Flute,** 1995, Blue Rubber/Squeeze. $1.00-1.50

Premiums:

❑ ❑ USA Pr9501 **Power Com,** 1995, Grey Watch/Blk Strap/Flips Open. $.50-1.00

❑ ❑ USA Pr9502 **Powermorpher Buckle,** 1995, Grey/Red Buckle with 3 Gold Coins/ 4p. $.50-1.00

❑ ❑ USA Pr9503 **Power Siren,** 1995, Blk/Grey Whistle. $.50-1.00

❑ ❑ USA Pr9504 **Alien Detector,** 1995, Purple Case/Blue Door. $.50-1.00

❑ ❑ USA Pr9526 **Display,** 1995, with 4 Premiums. $5.00-10.00

❑ ❑ USA Pr9543 **Crew Reference Sheet/Toys,** 1995, Blk/Wht Pic. $1.00-1.50

❑ ❑ USA Pr9544 **Crew Poster**, 1995. $1.50-3.00

❑ ❑ USA Pr9550 **Button**, 1995, Go for All 6/ Purple. $2.00-3.00

❑ ❑ USA Pr9564 **Translite/Sm**, 1995. $3.00-4.00

❑ ❑ USA Pr9575 **Wal-Mart: Power Ranger Bag**. $.50-1.00

Comments: National Distribution: USA - July 1-31, 1995.

Pr9530

Pr9525

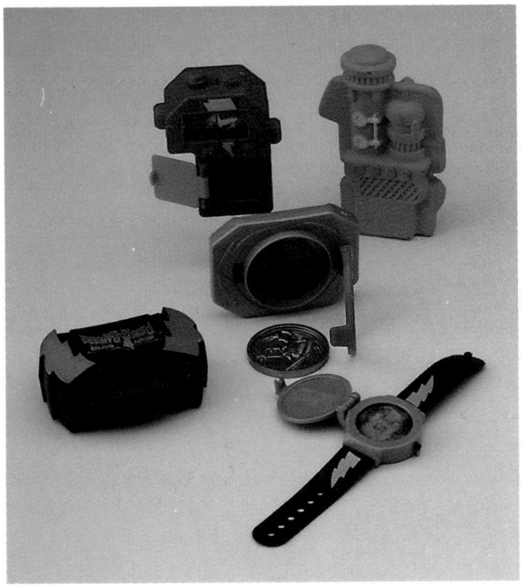

Top row, left to right: Pr9504, Pr9505
Center: Pr9502
Bottom row, left to right: Pr9503, Pr9501

Pr9526

Color Card

Pr9564

Sp9530

Space Rescue Happy Meal, 1995

Bag:

❑ ❑ USA Sp9530 **Hm Bag - Space Rescue**, 1995. $.25-.50

U-3 Premium:

❑ ❑ USA Sp9505 **U-3 Astro Viewer**, 1994, Grn/Purp/Wht Label. $1.00-1.50

Premiums:

❑ ❑ USA Sp9501 **Astro Viewer,** 1994, Grn/Purp/Pnk Label. $.50-1.00

❑ ❑ USA Sp9502 **Tele Communicator,** 1994, Org/Grn. $.50-1.00

❑ ❑ USA Sp9503 **Space Slate,** 1994, Blu/Purp/Org with Purp Pen/2p. $.50-1.00

❑ ❑ USA Sp9504 **Lunar Grabber,** 1994, Blu/Grn/Org. $.50-1.00

❑ ❑ USA Sp9526 **Display**, 1995, with 4 Premiums. $5.00-10.00

❑ ❑ USA Sp9543 **Crew Reference Sheet,** 1995, Blk/Wht Pic. $1.00-1.50

❑ ❑ USA Sp9544 **Crew Poster**, 1995. $1.50-3.00

❑ ❑ USA Sp9564 **Translite/Sm**, 1995. $3.00-4.00

Comments: National Distribution: USA - March 3-31, 1995. USA Sp9501 = Sp9505, loose out of package.

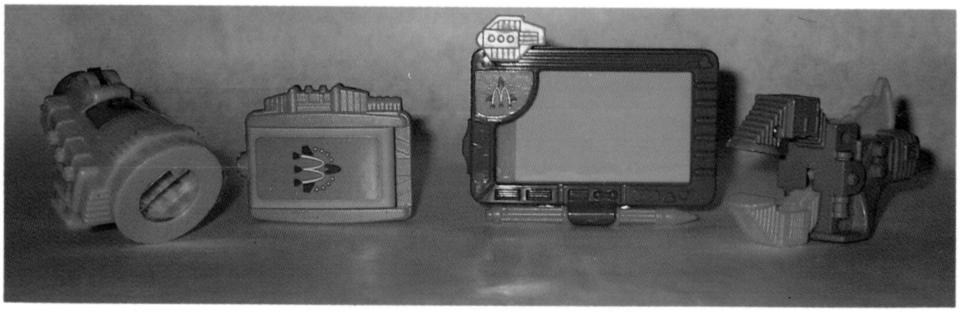

Left to right: Sp9501, Sp9502, Sp9503, Sp9504

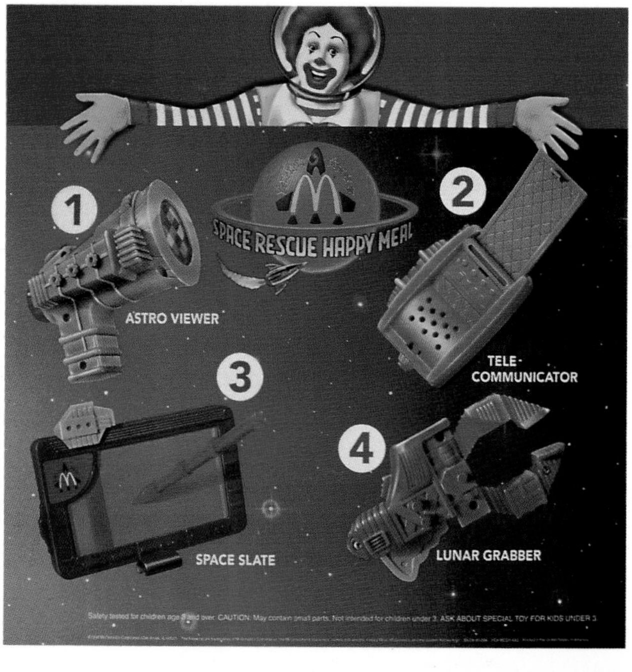

Sp9564

Spider-Man Happy Meal, 1995

Bag:

❑ ❑ USA Sm9530 **Hm Bag - Spiderman,** 1995. $.50-1.00

U-3 Premium:

❑ ❑ USA Sm9509 **U-3 Amazing Spider-Man,** 1995, Red/Blu Spider-Man/No Moveable Parts, same as Sm9501. $3.00-4.00

Premiums:

❑ ❑ USA Sm9501 **#1 Amazing Spider-Man,** 1995, Red/Blu Spider-Man No Moveable Parts . $2.50-3.50

❑ ❑ USA Sm9502 **#2 Scorpion Stingstriker Vehicle with Pliers,** 1995, Grn Scorpion Vehicle with Plier Claws. $2.50-3.50

❑ ❑ USA Sm9503 **#3 Dr. Octopus with Tentacles,** 1995, Yel/Grn Man with Gry Tentacles. $2.50-3.50

❑ ❑ USA Sm9504 **#4 Spider-Man Webrunner Red/Wht/Blu Vehicle,** 1995, Spider-Man in Wht/Red/Blu Spider Vehicle . $2.50-3.50

❑ ❑ USA Sm9505 **#5 Mary Jane Watson with Clip-on Dress,** 1995, Pnk Coat/Yel Shirt/W Red or Grn Clip-On Dress/3p. $2.50-3.50

❑ ❑ USA Sm9506 **#6 Venom Transport Vehicle,** 1995, Blk/Wht/Red Spider Vehicle. $2.50-3.50

❑ ❑ USA Sm9507 **#7 Spider-Sense Peter Parker Two Face/Half Face,** 1995, Brn Shirt/Blu Pants/Half Face. $2.50-3.50

❑ ❑ USA Sm9508 **#8 Hobgoblin Land Glider Vehicle,** 1995, Purp/Org/Gry Vehicle. $2.50-3.50

❑ ❑ USA Sm9526 **Display**, 1995, with 8 Premiums. $35.00-50.00

❑ ❑ USA Sm9543 **Crew Reference Sheet**, 1995, Blk/Wht Pic. $1.00-1.50

❑ ❑ USA Sm9544 **Crew Poster,** 1995. $1.50-3.00

❑ ❑ USA Sm9564 **Translite/Sm**, 1995. $5.00-7.00

Comments: National Distribution: USA - May 1-31, 1995. USA Sm9501 = Sm9509, loose out of package. Spider-Man character names and character likenesses are trademark and copyright of Marvel Entertainment Group, Inc.

Sm9501 Sm9508 Sm9502

Sm9507 Sm9506 Sm9504 Sm9503

Sm9526

Sm9530

Color Card

Sm9564

- ❑ ❑ USA To9510 **U-3 Mattel: Magic Nursery Doll/Boy,** 1993, Blu PJs/Candy Cane Cloth Body. $2.50-3.00
- ❑ ❑ USA To9511 **U-3 Mattel: Magic Nursery Doll/Girl,** 1993, Pnk PJs/Holly Cloth Body. $2.50-3.00

Premiums:

- ❑ ❑ USA To9501 **#1 Barbie : Holiday Barbie,** 1995, Grn/Wht Dressed Barbie in Wht/Gold Sleigh. $2.50-4.00

- ❑ ❑ USA To9502 **#2 57 Chevy Hot Wheels,** 1993, **Red 57 Chevy Hw Car with Blue Ramp/2p.** $1.00-1.50
- ❑ ❑ USA To9512 **#2 Gator Hot Wheels,** 1993, **Grn Hw Car/ Gator Graphics with Blue Ramp/2p.** $1.50-2.00

- ❑ ❑ USA To9503 **#3 Polly Pocket House,** 1995, Grn/Pnk/Wht House with Girl Fig Inside. $1.00-1.25
- ❑ ❑ USA To9504 **#4 Mighty Max Case,** 1995, Two Tone Blue Case/MM Fig Inside. $1.00-1.25
- ❑ ❑ USA To9505 **#5 Cabbage Patch Kids on Rocking Horse,** 1995, Pnk/Red Rocking Horse Case/Fig Inside. $1.00-1.25
- ❑ ❑ USA To9506 **#6 Hot Wheels: North Pole Explorer Vehicle,** 1995, Blu/Blk/Wht Explorer Truck/Purp Fig. $1.00-1.25
- ❑ ❑ USA To9507 **#7 Fisher-Price: Once upon a Dream Princess Figurine,** 1995, Red/Wht Fig with Wht Crown. $1.00-1.25
- ❑ ❑ USA To9508 **#8 Fisher-Price: Great Adventure Knight Figurine with Green Dragon,** 1995, Blk/Red Shield Fig with **Grn Dragon**/2p. $1.00-1.25

- ❑ ❑ USA To9526 **Display**, 1995, with 8 Premiums. $10.00-20.00
- ❑ ❑ USA To9543 **Crew Reference Sheet**, 1995, Blk/Wht Pictures. $1.00-1.50
- ❑ ❑ USA To9544 **Crew Poster**, 1995. $1.50-2.00
- ❑ ❑ USA To9564 **Translite/Sm**, 1995. $3.00-4.00

Comments: National Distribution: USA - December 1-31, 1995. USA To9311 Mighty Max, 1993, white skull face case with yellow figurine on inside/open close lid/marked McD ($1.00-1.50) was given out in some markets along with and in place of USA To9504 #4 Mighty Max two tone blue case. Magic Nursery Doll/Boy and Girl were repackaged from 1993 Totally Toy promotion. Loose out of package, the Magic Nursery Dolls (Boy or Girl) are the same premium.

To9530

Totally Toy Holiday/Mattel Happy Meal, 1995

Bag:

- ❑ ❑ USA To9530 **Hm Bag - Totally Toy Holiday**, 1995. $.25-.50

U-3 Premiums:

- ❑ ❑ USA Hw9509 **U-3 Key Force Car,** 1993, Red Car with Grey Tires/Purp Key/Grey Windshield (Same as USA To9313). $2.00-2.50

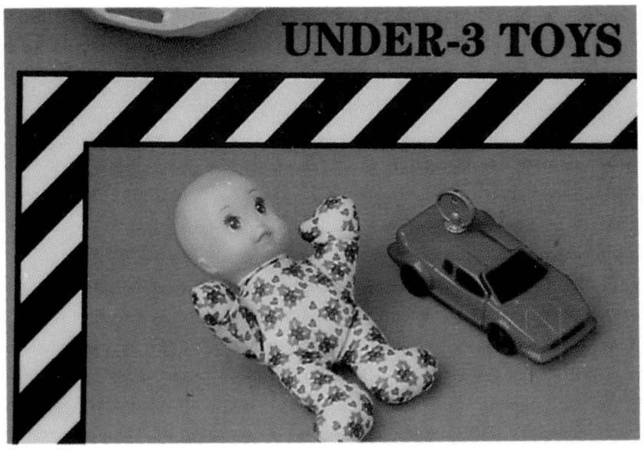

To9511 Hw9509

To9508 To9504 To9508

Top row, left to right: To9505, To9501
Bottom row, left to right: To9503, To9507

To9526

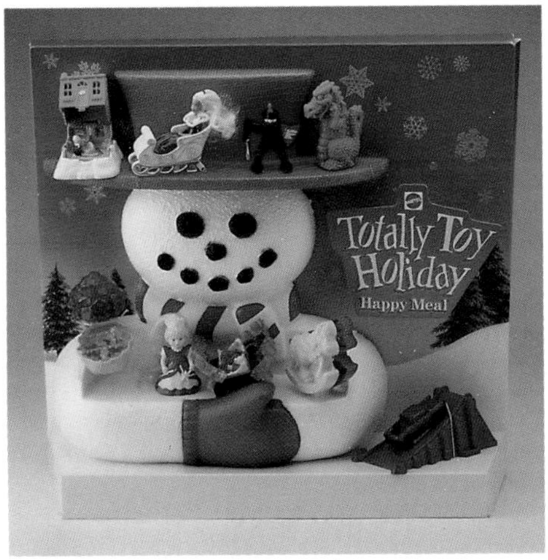

To9506 To9512 To9504

Color Card

To9543

To9564

Power Rangers Supplemental/Self-Liquidating Promotion, 1995

❑ ❑ USA Pr9531 **Wht Ranger/Falcon Ninjazord,** 1995, Wht/Gold Fig with Wht/Gold Falcon Carrier/2p. $2.00-4.00

❑ ❑ USA Pr9532 **Blk Ranger/Frog Ninjazord,** 1995, Blk/Wht Fig with Blk/Sil Frog Carrier/2p. $2.00-4.00

❑ ❑ USA Pr9533 **Blu Ranger/Wolf Ninjazord,** 1995, Blu/Wht Fig with Blu/Sil Wolf Carrier/2p. $2.00-4.00

❑ ❑ USA Pr9534 **Red Ranger/Ape Ninjazord,** 1995, Red/Wht Fig with Red/Blk/Gold Ape Carrier/2p. $2.00-4.00

❑ ❑ USA Pr9535 **Yel Ranger/Bear Ninjazord,** 1995, Yel/Wht Girl Fig with Blk/Yel Bear Carrier/2p. $2.00-4.00

❑ ❑ USA Pr9536 **Pnk Ranger/Crane Ninjazord,** 1995, Pnk/Wht Girl Fig with Wht/Pnk/Gold Airplane/2p. $2.00-4.00

❑ ❑ USA Pr9526 **Display**, 1995, with 6 Premiums. $5.00-15.00

Comments: National Distribution as self-liquidator (sold separately from Happy Meal): USA - July 1-31, 1995. Figurines and carriers were sold separately from Happy Meal for $1.59 each. Neither figurines nor Ninjazord carriers are marked with McDonald's logo. Packaging is marked, "McDonald's - Collect All 6."

Top row, left to right: Pr9536, Pr9531
Center row, left to right: Pr9533, Pr9534
Bottom row, left to right: Pr9535, Pr9532

USA Generic Promotions, 1995

❑ ❑ USA Ge9501 **Calendar/Ready, Set, Go!,** 1995, Paper with Stickers. $.50-1.00

❑ ❑ USA Ge9502 **Birthday Box: It's YOUR BIRTHDAY!,** 1995, red/org/yel/pnk/purp Birthday box. $1.00-2.00

❑ ❑ USA Ge9503 **Postcard,** 1995, with Stickers. $.25-.50

❑ ❑ USA Ge9504 **Booklet - Mystery of the Lost Polar Bear,** 1995, Paper. $.25-.50

❑ ❑ USA Ge9505 **Booklet - Mystery of the Lost Arches,** 1995, Paper. $.25-.50

❑ ❑ USA Ge9506 **Book Cover - Richard Scarry,** 1995, Wht/Blk Paper. $.25-.50

❑ ❑ USA Ge9507 **Booklet: Paint like Magic,** 1995, Ronald McDonald and the Lost Dog. $.25-.50

❑ ❑ USA Ge9508 **FTM: 1995-Issue 1 Out Of This World!** $.50-1.00

❑ ❑ USA Ge9509 **FTM: 1995-Issue 2 Go Wild!** $.50-1.00

❑ ❑ USA Ge9510 **FTM: 1995-Issue 3 Way To Grow** $.50-1.00

❑ ❑ USA Ge9511 **FTM: 1995-Issue 4 Let's Play Outside** $.50-1.00

❑ ❑ USA Ge9512 **FTM: 1995-Issue 5 The Greatest Halloween Party!** $.50-1.00

❑ ❑ USA Ge9513 **FTM: 1995-Issue 6 Holiday Magic!** $.50-1.00

☐ ☐ USA Ge9514 **1995 Calendar: Ready, Set, Go! 1995, One page calendar with stickers** $1.00-1.25
☐ ☐ USA Ge9515 **1995 Calendar: McDonald's Free Time Fun With Ronald McD/Friends/Coloring.** $1.00-1.25

☐ ☐ USA Ge9516 **Plate: Halloween - Four McNugget Buddies/Haunted House.** $3.00-4.00
☐ ☐ USA Ge9517 **Plate: Christmas.** $3.00-4.00

Comments: Regional Distribution: USA - 1995 as Fun Times Promotion.

McDonald's expanded into smaller sales units with McStop and McSnack operations in retail stores and limited space locations during 1995. Ronald McDonald Houses continued to serve the public and Ronald McDonald Children's Charities continued to focus on the needs of the needy in the communities. Forty years later, Ray Kroc's vision lived on.

Ge9502

Ge9509

Ge9511 Ge9512

1996

Aladdin and the King of Thieves Happy Meal, 1996
Babe Happy Meal, 1996
Barbie Dolls of the World VII/Hot Wheels VII HM, 1996
Eric Carle Finger Puppet Happy Meal, 1996
Fisher-Price Under-3 Promotion, 1996
Happy Meal Workshop Happy Meal, 1996
Littlest Pet Shop/Transformers Beast Wars I HM, 1996
Marvel Super Heroes Happy Meal, 1996
McNugget Buddies Halloween '96 Happy Meal, 1996
Muppet Treasure Island Happy Meal, 1996
101 [One Hundred and One] Dalmatians HM II, 1996
Space Jam Happy Meal, 1996
VR Troopers Happy Meal, 1996
Walt Disney Home Video Masterpiece Collection I Happy Meal (Act I), 1996
One Hundred and One Dalmatians Snow Domes Self-Liquidating Promotion, 1996
Space Jam Looney Tunes Characters Promotion, 1996
USA Generic Promotions, 1996

- **13th National O/O Convention**
- **"QSC and Me" - O/O advertising theme**

Aladdin and the King of Thieves Happy Meal, 1996

Bags & Boxes:

☐ ☐ USA AI9630 **Hm Bag - Aladdin/Jasmine with 3 Thieves after Gift**, 1995. $.50-1.00

☐ ☐ USA AI9631 **Hm Bag - Vanishing Island/Do You Know the Secret,** 1995. $.50-1.00

☐ ☐ USA AI9632 **Hm Box - Aladdin/Abu**, 1995. $15.00-20.00

☐ ☐ USA AI9633 **Hm Box - Jasmine/Aladdin on Rope**, 1995. $15.00-20.00

AI9632

AI9633

U-3 Premium:

☐ ☐ USA AI9609 **U-3 Abu,** 1996, Brown Squeeze Squirter/Rubber Monkey Sitting with Hands Crossed. $2.00-3.00

AI9609

Premiums: Figures with Dioramas

☐ ☐ USA AI9601 **#1 Cassim with Diorama,** 1996, Standing with Dark Blue Cape/Black Wrap/Grey Boots/2p. $1.00-1.50

☐ ☐ USA AI9602 **#2 Abu with Diorama,** 1996, Monkey on Carpet with Backdrop/2p. $1.00-1.50

☐ ☐ USA AI9603 **#3 Jasmine with Diorama,** 1996, with Wht Dress/Gold Trim/Diorama/2p. $1.00-1.50

☐ ☐ USA AI9604 **#4 Lago with Diorama,** 1996, Red Bird on Blue Money Cart/Diorama/2p. $1.00-1.50

☐ ☐ USA AI9605 **#5 Genie with Diorama,** 1996, Blue Genie on Wht Cloud/2p. $1.00-1.50

☐ ☐ USA AI9606 **#6 Sa'luk with Diorama,** 1996, Blk/Purp Bare Chested/Gold Wrist Band. $1.00-1.50

☐ ☐ USA AI9607 **#7 Aladdin with Diorama,** 1996, Wht Coat/Gold Trim/Hand to Waist/2p. $1.00-1.50

☐ ☐ USA AI9608 **#8 Maître D'Genie,** 1996, Purp Fig/Blk Long Coat/Wht Wedding Cake/2p. $1.00-1.50

☐ ☐ USA AI9626 **Display**, 1995, with 8 Premiums. $15.00-25.00

☐ ☐ USA AI9627 **Color Card.** $2.00-3.00

☐ ☐ USA AI9643 **Crew Reference Sheet**, 1995, Blk/Wht Pic. $.50-1.00

☐ ☐ USA AI9644 **Crew Poster**, 1995. $1.50-2.00

☐ ☐ USA AI9664 **Translite/Sm**, 1995. $3.00-5.00

Comments: National Distribution: USA - August 16-September 12, 1996. Each toy came with its own paper adventure scene/diorama. Happy Meal boxes were test marketed along with national distributed Happy Meals bags.

Left: AI9630
Right: AI9631

AI9601 AI9602 AI9603

AI9604 AI9605 AI9606

Top row, left to right: AI9605 AI9608
Bottom row: AI9602

AI9607 AI9608

AI9607 AI9603

AI9606 AI9601 AI9604

AI9626

AI9627

AI9664

Babe Happy Meal, 1996

Bags & Boxes:

❑ ❑ USA Bb9630 **Hm Bag, 1995, #1 - I'm a Sheep Pig!**, 1995. $.50-1.00

❑ ❑ USA Bb9631 **Hm Bag, 1995, #2 - You Can Be Whatever You Want to Be!**, 1995. $.50-1.00

❑ ❑ USA Bb9632 **Hm Box, 1996, Fly the Dog**, 1995. $15.00-25.00

❑ ❑ USA Bb9633 **Hm Box, 1996, Babe the Pig**, 1995. $15.00-25.00

Premiums: Stuffed Barnyard Animals

❑ ❑ USA Bb9601 **#1 Babe the Pig,** 1995, Stuffed/Plush Pig/Pink. $1.00-1.50

❑ ❑ USA Bb9602 **#2 Cow,** 1995, Stuffed/Plush Cow/Blk-Wht. $1.00-1.50

❑ ❑ USA Bb9603 **#3 Maa the Ewe,** 1995, Stuffed/Plush Sheep/Wht. $1.00-1.50

❑ ❑ USA Bb9604 **#4 Fly the Dog,** 1995, Stuffed/Plush Dog/Blk-Wht. $1.00-1.50

❑ ❑ USA Bb9605 **#5 Ferdinand the Duck,** 1995, Stuffed/Plush Wht Duck. $1.00-1.50

❑ ❑ USA Bb9606 **#6 Duchess the Cat,** 1995, Stuffed/Plush Furry Grey Cat. $1.00-1.50

❑ ❑ USA Bb9607 **#7 Mouse,** 1995, Stuffed Mouse/Plush Sitting Upright. $1.00-1.50

❑ ❑ USA Bb9626 **Display**, 1995, with 7 Premiums. $10.00-15.00

❑ ❑ USA Bb9643 **Crew Reference Sheet**, 1995, Blk/Wht Pic. $.50-1.00

❑ ❑ USA Bb9644 **Crew Poster**, 1995. $1.50-2.00

❑ ❑ USA Bb9664 **Translite/Sm**, 1995. $3.00-5.00

Comments: National Distribution: USA - June 14-July 11, 1996. No U-3 was distributed. All toys were safety tested for children of all ages. Two Happy Meal boxes were test marketed. The Babe the Pig plush was distributed in Week 1 and Week 2.

Bag flat layout sheet.

Bb9633 Bb9632

Bb9664

Left to right: Bb9601, Bb9602, Bb9603, Bb9604, Bb9605, Bb9606

Bb9626

Bb9643

Crew Reference Card

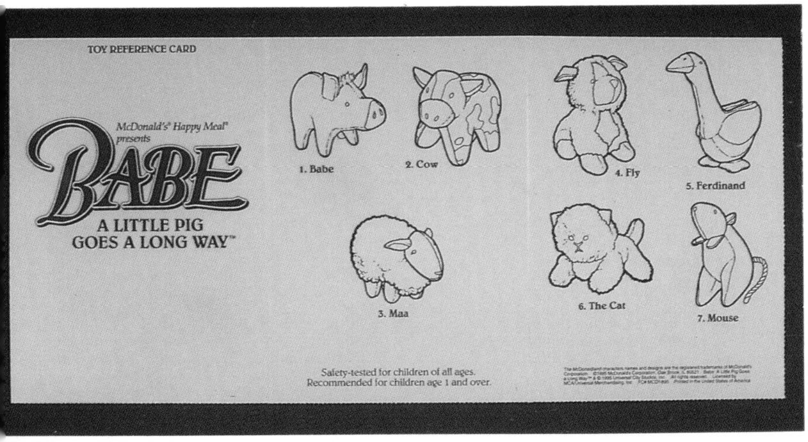

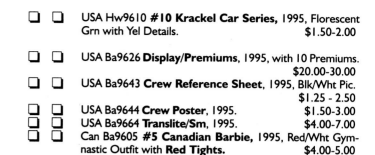

☐ ☐ USA Hw9610 **#10 Krackel Car Series,** 1995, Florescent Grn with Yel Details. $1.50-2.00

☐ ☐ USA Ba9626 **Display/Premiums**, 1995, with 10 Premiums. $20.00-30.00

☐ ☐ USA Ba9643 **Crew Reference Sheet**, 1995, Blk/Wht Pic. $1.25 - 2.50

☐ ☐ USA Ba9644 **Crew Poster**, 1995. $1.50-3.00

☐ ☐ USA Ba9664 **Translite/Sm**, 1995. $4.00-7.00

☐ ☐ Can Ba9605 **#5 Canadian Barbie,** 1995, Red/Wht Gymnastic Outfit with **Red Tights.** $4.00-5.00

Comments: National Distribution: USA July 12-August 15, 1996. USA distributed Olympic Looking Barbie with blue tights. Canada distributed Olympic Looking Barbie with red tights (no medal hanging from neck). Canadian boxes are slightly different from USA boxes, language variations.

Barbie Dolls of the World/Hot Wheels VII Happy Meal, 1996

Boxes:

☐ ☐ USA Ba9610 **Hm Box - USA Barbie Is Running Her Victory Lap...,** 1995. $.50-1.00

☐ ☐ USA Ba9611 **Hm Box - USA Barbie Looks Great with Her Gold Medal...,** 1995. $.50-1.00

☐ ☐ USA Hw9612 **Hm Box - Danger/This Loop the Loop Is Loopy!,** 1995. $.50-1.00

☐ ☐ USA Hw9613 **Hm Box - Orange Roadster/Pardon My Dust!,** 1995. $.50-1.00

U-3 Premiums:

☐ ☐ USA Ba9617 **U-3 Barbie Square Window Slide,** 1995, Pnk/Wht with Red/Wht/Purp Windows/1p. $2.00-2.50

☐ ☐ USA Hw9618 **U-3 HW Rubber Tire,** 1995, Blu/Silver Squeeze Tire/1p. $1.00-2.50

Premiums: Dolls

☐ ☐ USA Ba9601 **#1 Dutch Barbie,** 1995, Blu/Wht Striped Skirt/Wht Hat/Blonde Braids. $1.50-2.00

☐ ☐ USA Ba9602 **#2 Kenyan Barbie,** 1995, Red Fabric Cape/Yel Base/Red Plastic Dress/2p. $1.50-2.00

☐ ☐ USA Ba9603 **#3 Japanese Barbie,** 1995, Lt Purp Fabric Kimono/Blk Hair. $1.50-2.00

☐ ☐ USA Ba9604 **#4 Mexican Barbie,** 1995, Wht/Red/Green Flowered Fabric Dress. $1.50-2.00

☐ ☐ USA Ba9605 **#5 USA,** 1995, Red/Wht Gymnastic Outfit with **Blu Tights.** $2.00-2.50

Premiums: Hot Wheels Vehicles

☐ ☐ USA Hw9606 **#6 Flame Series,** 1995, Metallic Blu with Org Flames. $1.50-2.00

☐ ☐ USA Hw9607 **#7 Roarin Rod Series,** 1995, Extended Length/Wht with Blk Zebra Stripes. $1.50-2.00

☐ ☐ USA Hw9608 **#8 Dark Rider Series,** 1995, Black/Batman Style Car. $1.50-2.00

☐ ☐ USA Hw9609 **#9 Hot Hubs Series,** 1995, Org/Exposed Silver Engine. $1.50-2.00

Ba9610 Ba9611

Hw9612 Hw9613

Left: Ba9617
Right: Hw9618

Top: Ba9603
Bottom row, left to right: Ba9605, Ba9604, Ba9601, Ba9602

Ba9664

Left to right: Hw9606, Hw9607, Hw9608, Hw9609, Hw9610

Ba9626

Er9633 Er9632

Eric Carle Finger Puppet Happy Meal, 1996

Bags & Boxes:

- ❑ ❑ USA Er9630 **Hm Bag - I Am the Grouchy Ladybug,** 1996. $.50-1.00
- ❑ ❑ USA Er9631 **Hm Bag - I Am the Very Hungry Caterpillar**, 1996. $.50-1.00
- ❑ ❑ USA Er9632 **Hm Box - Ladybug**, 1996. $12.00-15.00
- ❑ ❑ USA Er9633 **Hm Box - Caterpillar**, 1996. $12.00-15.00

Premiums:

- ❑ ❑ USA Er9601 **#1 The Very Quiet Cricket,** 1996, Dk Blue Head with Purple Body/Clip **Button** on bottom. $1.00-1.50
- ❑ ❑ USA Er9602 **#2 The Grouchy Ladybug,** 1996, Red Wings/Peg on Bottom moves wings. $1.00-1.50
- ❑ ❑ USA Er9603 **#3 The Very Busy Spider**, 1996, Wht Base/Finger Moves Head & Body. $1.00-1.50
- ❑ ❑ USA Er9604 **#4 The Very Hungry Caterpillar**, 1996, Red Apple/Finger Moves Worm's Head & Body. $1.00-1.50
- ❑ ❑ USA Er9605 **#5 A House for Hermit Crab**, 1996, Wht Snail Shell/Finger Moves Crab's Body. $1.00-1.50
- ❑ ❑ USA Er9606 **#6 The Very Lonely Firefly**, 1996, Red Wings/Grn Head/Finger Moves Firefly. $1.00-1.50

- ❑ ❑ USA Er9626 **Display/Premiums**, 1996, with 6 Premiums. $5.00-15.00
- ❑ ❑ USA Er9643 **Crew Reference Sheet**, 1995, Blk/Wht Pic. $.50-1.00
- ❑ ❑ USA Er9644 **Crew Poster**, 1996. $1.00-2.00
- ❑ ❑ USA Er9664 **Translite/Sm**, 1996. $1.00-3.00

Comments: National Distribution: USA - September 20-October 10, 1996. In conjunction with Eric Carle Finger Puppet Happy Meal, McDonald's began the U-3 Fisher Price toddler toy distribution. Twenty-four different generic type under-3 toys were distributed.

Top to bottom, left to right:
Er9604
Er9602, Er9603
Er9605, Er9601
Er9606

Er9626

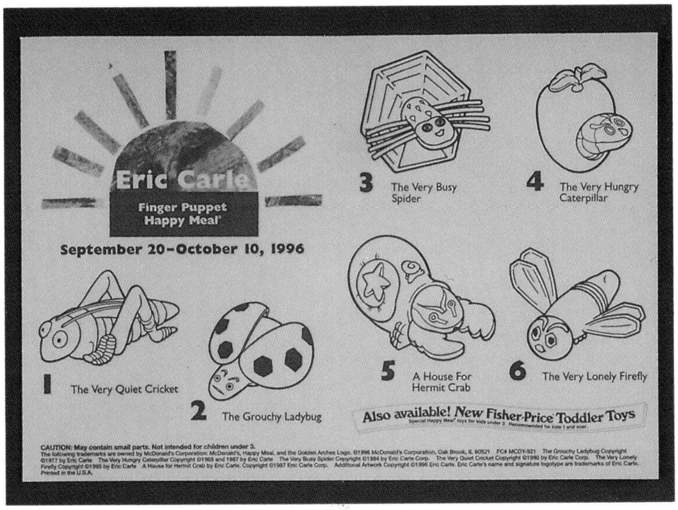

Er9643

Er9664

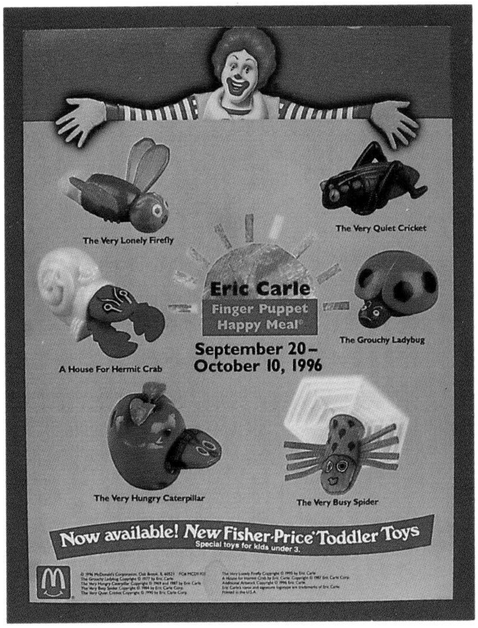

Color Card

Fisher-Price Under-3 Promotion, 1996

Group A Premiums:

❑ ❑ USA Fp9601 **Ronald at the Drive-Thru/Yellow Building/Red Roof,** 1996. $3.00-4.00

❑ ❑ USA Fp9602 **Grimace Inside Purple Rolling Ball,** 1996. $3.00-4.00

❑ ❑ USA Fp9603 **Birdie in Aqua Pop Car with Pink Wheels,** 1996. $3.00-4.00

❑ ❑ USA Fp9604 **Yellow/Red "M" Shaped Key With White Ring,** 1996. $3.00-4.00

Group B Premiums:

❑ ❑ USA Fp9605 **White Train Engine with Blue Wheels,** 1996, Red/Yellow Spinner on Top. $3.00-4.00

❑ ❑ USA Fp9606 **Barn Puzzle Square,** 1996, Yellow and Red Sides. $3.00-4.00

❑ ❑ USA Fp9607 **Boom Box Radio,** 1996, Yellow Front/Green Back. $3.00-4.00

❑ ❑ USA Fp9608 **Peg in a Barrel,** 1996, White or Red Side/House. Shaped. $3.00-4.00

Group C Premiums:

❑ ❑ USA Fp9609 **Doghouse with Puppy inside Window,** 1996, Red Roof/Blue Front. $3.00-4.00

❑ ❑ USA Fp9610 **Yellow Round Open Ball/Yellow/Red/Blue/Twirler,** 1996, Hands Grasp Ball Shape. $3.00-4.00

❑ ❑ USA Fp9611 **Lime Green Jeep with Purple Wheels,** 1996, No Driver, No Passengers, Blue Seats. $3.00-4.00

❑ ❑ USA Fp9612 **Book on Cows,** 1996, Washable Plastic Type/Red/White/Yellow/Blue. $3.00-4.00

Group D Premiums:

❑ ❑ USA Fp9613 **Chatter Telephone/Wheels,** 1996, White Phone/Yellow Dial/Red Receiver. $3.00-4.00

❑ ❑ USA Fp9614 **Rolling Blue Ball with Dog Inside,** 1996. $3.00-4.00

❑ ❑ USA Fp9615 **Red Clock with Blue Roof/Yellow Hands,** 1996. $3.00-4.00

❑ ❑ USA Fp9616 **Musical Ball - Yellow/Blue/Red,** 1996. $3.00-4.00

Group E Premiums:

- ❑ ❑ USA Fp9617 **Blue/Red Roof Dog House with Brn Eye Dog Inside,** 1996. $3.00-4.00
- ❑ ❑ USA Fp9618 **White Dog with Brown Spots on Red Wheels,** 1996, Gold Dog Tags. $3.00-4.00
- ❑ ❑ USA Fp9619 **Poppity Red Car with Yellow Wheels,** 1996, Red Car with Yellow Wheels/People Inside. $3.00-4.00
- ❑ ❑ USA Fp9620 **McDonald's Truck,** 1996, Red Cab/White Truck Bed/Blue Wheels. $3.00-4.00

Group F Premiums:

- ❑ ❑ USA Fp9621 **Balls in a Yellow Ball**, 1996, Yellow Ball With Red and white Balls Inside. $3.00-4.00
- ❑ ❑ USA Fp9622 **School Bus,** 1996, Yellow Bus with Blue Wheels/Ronald McDonald Driving. $3.00-4.00
- ❑ ❑ USA Fp9623 **Horse,** 1996, White with Red Reins. $3.00-4.00
- ❑ ❑ USA Fp9624 **Lawn Mower Popper,** 1996, Push Long Handle/Items Inside Pop Up And Down. $3.00-4.00

Fp9612 Fp9609

Comments: National Distribution: USA - September 1996-August 1997. McDonald's' standardization move resulted in a generic type Fisher-Price U-3 toy distributed for children under the age of three in the USA, Canada, and Mexico. A combination of eight, twelve, or more of the twenty-four announced Fisher-Price U-3 toys was distributed. Variations of the above toys exist with the molds being made backwards/reversed. That is, an "M" key on a ring exists with a red front/yellow back and white ring at top instead of USA Fi9604. For identification purposes, the back of the toy is considered where the screws can be viewed. This mold variation exists for several of the U-3 toys. The primary basic toy is listed above. Prices on the various toys and/or variations are the same. The new package used was red, white, yellow, and blue. The front of the package has Ronald McDonald holding up three fingers to indicate the age of three. A table tent, "What's Gotten into Happy Meals?" accompanied the initial promotion along with a trayliner announcing the introduction of the Fisher-Price toys. The U-3 poster displayed at the stores does not include USA Fp9624 Lawn Mower Popper. This U-3 was initially recalled due to misspelling of "Fishr-Price" instead of "Fisher-Price" on the reverse side. The U-3 toy was reprinted with the correct spelling and distributed in the last box, Group F premiums.

Fp9613 Fp9614 Fp9615 Fp9616

Fp9610 Fp9611

Fp9602 Fp9603 Fp9604 Fp9601

Fp9608 Fp9607 Fp9606 Fp9605

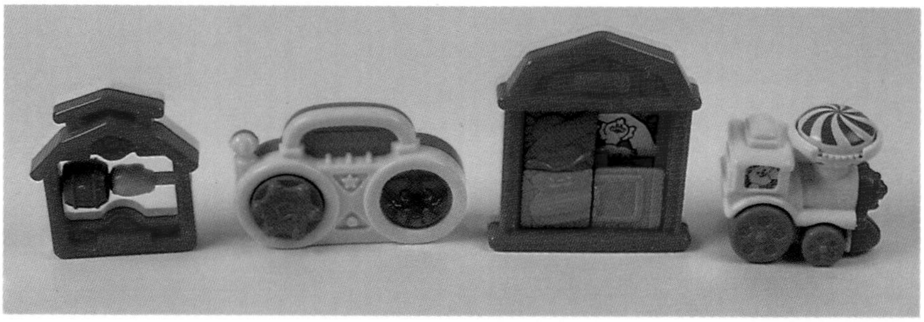

Fp9617 Fp9618 Fp9619 Fp9620

Fp9623 Fp9622 Fp9621 Fp9624

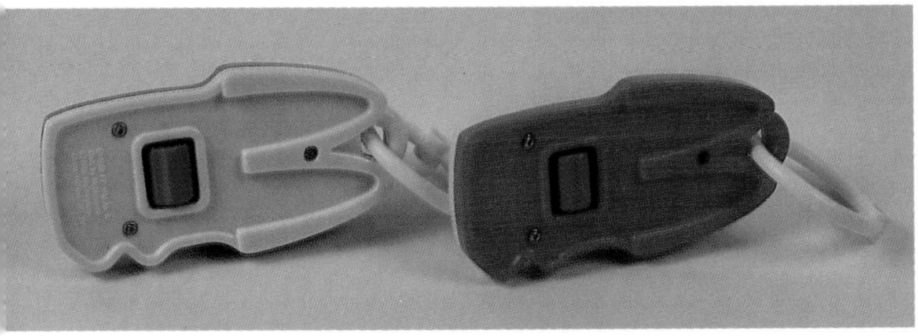

Fp9604 variation.

Fp9606 variation.

Fp9607 variation.

Fp9608 variation.

Fp9620

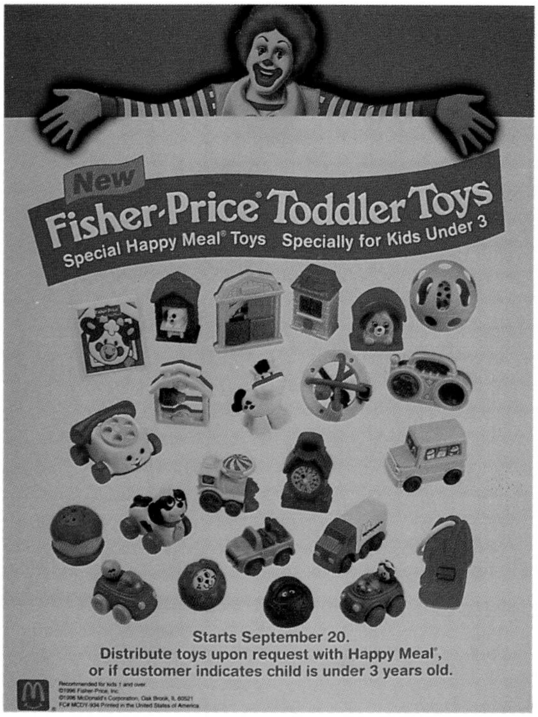
New
Fisher-Price Toddler Toys
Special Happy Meal Toys Specially for Kids Under 3
Starts September 20.
Distribute toys upon request with Happy Meal,
or if customer indicates child is under 3 years old.
Recommended for kids 1 and over
©1996 Fisher-Price, Inc.
©1996 McDonald's Corporation, Oak Brook, IL 60521
FC# MCDY-934 Printed in the United States of America

New
Fisher-Price
Toddler Toys

Fisher-Price
UNDER-3 TOY
JOUET POUR MOINS DE 3 ANS
MENORES DE 3 ANOS PREMIO
See back for safety information.
Instructions touchant la sécurité au dos du sac
Véase la información sobre seguridad al dorso.

Special Happy Meal Toys
Specially for Me
New
Fisher-Price Toddler Toys
Available designs may vary.

Special Happy Meal
Toddler Toys
by
Fisher-Price

Ask About New
Fisher-Price Toddler Toys
Special Happy Meal Toys for Kids Under 3
Available designs may vary.

Happy Meal Workshop Happy Meal, 1996

Boxes:

❑ ❑ USA Wo9610 **Hm Box - Ronald/Scratch to Win**, 1995. $.50-1.00

❑ ❑ USA Wo9611 **Hm Box - Ronald/Birdie/Scratch to Win**, 1995. $.50-1.00

U-3 Premium:

❑ ❑ USA Ea9405 **Tool Carrier**, 1993, Blu with Yel Strap/Red Shovel/3p. $.50-1.00

❑ ❑ USA Wo9626 **Display**, 1995, with 1 Box. $5.00-8.00

❑ ❑ USA Wo9664 **Translite/Sm**, 1995. $2.00-3.00

Comments: National Distribution: USA - January 5-18, 1996. Premiums from earlier Happy Meal promotions (USA and international) were used. No new premiums were specifically created for this promotion. Each Happy Meal box contained a scratch-off black square. If the scratch-off square said, "You Win," the customer had to complete a Happy Meal workshop game form and mail in the front panel of the Happy Meal box. Each prize package, sent by mail, included two sets of washable McMarkers (tank style and fine point): Sanford Washable McMarker 8-Color Set/ Sanford Washable Scented McMarker 10 Color Set and one "Write, Draw and Scribble" McDonaldland Stuart Hall Scribble/Activity Pad. The same markers and scribble pad could be purchased in retail stores in the USA. Retail value of all three items: $15.00. The U-3 Premium was a repeat from USA Earth Days Happy Meal, 1994.

Wo9664

Wo9610 Wo9611

Littlest Pet Shop/Transformers Beast Wars I Happy Meal, 1996

Boxes:

❑ ❑ USA Li9610 **Hm Box - What Are a Cat's Favorite Jewels?**, 1995. $.50-1.00

❑ ❑ USA Li9611 **Hm Box - Why Did the Littlest Pet Shop Friends Stay...**, 1995. $.50-1.00

❑ ❑ USA Li9612 **Hm Box - Transformers - Manta Ray and Beetle**, 1995. $.50-1.00

❑ ❑ USA Li9613 **Hm Box - Transformers - Panther and Rhino**, 1995. $.50-1.00

U-3 Premiums:

❑ ❑ USA Li9609 **U-3 Sphere,** 1996, Yellow Rolling Sphere/Wheel with Brn Animal in Center. $1.00-2.00

❑ ❑ USA Li9610 **U-3 Mighty Max Lion,** 1996, Yel M Max Lion/Opens to Blk/Red Transformer. $1.00-2.00

Premiums:

❑ ❑ USA Li9601 **#1 Swan,** 1996, Pink/Purp Swan with Wings. $1.00-1.50

❑ ❑ USA Li9602 **#2 Unicorn,** 1996, Purple Unicorn with Pink Tail. $1.00-1.50

❑ ❑ USA Li9603 **#3 Dragon,** 1996, Yel Dragon with Org Wings. $1.00-1.50

❑ ❑ USA Li9604 **#4 Tiger,** 1996, White Tiger with Pink Fur. $1.00-1.50

❑ ❑ USA Li9605 **#5 Manta Ray,** 1996, Dk Blue/Lt Blu Ray with Movable Head. $1.00-1.50

❑ ❑ USA Li9606 **#6 Beetle,** 1996, Maroon/Grn/Grn Beetle with Movable Head. $1.00-1.50

❑ ❑ USA Li9607 **#7 Panther,** 1996, Blk/Blu/Red Panther with Movable Head. $1.00-1.50

❑ ❑ USA Li9608 **#8 Rhino,** 1996, Grey/Red Rhino with Movable Head. $1.00-1.50

❑ ❑ USA Li9626 **Display/Premiums**, 1995, with 8 Premiums. $5.00-15.00
❑ ❑ USA Li9643 **Crew Reference Sheet**, 1995, Blk/Wht Pic. $.50-1.00
❑ ❑ USA Li9644 **Crew Poster**, 1995. $1.00-2.00
❑ ❑ USA Li9664 **Translite/Sm**, 1995. $3.00-4.00

Comments: National Distribution: USA - March 15-April 11, 1996.

Li9610 Li9609

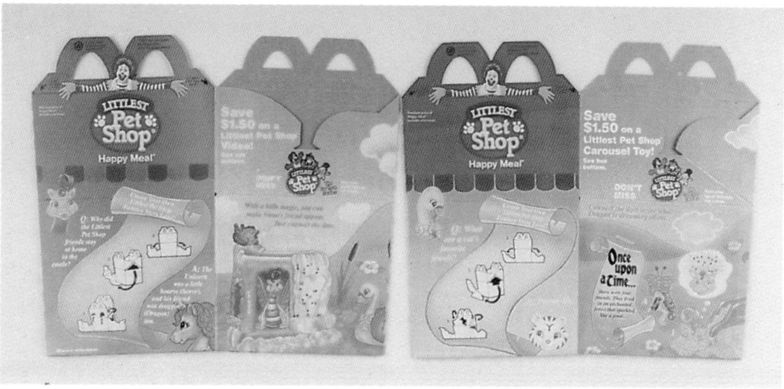

Li9611 Li9610

Top row, left to right: Li9610, Li9606
Bottom row, left to right: Li9607, Li9605

Li9612 Li9613

Li9608

Top row: Li9601
Bottom row, left to right: Li9603, Li9604, Li9602

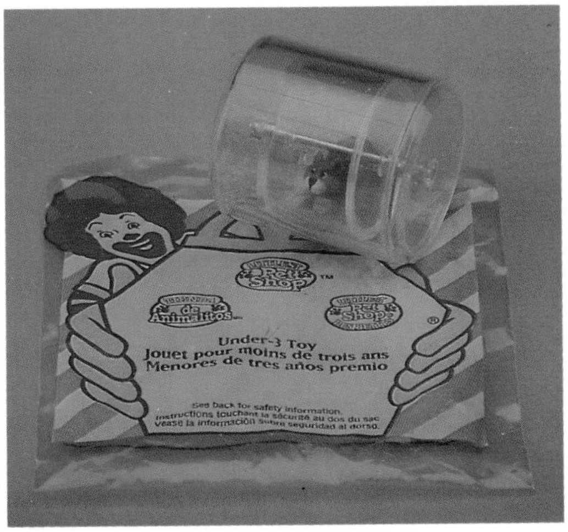

Li9609

Color Card

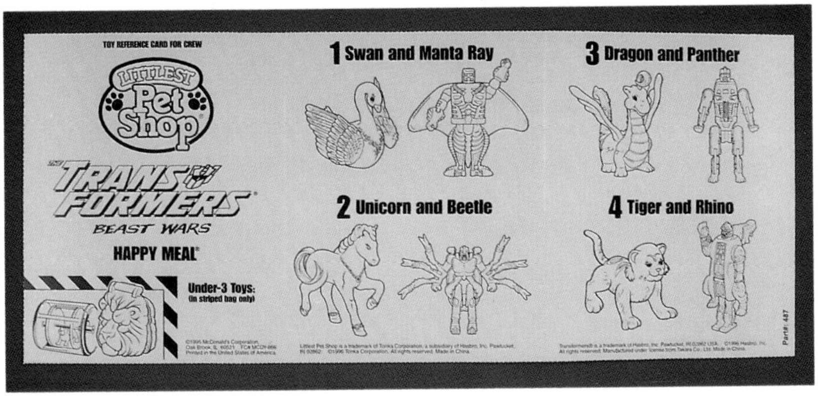

Li9643

Li9664

Marvel Super Heroes Happy Meal, 1996

Bags & Boxes:

❑ ❑ USA Ma9630 **Hm Bag - Marvel-Ous Offer in Wht/Unscramble the Red and Blue Letters**, 1996. $.50-1.00

❑ ❑ USA Ma9631 **Hm Bag - Marvel-Ous Offer in Yel/Which Line Leads to Jubilee?**, 1996. $.50-1.00

Ma9630 Ma9631

❑ ❑ USA Ma9610 **Hm Box - Which Line Leads to Wolverline?**, 1996. $12.00-15.00

❑ ❑ USA Ma9611 **Hm Box - Unscramble the Red and Blue Letters**, 1996. $12.00-15.00

U-3 Premium:

❑ ❑ USA Ma9609 **U-3 Spider-Man Ball**, 1996. $1.00-2.00

Premiums:

- ❑ ❑ USA Ma9601 **#1 Spider-Man Vehicle,** 1996, Car with Open/Close Web Throw. $1.00-1.50
- ❑ ❑ USA Ma9602 **#2 Storm,** 1996, Storm in Parking Cloud. $1.00-1.50
- ❑ ❑ USA Ma9603 **#3 Wolverine,** 1996, Wolverine in a Jet with Retractable Claws. $1.00-1.50
- ❑ ❑ USA Ma9604 **#4 Jubilee,** 1996, Jubilee on a Scooter with an Optical Illusion Shield. $1.00-1.50
- ❑ ❑ USA Ma9605 **#5 Invisible Woman,** 1996, Woman Changes Colors in Cold Water. $1.50-2.00
- ❑ ❑ USA Ma9606 **#6 Thing,** 1996, Vehicle Bursts Open to Reveal Thing. $1.00-1.50
- ❑ ❑ USA Ma9607 **#7 Hulk,** 1996, Hulk Figurine. $1.50-2.00
- ❑ ❑ USA Ma9608 **#8 Human Torch,** 1996, Human Torch Figurine. $1.00-1.50

- ❑ ❑ USA Ma9626 **Display/Premiums**, 1995, with 8 Premiums. $20.00-35.00
- ❑ ❑ USA Ma9643 **Crew Reference Sheet**, 1995, Blk/Wht Pic. $.50-1.00
- ❑ ❑ USA Ma9644 **Crew Poster**, 1995. $1.00-2.00
- ❑ ❑ USA Ma9664 **Translite/Sm**, 1995. $3.00-5.00

Comments: National Distribution: USA - May 17 - June 13, 1996. USA Happy Meal boxes Ma9610/11 were test marketed/distributed in Boones Mill, Virginia. Each box had a paper punch-out light switch cover.

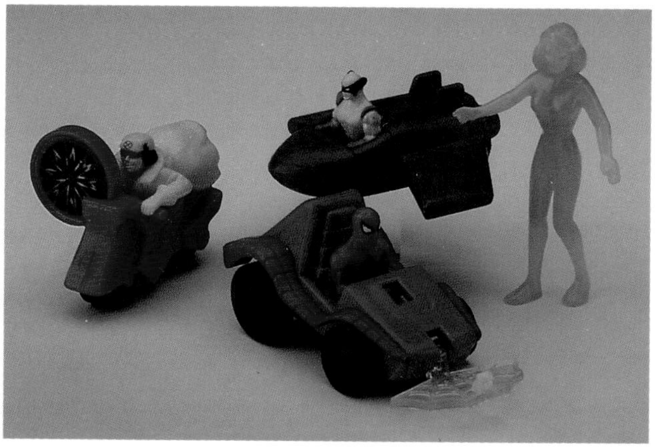

Ma9604 Ma9603 Ma9601 Ma9605

Ma9611 Ma9610

Ma9608 Ma9602 Ma9606 Ma9607

Ma9609

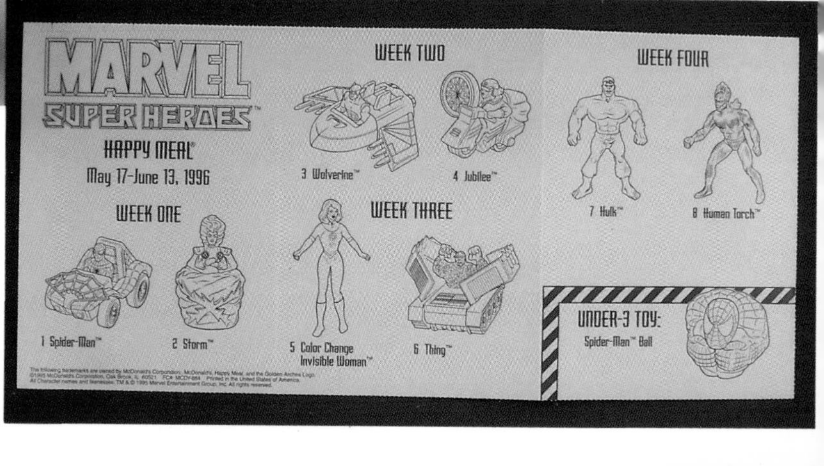

Ma9643

Ma9664

Halloween '96/McNugget Buddies Halloween '96 Happy Meal, 1996

Boxes:

❑ ❑ USA Ha9610 **Hm Box - One Eyed Yellow Monster/ Jeepers Creepers/W Coupon,** 1996. $.50-1.00

❑ ❑ USA Ha9611 **Hm Box - Two Eyed Green Dragon/You'll Go Batty,** 1996. $.50-1.00

Premiums:

❑ ❑ USA Ha9601 **#1 Spider McNugget,** 1995, Purp Spider Legs Base with "M"/Purple Hat/Purp Eyelashes McNugget/ 3p. $1.00-1.50

❑ ❑ USA Ha9602 **#2 Rock Star McNugget,** 1996, Grn Florescent Hat/Blk Shoes Base with Yel "M"/Blk Eyelashes/ 3p. $1.00-1.50

❑ ❑ USA Ha9603 **#3 Fairy Princess McNugget,** 1995, Yel Hair with Silver Crown with "M"/Metallic Grn Base/Blu Eyelashes/ 3p. $1.00-1.50

❑ ❑ USA Ha9604 **#4 Dragon McNugget,** 1996, Grn Dragon Hat/Grn Dragon Feet with Yel "M"/Red Mouth McNugget/ 3p. $1.00-1.50

❑ ❑ USA Ha9603 **#5 Alien Monster McNugget,** 1995, Org Hat/Pnk with 4 Arms Base/2 Teeth McNugget/3p. $1.00-1.50

❑ ❑ USA Ha9604 **#4 Ronald McNugget,** 1996, Red Hair/Yel Clown Base with Red Shoes/Red Smile McNugget/3p. $2.00-2.50

❑ ❑ USA Ha9627 **Fisher-Price Dragon/Knight,** 1996, Black Knight/Red Florescent Dragon/2p. $4.00-5.00

❑ ❑ USA Ha9626 **Display,** 1996, with 6 Premiums. $25.00-35.00

❑ ❑ USA Ha9643 **Crew Reference Sheet,** 1996, Blk/Wht Pic. $1.00-1.50

❑ ❑ USA Ha9644 **Crew Poster,** 1995. $1.00-2.00

❑ ❑ USA Ha9664 **Translite/Sm,** 1995. $3.00-5.00

Comments: National Distribution: USA - October 11-October 31, 1996. The generic Fisher Price U-3 toys were distributed, with no McDonald's markings on the top and base. McNugget marked, "1995 Or 1996 McDonald's Corp. China/Chine Sn." The first box distributed had a Fisher-Price coupon redeemable at Toys R Us for a free Knight and Dragon. The Black Knight and Red Dragon came sealed in McDonald's style packaging for toys, without McDonald's markings on package or toys. The Knight was the same one given as a premium during Christmas 1995, Totally Toys Happy Meal (Great Adventures Knight figurine). The Dragon was a different color: florescent red instead of the Totally Toys Happy Meal green color.

Ha9610 Ha9611

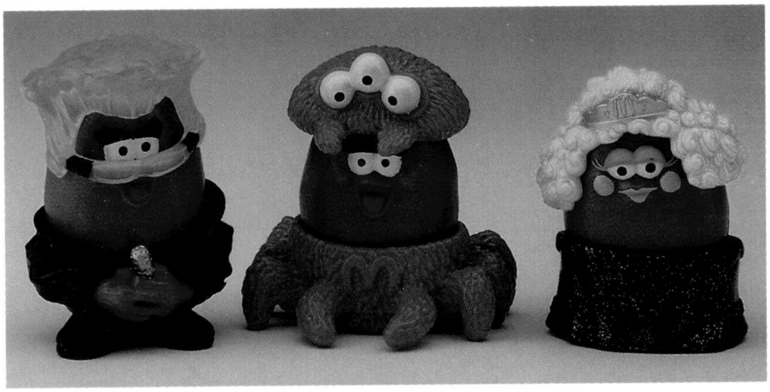

Ha9602 Ha9601 Ha9603

Ha9606 Ha9604 Ha9605

Ha9664

Ha9627

Ha9643

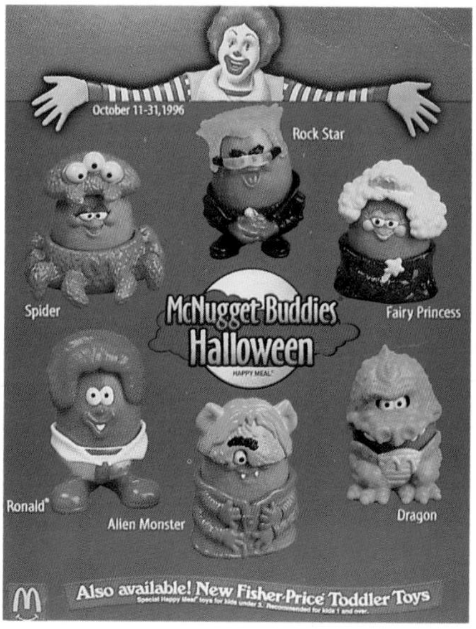

Muppet Treasure Island Happy Meal, 1996

Bag:
❑ ❑ USA Mu9630 **Hm Bag - Muppet Treasure Island**, 1995. $.25-.50

U-3 Premium:
❑ ❑ USA Mu9605 **U-3 Book for Bath: Muppet Treasure Island,** 1995, White Plastic Story Book/Floats. $1.00-2.00

Premiums:
❑ ❑ USA Mu9601 **#1 Miss Piggy Tub Toy,** 1995, M Piggy in Grn Tub/Dress Changes Color. $1.00-1.25
❑ ❑ USA Mu9602 **#2 Kermit in Boat,** 1995, Kermit with Blk Cannon/Brn Boat/Squirts Water. $1.00-1.25
❑ ❑ USA Mu9603 **#3 Gonzo in Paddle Wheel Boat,** 1995, Gonzo in Purp Boat with Grn Moving Wheel. $1.00-1.25
❑ ❑ USA Mu9604 **#4 Fozzie in Barrel,** 1995, Fossie in Blue Barrel/Bobs up and Down. $1.00-1.25

❑ ❑ USA Mu9626 **Display**, 1995, with 4 Premiums. $5.00-10.00
❑ ❑ USA Mu9643 **Crew Reference Sheet**, 1995, Blk/Wht Pic. $.50-1.00
❑ ❑ USA Mu9644 **Crew Poster**, 1995. $1.00-2.00
❑ ❑ USA Mu9664 **Translite/Sm**, 1995. $3.00-4.00

Comments: National Distribution: USA - February 16 - March 14, 1996.

Mu9643

Mu9644

Mu9601 Mu9603 Mu9602 Mu9604

Mu9605

Mu9664

101 [One Hundred and One] Dalmatians Happy Meal II, 1996

Bags & Boxes:
- ❑ ❑ USA On96130 **Hm Bag - 2 Dalmatians with Puppy Pages and Doggone Deals Coupon.** $.50.-1.00
- ❑ ❑ USA On96131 **Hm Bag - 1 Dalmatian,** 1996. $.50-1.00
- ❑ ❑ USA On96132 **Hm Box - Santa Cap/Candy Cane/One Dalmatian,** 1996. $5.00-8.00
- ❑ ❑ USA On96133 **Hm Box - Mickey's Ears/One Dalmatian, 1996.** $5.00-8.00

Row 1 - Poster:
- ❑ ❑ USA On9601 **Gold Wrap - Wrapped in Gold Ribbon.** $3.00-4.00
- ❑ ❑ USA On9602 **Orange Collar / 1 Ear Spotted.** $3.00-4.00
- ❑ ❑ USA On9603 **In Blue/Brn Truck/Hiding Eyes/Light Green Collar.** $3.00-4.00
- ❑ ❑ USA On9604 **Wearing Brown Derby Hat with Blue Band/Sitting up/Green Collar.** $4.00-5.00
- ❑ ❑ USA On9605 **Toy Soldier in Mouth - Org Collar with Toy Soldier Nutcracker/Soldier in Mouth.** $3.00-4.00
- ❑ ❑ USA On9606 **Dark Blue Collar/1 All Black Ear/1 Spotted Ear.** $3.00-4.00
- ❑ ❑ USA On9607 **Green Wreath on Tail/Light Green Collar.** $3.00-4.00
- ❑ ❑ USA On9608 **Standing/Pink Collar/Green Holly with Yellow Jingle Bells on Tail.** $3.00- 4.00

Row 2 - Poster:
- ❑ ❑ USA On9609 **Pink/Fuchsia Collar/2 Solid Black Ears.** $3.00-4.00
- ❑ ❑ USA On9610 **Wearing Cowboy Hat - Dark Green Collar/Brn Cowboy Hat with Red Band.** $5.00-8.00
- ❑ ❑ USA On9611 **In Pink Tea Pot.** $12.00-15.00
- ❑ ❑ USA On9612 **Blue Mitten in Mouth - Yellow Collar.** $3.00-4.00
- ❑ ❑ USA On9613 **Newspaper in Mouth - Green Collar.** $3.00-4.00
- ❑ ❑ USA On9614 **Wrapped in Yellow/Green Scarf/Sweater/ No Collar.** $3.00-4.00
- ❑ ❑ USA On9615 **Brown Bucket on tail/Orange Collar.** $3.00-4.00
- ❑ ❑ USA On9616 **Wearing Green Santa Hat/Holding Bone/ Standing/Blue Collar.** $3.00-4.00

Row 3 - Poster:
- ❑ ❑ USA On9617 **Plain Green Collar/ Mouth open/Spotted Ears.** $3.00-4.00
- ❑ ❑ USA On9618 **In Pink Baby Buggy with Turq Wheels/ Blue Collar/Hiding Eyes.** $5.00-8.00
- ❑ ❑ USA On9619 **In Newspaper/White London Herald Newspaper House.** $7.00-10.00

On9630

On9631

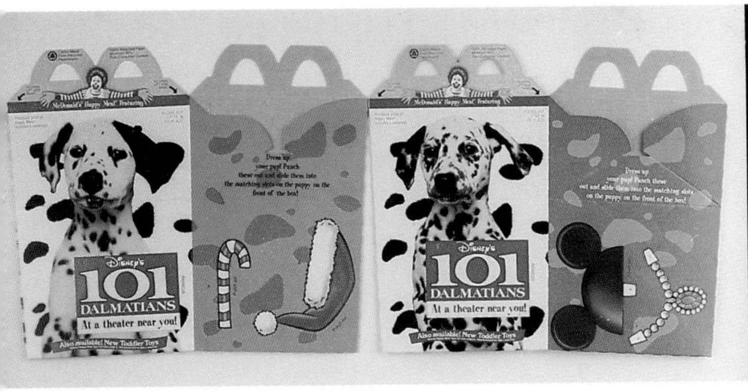

On9632 On9633

On9609 On9610 On9611 On9612

On9601 On9603 On9602 On9604

On9613 On9614 On9615 On9616

On9605 On9607 On9606 On9608

On9617 On9618 On9619 On9620

❑ ❑ USA On9620 **Wrapped in Red Scarf with Yellow Tassels.** $3.00-4.00
❑ ❑ USA On9621 **Blue Collar/Sitting/Red Christmas Lights Around Face.** $5.00-6.00
❑ ❑ USA On9622 **On Heavy Red 101 Dalmatian Drum/Purple Collar.** $7.00-10.00
❑ ❑ USA On9623 **Plain Yellow Collar /Spotted Ears.** $3.00-4.00
❑ ❑ USA On9624 **Black Rings around Eye/Dark Purple Collar/Black Eye/2 Solid Black Ears.** $3.00-4.00
❑ ❑ USA On9625 **In Red Present/Orange Collar.** $5.00-8.00
❑ ❑ USA On9626 **With Red/White Candy Cane in Mouth/Sitting/Green Collar.** $3.00-4.00
❑ ❑ USA On9627 **Holding Red Book on Belly/Green Collar/Black Eye.** $3.00-4.00
❑ ❑ USA On9628 **In Yellow Cookie Jar/Green Collar.** $8.00-15.00

Row 4 - Poster:
❑ ❑ USA On9629 **Holding Brown Shoe in Mouth/Purple Collar/1 Solid Black Ear.** $3.00-4.00
❑ ❑ USA On9630 **In Yellow Present /Blue Collar/Red Santa Hat.** $5.00-8.00
❑ ❑ USA On9631 **With Green Candy Cane in Mouth/Holding Bone - Standing with Purp Collar.** $3.00-4.00
❑ ❑ USA On9632 **Light Blue Collar/White Ear/Right Paw up with 1 Spotted Ear.** $3.00-4.00
❑ ❑ USA On9633 **In Red Stocking/Grn Collar/White Bone in Mouth/Black Eye.** $3.00-4.00
❑ ❑ USA On9634 **Wearing Black Cruella Hat/Sitting with Red Collar.** $3.00-4.00
❑ ❑ USA On9635 **Dark Purple Collar/1 White Ear.** $5.00-8.00
❑ ❑ USA On9636 **Bluebird on Head/Red-Orange Collar.** $5.00-8.00
❑ ❑ USA On9637 **Wrapped in Blue Scarf/Purple Tassels.** $3.00-4.00
❑ ❑ USA On9638 **In White DeVil Car /Orange Collar.** $7.00-10.00
❑ ❑ USA On9639 **Yellow Bow on Tail/Standing/Purple Collar/1 Black Foot.** $3.00-4.00
❑ ❑ USA On9640 **In Green Wreaths with Red Bow/Wearing Red Santa Hat/Blue Collar.** $5.00-8.00
❑ ❑ USA On9641 **Holding Cookie/Standing with Blue Collar.** $3.00-4.00

Row 5 - Poster:
❑ ❑ USA On9642 **Laying Flat/Black-White Tennis Shoe in Mouth/Blue Collar.** $3.00-4.00
❑ ❑ USA On9643 **On Heavy Red Christmas Ball Decorated with Green Tree/Yellow Collar.** $7.00-10.00
❑ ❑ USA On9644 **Wearing Indiana Jones Hat - with Dk Pink Collar.** $5.00-8.00
❑ ❑ USA On9645 **With Org Candle in Mouth/Dark Purple Collar.** $3.00-4.00
❑ ❑ USA On9646 **Wrapped in Green Ribbon/1 Black Ear/No Collar.** $3.00-4.00
❑ ❑ USA On9647 **Laying with Yellow Teddy Bear on Stomach/Orange Collar.** $8.00-15.00
❑ ❑ USA On9648 **In Green Bus/Purple Collar.** $4.00-7.00
❑ ❑ USA On9649 **Wrapped in Silver Ribbon/2 Spots on One Ear/No Collar.** $3.00-4.00
❑ ❑ USA On9650 **In Lavender Book.** $10.00-15.00
❑ ❑ USA On9651 **Wearing Mickey Mouse Ears/with "Fidget" Name Back of Hat/Lt Blu Collar.** $10.00-15.00
❑ ❑ USA On9652 **In Blue Baby Buggy with Yellow Wheels/Red Collar.** $5.00-8.00

On9621 On9622 On9623 On9624

On9625 On9627 On9626 On9628

On9629 On9630 On9631 On9632

On9633 On9634 On9636 On9635

On9646 On9648 On9647 On9649

On9637 On9638 On9640 On9641 On9639

On9650 On9652 On9651

Left to right: On9642, On9644, On9643, On9645

Row 6 - Poster:

❑ ❑ USA On9653 **Wrapped in Aqua Garland with Purple Ornaments/Spotted Head/No Collar.** $3.00-4.00

❑ ❑ USA On9654 **Wrapped in Green Wreath with Yellow Ribbon/Candy Cane in Mouth.** $4.00-5.00

❑ ❑ USA On9655 **Wearing Blue Bobby Hat/Red Collar.** $3.00-4.00

❑ ❑ USA On9656 **Wearing Crown on Head/Lavender Collar.** $5.00-8.00

❑ ❑ USA On9657 **In Red Bus/Light Green Collar.** $3.00-4.00

❑ ❑ USA On9658 **In Bobby Hat/Red Collar.** $5.00-8.00

❑ ❑ USA On9659 **Laying Down/Playing Yellow Trumpet/Horn/Holly on Horn/Red Collar.** $3.00-4.00

❑ ❑ USA On9660 **Wrapped in Red Garland/Green Ornaments/No Collar.** $3.00-4.00

❑ ❑ USA On9661 **In Blue Present/Bone in Mouth/Silver Ribbon/Purple Collar.** $5.00-8.00

❑ ❑ USA On9662 **Leash Wrapped Around Face/Green Collar.** $5.00-6.00

❑ ❑ USA On9663 **In Silver Paint Can with Purple Paint.** $7.00-10.00

❑ ❑ USA On9664 **Holding Bone in Mouth/Light Green Collar.** $3.00-4.00

Row 7 - Poster:

❑ ❑ USA On9665 **On Soccer Ball/Yellow Collar.** $5.00-8.00

❑ ❑ USA On9666 **Solid Black Tail Painted on/Fuchsia/Red collar/No Spots on Ears.** $3.00-4.00
❑ ❑ USA On9667 **Holding Dog Dish in Mouth/Green Collar.** $3.00-4.00
❑ ❑ USA On9668 **Green Frog on Head/Pink Fuchsia Collar.** $5.00-8.00
❑ ❑ USA On9669 **Blue Top Hat on Tail/Green Collar.** $3.00-4.00
❑ ❑ USA On9670 **Butterfly on Head/Green/Teal Collar.** $5.00-8.00
❑ ❑ USA On9671 **Red Flower/Bow on Nose/ Yellow Collar.** $3.00-.00
❑ ❑ USA On9672 **Holding Blue Can of Dog Treats/Yellow Collar.** $3.00-4.00
❑ ❑ USA On9673 **Red Bow on Tail/Blue Collar.** $3.00-4.00
❑ ❑ USA On9674 **Holding Red Dog Dish/Purple Collar.** $3.00-4.00
❑ ❑ USA On9675 **Stick in Mouth/Pinkish-Lavender Collar.** $3.00-4.00
❑ ❑ USA On9676 **In Red Doghouse/Green Roof.** $4.00-5.00

Row 8 - Poster:
❑ ❑ USA On9677 **Holding Purple Present/Lime Green Collar.** $3.00-4.00
❑ ❑ USA On9678 **In Green Stocking/Red-White Candy Cane in Mouth/Blue Collar.** $3.00-4.00
❑ ❑ USA On9679 **Wearing Black Palace Hat/Purple Collar.** $3.00-4.00
❑ ❑ USA On9680 **Leash in Mouth/Orange Collar.** $3.00-4.00
❑ ❑ USA On9681 **Holding Green Bell/Red Holly/Fuchsia Collar.** $3.00-4.00
❑ ❑ USA On9682 **Purple Bow on Head/Blue Collar.** $5.00-6.00
❑ ❑ USA On9683 **In Brown Barrel/Blue Collar.** $5.00-8.00
❑ ❑ USA On9684 **In Purple Umbrella/Green Collar.** $15.00-20.00
❑ ❑ USA On9685 **Wearing Grey Wig/Fuchsia Collar.** $5.00-6.00
❑ ❑ USA On9686 **On Green Turtle/Red-Orange Collar.** $15.00-20.00
❑ ❑ USA On9687 **Pushing Blu/Wht Soccer Ball/Orange Collar.** $3.00-4.00
❑ ❑ USA On9688 **Red Ornament on nose/Purple Collar.** $3.00-4.00
❑ ❑ USA On9689 **Orange Maple Leaf on Head/Fuchsia Collar.** $5.00-8.00

On9653 On9654 On9656 On9655

On9657 On9658 On9659 On9660

On9661 On9662 On9663 On9664

On9665 On9666 On9667 On9668

On9669 On9670 On9671 On9672

On9681 On9683 On9682 On9684

On9673 On9674 On9676 On9675

On9685 On9686 On9689 On9687 On9688

On9677 On9678 On9679 On9680

Row 9 - Poster:

- ❑ ❑ USA On9690 **Wearing Green Santa Stocking/Red Collar.** $3.00-4.00
- ❑ ❑ USA On9691 **Wearing Purple Beret/Yellow Collar.** $5.00-8.00
- ❑ ❑ USA On9692 **In Black Rubber Tire/Red Collar.** $7.00-10.00
- ❑ ❑ USA On9693 **Wearing Blue Baseball Cap/Orange Collar.** $3.00-4.00
- ❑ ❑ USA On9694 **Gold Present in Mouth/Blue Collar.** $3.00-4.00
- ❑ ❑ USA On9695 **Green Wreath around Nose/Yellow Collar.** $3.00-4.00
- ❑ ❑ USA On9696 **Green Cricket on Head/Purple Collar.** $5.00-8.00
- ❑ ❑ USA On9697 **Pink Present on Tail/Yellow Collar.** $3.00-4.00
- ❑ ❑ USA On9698 **Brown Purse in Mouth/Red Collar.** $3.00-4.00
- ❑ ❑ USA On9699 **Red Santa Hat on Tail/Purple Collar.** $3.00-4.00
- ❑ ❑ USA On96100 **Wearing Orange Hunting Cap/Lime Green Collar.** $3.00-4.00
- ❑ ❑ USA On96101 **In Red Car/Purple Collar.** $3.00-4.00

Variation:
- ❑ ❑ USA On96102 **Green Present in Mouth/Blue Collar.** $20.00-25.00

- ❑ ❑ USA On96126 **Display**/Store/Premiums, 1996, with Premiums. $95.00-140.00
- ❑ ❑ USA On96127 **Display**/Purchased/101 Premiums, 1996, with 101 Different Premiums. $425.00-500.00
- ❑ ❑ USA On96144 **Crew Poster**, 1996. $4.00-5.00
- ❑ ❑ USA On96145 **101 Dalmatians Poster,** 1996, Blue with 101 Dalmatians Pictured/6 Different Reverse Sides. $2.00-3.00
- ❑ ❑ USA On96146 **101 Dalmatians Cookie Package**, 1996. $1.00-1.50
- ❑ ❑ USA On96147 **Trayliner,** 1996. $.25-.50
- ❑ ❑ USA On96164 **Translite/Sm**, 1996. $5.00-7.00

Comments: National Distribution: USA/Canada/Mexico - November 27, 1996-January 2, 1997. A series of 101 different puppy figures based on Walt Disney's *101 Dalmatians* movie, these toys came packaged in opaque (non see-through) white polybags with random distribution. There were approximately ten designs per case with two cases being used per week; a total of ten mixes of premiums (mix a-j) were distributed over a five week period. In Week #2, a twelve page activity book was applied to the Happy Meal bag. Fisher-Price Toddler toys were available for children under three. 101 Dalmatians posters were given out to collectors to view the whole set of 101 toys. 101 Dalmatians cookie packages were sold for $.49-.69 in conjunction with the Happy Meal promotion. 101 Dalmatians dog descriptions follow the order of toys on the 101 Dalmatians poster given out in the stores. Variation may reflect the 101 Dalmatians being distributed internationally. Internationally (in the UK), for example, the Mickey's Ears Dalmatian did not have the name Fidget on the reverse side. Slight color variations are occurring on several toys; these are not considered toy variations due to the large number of toys produced for one Happy Meal promotion. A phenomenal number of 101 Dalmatians were produced, 77 million. This number was surpassed by the Teenie Beanie Babies I Happy Meal where 100 million toys were produced and distributed through the stores in under two weeks. The 101 Dalmatians Happy Meal promotion was a very successful promotion, both within the USA and worldwide. On the variation, Dog with Green Package in Mouth, the color of the collar varies; the package is originally painted green and not two-tone.

On9694 On9695 On9696 On9697

On9698 On9699 On96101 On96100

On9694 On96102

Head switching variations.

On9690 On9691 On9692 On9693

On96126

On96145

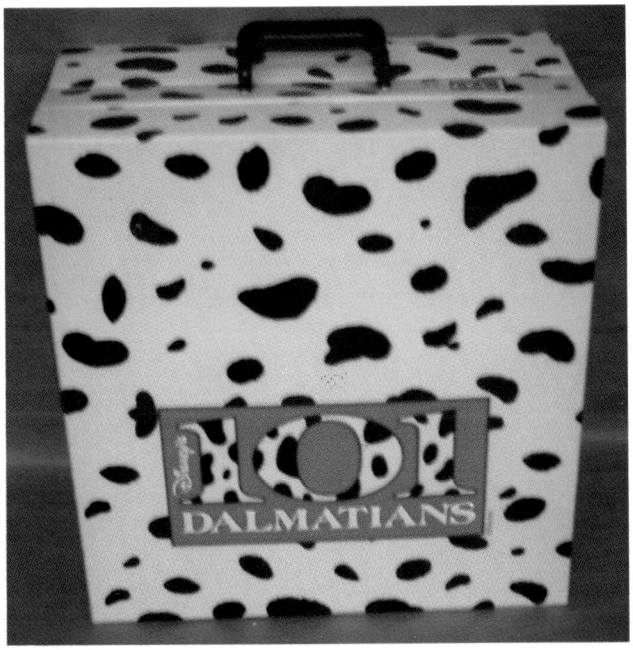

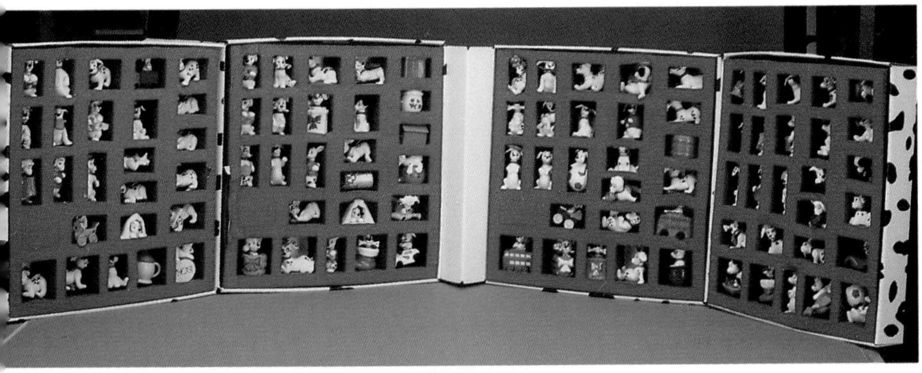

On96127. Collector case of 101 Dalmations.

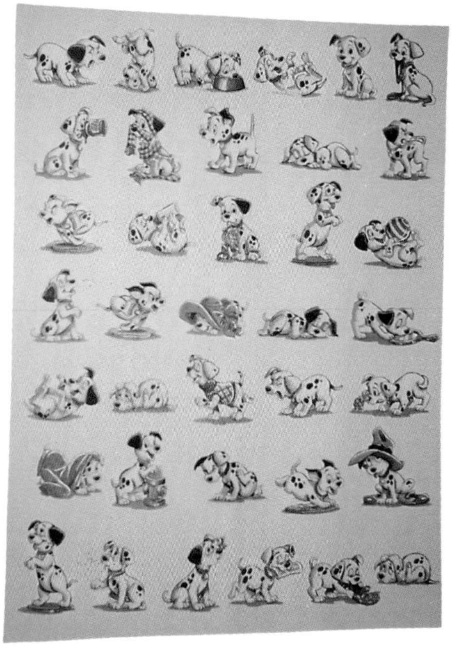

Projected premium layout boards.

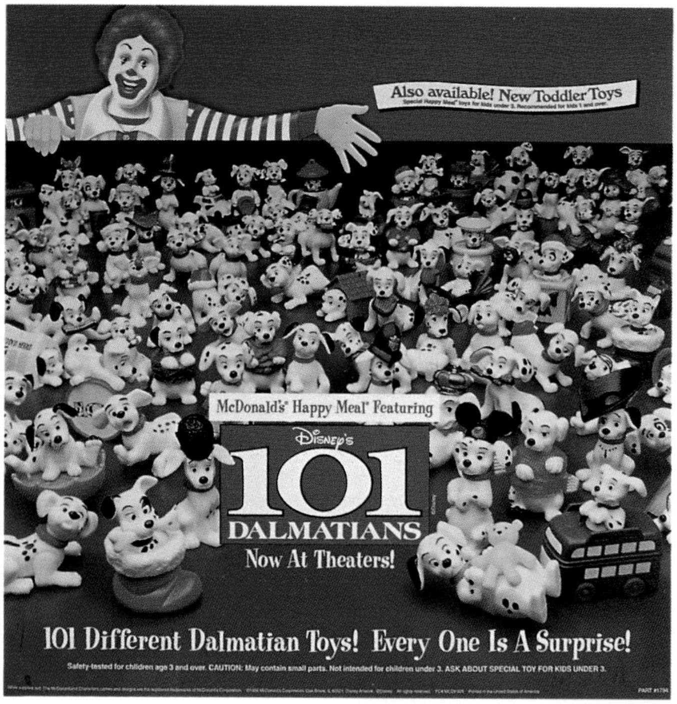

On96164

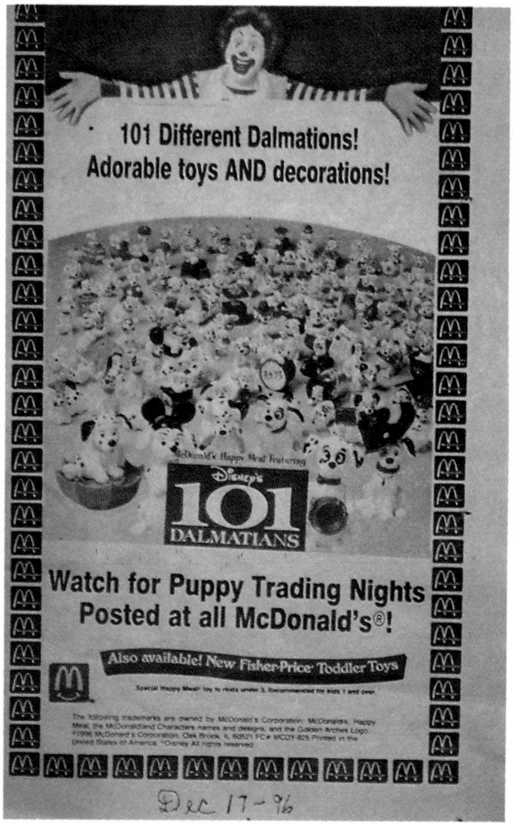

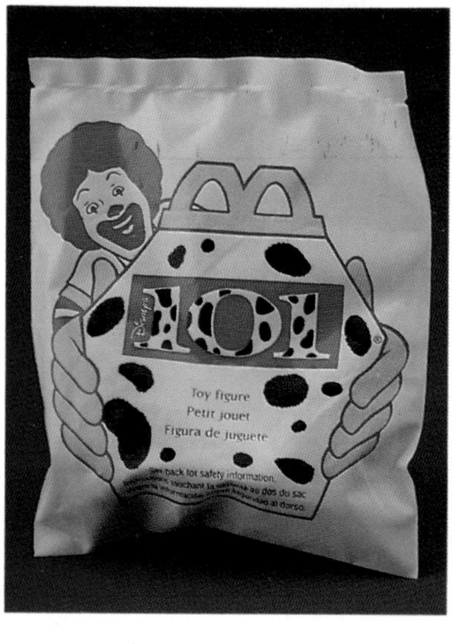

Alternative 101 Dalmatians Checklist

(Arranged according to type of position and collar color with numbers relating to position on the posters)

Wearing Collars Only:

❑ ❑ **# 2** Orange Collar. $3.00-4.00
❑ ❑ **# 6** Dark Blue Collar, 1 All Black Ear. $3.00-4.00
❑ ❑ **# 32** Light Blue Collar, 1 Spotted Ear. $3.00-4.00
❑ ❑ **# 9** Light Pink/Fuchsia-Purplish Collar, 2 Blk Ears. $3.00-4.00
❑ ❑ **# 66** Fuchsia-red Collar, Solid Painted-on Black Tail. $3.00-4.00
❑ ❑ **# 17** Green Collar. $3.00-4.00
❑ ❑ **# 23** Yellow Collar. $3.00-4.00
❑ ❑ **# 24** Dark Purple Collar, 1 Black Eye. $3.00-4.00
❑ ❑ **# 35** Dark Purple Collar with 1 White Ear. $3.00-4.00

Puppies in Vehicles:

❑ ❑ **# 3** In Blue Truck, Light Green Collar. $3.00-4.00
❑ ❑ **# 18** In Pink Doll Carriage, Blue Collar. $5.00-8.00
❑ ❑ **# 38** In White DeVil Car, Orange Collar. $7.00-10.00
❑ ❑ **# 48** In Green Bus, Purple Collar. $4.00-7.00
❑ ❑ **# 52** In Blue Doll Carriage, Red Collar. $5.00-8.00
❑ ❑ **# 57** In Red Bus, Green Collar. $3.00-4.00
❑ ❑ **# 101** In Red Car, Purple Collar. $3.00-4.00

Wearing a Hat:

❑ ❑ **# 4** Wearing Brown Bowler Hat, Green Collar. $4.00-5.00
❑ ❑ **#10** Wearing Brown Cowboy hat, Dark Green Collar. $5.00-8.00
❑ ❑ **#35** Wearing Cruella's Black Hat, Red Collar. $5.00-8.00
❑ ❑ **#44** Wearing Tan Indiana Jones Hat, Dark Pink Collar. $5.00-8.00
❑ ❑ **#51** Wearing Mickey Mouse Ears, "Fidget" Name, Light Blue Collar. $10.00-15.00
❑ ❑ **#55** Wearing Blue Bobby Hat, Red Collar. $3.00-4.00
❑ ❑ **#56** Wearing Purple Crown, Purple Collar. $5.00-8.00
❑ ❑ **#79** Wearing Black Bobby Hat, Purple Collar. $3.00-4.00
❑ ❑ **#91** Wearing Purple Beret, Yellow Collar. $5.00-8.00
❑ ❑ **#93** Wearing Blue Baseball Cap, Orange Collar. $3.00-4.00
❑ ❑ **#100** Wearing Orange Hunting Hat, Light Green Collar. $3.00-4.00

Holding Something:

❑ ❑ **#16** Holding Bone, Wearing Green Santa Hat, Blue Collar. $3.00-4.00
❑ ❑ **#27** Holding Red Book, Green Collar. $3.00-4.00
❑ ❑ **#41** Holding Brown Cookie, Blue Collar. $3.00-4.00
❑ ❑ **#47** Holding Yellow Bear, Orange Collar. $8.00-15.00
❑ ❑ **#59** Holding Yellow Horn, Red Collar. $3.00-4.00
❑ ❑ **#72** Holding Blue Can, Yellow Collar. $3.00-4.00
❑ ❑ **#74** Holding Red Bowl, Purple Collar. $3.00-4.00
❑ ❑ **#77** Holding Purple Present, Lime Green Collar. $3.00-4.00
❑ ❑ **#81** Holding Green Bell, Fuchsia Collar. $3.00-4.00
❑ ❑ **#87** Holding Blue and White Soccer Ball, Orange Collar. $3.00-4.00

With Scarves and/or Ribbons:

❑ ❑ **# 1** Wrapped in Gold Ribbon. $3.00-4.00
❑ ❑ **#14** Wrapped in Yellow & Green Scarf. $3.00-4.00
❑ ❑ **#20** Wrapped in Red Scarf. $3.00-4.00
❑ ❑ **#37** Wrapped in Blue Scarf. $3.00-4.00
❑ ❑ **#46** Wrapped in Green Ribbon. $3.00-4.00
❑ ❑ **#49** Wrapped in Silver Ribbon. $3.00-4.00
❑ ❑ **#53** Wrapped in Turquoise Garland With Purple Ornaments. $3.00-4.00
❑ ❑ **#60** Wrapped in Red Garland With Green Ornaments. $3.00-4.00

On Top of Something:

❑ ❑ **#22** On 101 Dalmatians Drum, Purple Collar. $7.00-10.00
❑ ❑ **#43** On Red Ornament, Yellow Collar. $7.00-10.00
❑ ❑ **#65** On Blue & White Soccer Ball, Yellow Collar. $5.00-8.00
❑ ❑ **#84** In Purple Umbrella, Green Collar. $15.00-20.00
❑ ❑ **#86** On Green Turtle, Red-Orange Collar. $15.00-20.00
❑ ❑ **#92** In Black Tire, Red Collar. $7.00-10.00

Inside of Something:

❑ ❑ **#11** In Pink Teapot. $12.00-15.00
❑ ❑ **#19** In London Herald Newspaper. $7.00-10.00
❑ ❑ **#25** In Red Present, Orange Collar. $5.00-8.00
❑ ❑ **#28** In Yellow Cookie Jar, Green Collar. $8.00-15.00
❑ ❑ **#30** In Yellow Present, Blue Collar. $5.00-8.00
❑ ❑ **#33** In Red Stocking, Green Collar. $3.00-4.00
❑ ❑ **#40** In Red Box, Blue Collar. $5.00-8.00
❑ ❑ **#50** In 101 Lavender Book $10.00-15.00
❑ ❑ **#54** In Green Wreaths with Yellow Bow. $4.00-5.00
❑ ❑ **#58** In Blue Bobby Hat, Red Collar. $5.00-8.00
❑ ❑ **#61** In Blue Present, Purple Collar. $5.00-8.00
❑ ❑ **#63** In Silver Paint Can, Purple Paint. $7.00-10.00
❑ ❑ **#76** In Red Dog House. $4.00-5.00
❑ ❑ **#78** In Green Stocking, Blue Collar. $3.00-4.00
❑ ❑ **#83** In Brown Barrel, Blue Collar. $5.00-8.00

Something in Mouth:

❑ ❑ **# 5** Nutcracker Soldier in Mouth, Orange Collar. $3.00-4.00
❑ ❑ **# 8** Turquoise Leash in Mouth, Orange Collar. $3.00-4.00
❑ ❑ **#12** Blue Mitten in Mouth, Yellow Collar. $3.00-4.00
❑ ❑ **#13** Newspaper in Mouth, Green Collar. $3.00-4.00
❑ ❑ **#26** Red and White Candy Cane in Mouth, Green Collar. $3.00-4.00
❑ ❑ **#29** Brown Shoe in Mouth, Purple Collar. $3.00-4.00
❑ ❑ **#31** Green and White Candy Cane in Mouth, Purple Collar. $3.00-4.00
❑ ❑ **#42** Black and White Tennis Shoe in Mouth, Blue Collar. $3.00-4.00
❑ ❑ **#45** Yellow Candle in Mouth, Purple Collar. $3.00-4.00
❑ ❑ **#64** Bone in Mouth, Green Collar. $3.00-4.00
❑ ❑ **#67** Red Bowl in Mouth, Green Collar. $3.00-4.00
❑ ❑ **#75** Brown Stick in Mouth, Light Purple Collar. $3.00-4.00
❑ ❑ **#94** Gold Present in Mouth, Blue Collar. $3.00-4.00
❑ ❑ **#98** Brown Purse in Mouth, Red Collar. $3.00-4.00
❑ ❑ **#102** Green Present in Mouth, Yellow Collar (Variation). $20.00-25.00

Something on Nose or Face:

❑ ❑ **#21** String of Lights Around Nose, Blue Collar. $5.00-6.00
❑ ❑ **#62** Brown Leash Around Face, Green Collar. $5.00-6.00
❑ ❑ **#71** Red Bow on Nose, Lime Green/Yellow Collar. $3.00-4.00
❑ ❑ **#88** Red Ornament on Nose, Purple Collar. $3.00-4.00
❑ ❑ **#95** Wreath around Nose, Yellow Collar. $3.00-4.00

Something on Tail or Bottom:

☐ ☐ **# 7** Green Wreath on Tail, Light Green Collar. $3.00-4.00

☐ ☐ **# 8** Jingle Bells with Holly on Tail, Pink Collar. $3.00-4.00

☐ ☐ **#15** Brown Bucket on Tail, Orange Collar. $3.00-4.00

☐ ☐ **#39** Yellow Bow on Tail, Purple Collar. $3.00-4.00

☐ ☐ **#69** Blue Top Hat on Tail, Green Collar. $3.00-4.00

☐ ☐ **#73** Red Bow on Tail, Blue Collar. $3.00-4.00

☐ ☐ **#90** Green Stocking on Tail, Red Collar. $3.00-4.00

☐ ☐ **#97** Pink Gift on Tail, Yellow Collar. $3.00-4.00

☐ ☐ **#99** Red Santa Hat On Tail, Purple Collar. $3.00-4.00

Something on Head:

☐ ☐ **#36** Blue Bird on Head, Red/Orange Collar. $5.00-8.00

☐ ☐ **#68** Green Frog on Head, Pink Collar. $5.00-8.00

☐ ☐ **#70** Orange Butterfly on Head, Teal Collar. $5.00-8.00

☐ ☐ **#82** Purple bow on head, blue collar $5.00-6.00

☐ ☐ **#85** Gray Wig on Head, Dark Pink/Fuchsia Collar. $5.00-6.00

☐ ☐ **#89** Orange Maple Leaf on Head, Fuchsia Collar. $5.00-8.00

☐ ☐ **#96** Green Cricket on Head, Purple Collar. $5.00-8.00

Comments: 101 Dalmatians were distributed in the USA stores. The variation, #102, may just be a painting color mistake and not a planned figurine variation. Other variations might exist due to quality control mistakes.

Space Jam Happy Meal, 1996

Bag:

☐ ☐ USA Sp9630 **Hm Bag - Time Out!** $.50-1.00

☐ ☐ USA Sp9631 **Hm Bag - We're the Tune Squad.** $.50-1.00

☐ ☐ USA Sp9632 **Hm Box - Time Out Doc!** $15.00-20.00

☐ ☐ USA Sp9633 **Hm Box - We're Little Nerdlucks.** $15.00-20.00

Premiums:

☐ ☐ USA Sp9601 **#1 Lola Bunny - Lady Basketball Player with Org Basketball on Brown Base.** $1.00-1.50

☐ ☐ USA Sp9602 **#2 Bugs Bunny - Shooting Basket/Red Pole on Brown Base.** $1.00-1.50

☐ ☐ USA Sp9603 **#3 Marvin the Martian - Grn/Blk Martian Standing on Top of Org Ball on Brown Base.** $1.00-1.50

☐ ☐ USA Sp9604 **#4 Daffy Duck - Standing on Top of Orange Ball on Brown Base.** $1.00-1.50

☐ ☐ USA Sp9605 **#5 Tasmanian Devil - Shooting Ball into White Hoop on Brown Base.** $1.00-1.50

☐ ☐ USA Sp9606 **#6 Monstar - Green/Black Player with Arms Raised on Brown Base.** $1.00-1.50

☐ ☐ USA Sp9607 **#7 Sylvester & Tweety - Sylvester & Tweety on Orange Ball on Brown Base.** $1.00-1.50

☐ ☐ USA Sp9608 **#8 Nerdlucks - Purple/Blue Totem Pole Style Player on Brown Base.** $1.00-1.50

☐ ☐ USA Sp9626 **Display**, 1996, with 8 Premiums. $5.00-10.00

☐ ☐ USA Sp9643 **Crew Reference Sheet**, 1996, Blk/Wht Pic. $.50-1.00

☐ ☐ USA Sp9644 **Crew Poster**, 1996. $1.00-2.00

☐ ☐ USA Sp9664 **Translite/Sm**, 1996. $3.00-4.00

Comments: National Distribution: USA - November 1-26, 1996. Promotion coincided with release of Michael Jordan's *Space Jam* movie by Warner Brothers.

Sp9631 Sp9630

Sp9632 Sp9633

Left to right: Sp9601, Sp9602, Sp9607, Sp9603

Left to right: Sp9608, Sp9604, Sp9605, Sp9606

Sp9643

Sp9626

Sp9664

Color Card

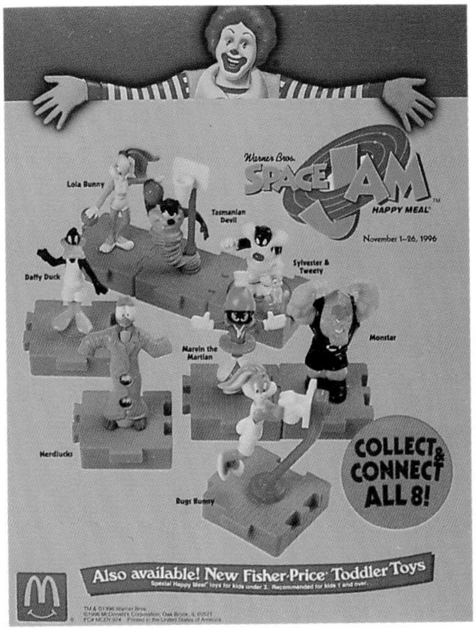

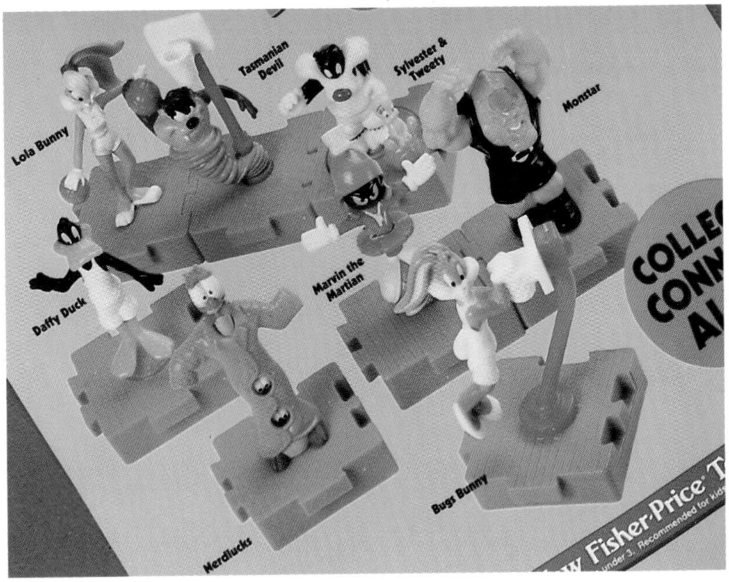

VR Troopers Happy Meal, 1996

Bag:
❑ ❑ USA Vr9630 **Hm Bag - VR Troopers,** 1995. $.50-1.00

U-3 Premium:
❑ ❑ USA Vr9605 **U-3 VR Troopers Sphere,** 1995. $1.00-1.50

Premiums:
❑ ❑ USA Vr9601 **#1 Visor,** 1995, Metal/silver color plastic Eyewear. $.50-1.00
❑ ❑ USA Vr9602 **#2 Virtualizer,** 1995, Pendant with 2 Lenses. $.50-1.00
❑ ❑ USA Vr9603 **#3 Wrist Spinner,** 1995, Wristband with 2 Holographic Discs/3p. $.50-1.00
❑ ❑ USA Vr9604 **#4 Kaleidoscope,** 1995, Camera Shaped. $.50-1.00

❑ ❑ USA Vr9626 **Display**, 1995, with 4 Premiums. $5.00-10.00
❑ ❑ USA Vr9643 **Crew Reference Sheet**, 1995, Blk/Wht Pic. $.50-1.00
❑ ❑ USA Vr9644 **Crew Poster**, 1995. $1.00-2.00
❑ ❑ USA Vr9664 **Translite/Sm**, 1995. $3.00-4.00

Comments: National Distribution: USA - January 19-February 15, 1996.

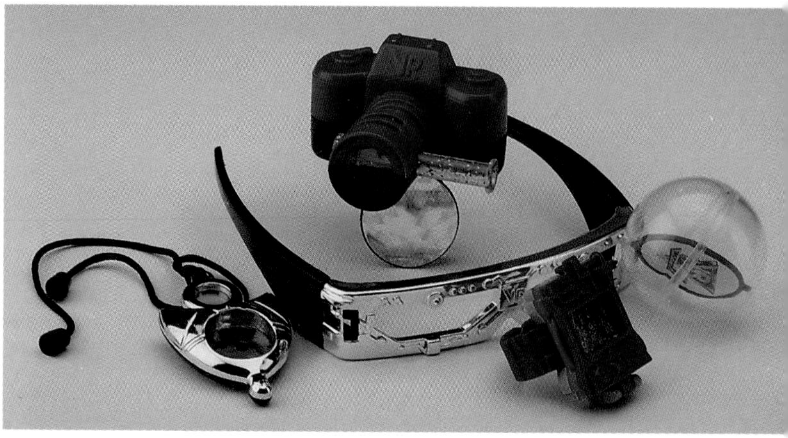

Top row: Vr9604
Bottom row, left to right: Vr9602, Vr9601, Vr9603, Vr9605

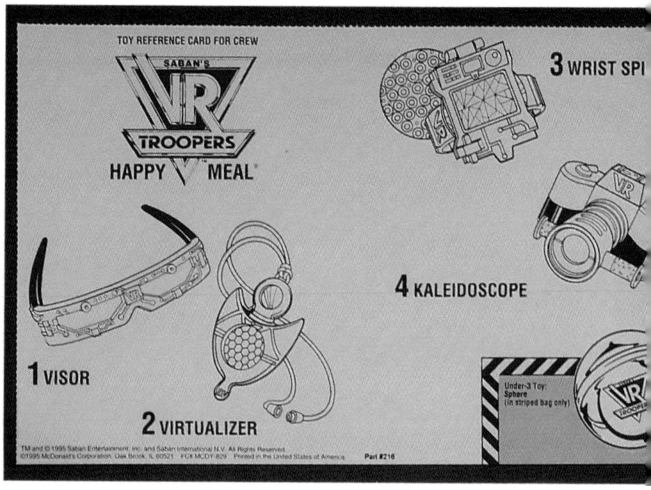

Vr9643

Vr9630

Vr9664

Vr9605

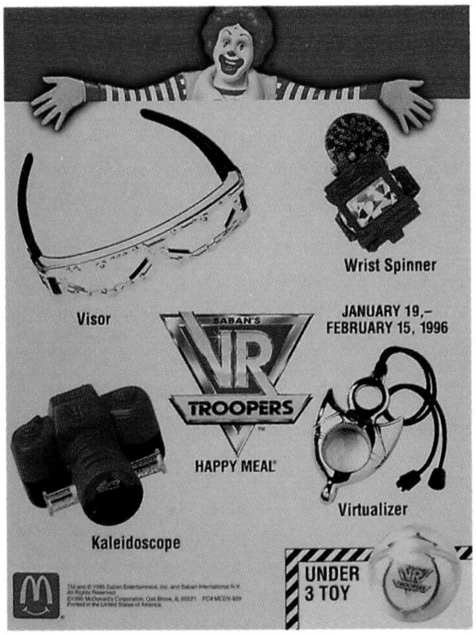

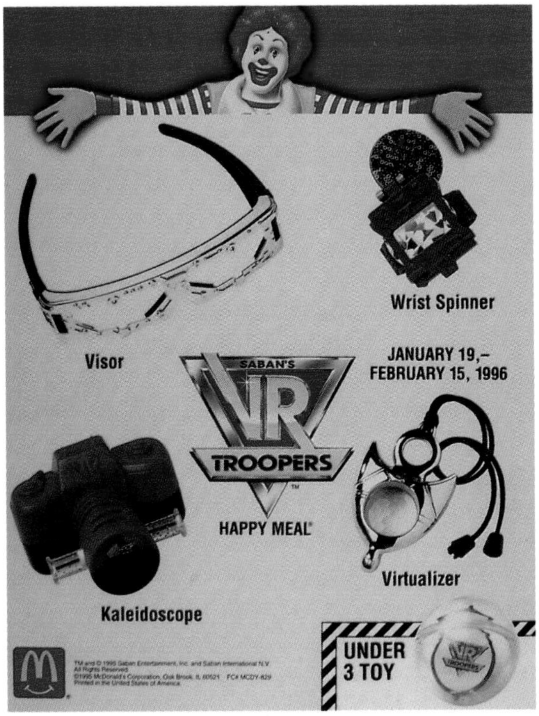

Walt Disney Home Video Masterpiece Collection I Happy Meal (Act I), 1996

Bag:

❑ ❑ USA Wa9630 **Hm Bag - Walt Disney Home Video Masterpiece Collection,** 1996. $.50-1.00

U-3 Premium:

❑ ❑ USA Wa9609 **U-3 Dumbo,** 1996, Dumbo Water Squirter. $4.00-5.00

Premiums:

❑ ❑ USA Wa9601 **#1 Cinderella,** 1996, Cinderella with Rooted Hair/Video Box. $2.00-3.00

❑ ❑ USA Wa9602 **#2 Robin Hood with Gold Money Bag,** 1996, with Plush Tail/Gold Bag/**White Mouth**/Video Box. $2.00-3.00

❑ ❑ USA Wa9609 **#2 Robin Hood with Pea Green Money Bag,** 1996, with Plush Tail/Pea Green Bag/**Grey Mouth**/Video Box. $3.00-5.00

❑ ❑ USA Wa9603 **#3 Pocahontas,** 1996, Pocahontas with Rooted Hair/Comb/2p/Video Box. $2.00-3.00

❑ ❑ USA Wa9604 **#4 Aladdin,** 1996, Aladdin with Moveable Arms, Head/Waist/Video Box. $2.00-3.00

❑ ❑ USA Wa9605 **#5 Snow White,** 1996, Snow White with Rooted Hair/Video Box. $2.00-3.00

❑ ❑ USA Wa9606 **#6 Merlin,** 1996, Sword in the Stone Merlin with Rooted Beard/Video Box. $2.00-3.00

❑ ❑ USA Wa9607 **#7 Alice in Wonderland,** 1996, Alice with Rooted Hair and Comb/2p/Video Box. $2.00-3.00

❑ ❑ USA Wa9608 **#8 Scat Cat,** 1996, Aristocats Scat Cat with Plush Stomach/Video Box. $2.00-3.00

❑ ❑ USA Wa9626 **Display/Premiums**, 1995, with 8 Premiums. $20.00-35.00

❑ ❑ USA Wa9643 **Crew Reference Sheet**, 1995, Blk/Wht Pic. $.50-1.00

❑ ❑ USA Wa9644 **Crew Poster**, 1995. $2.00-3.00

❑ ❑ USA Wa9664 **Translite/Sm**, 1995. $4.00-6.00

Comments: National Distribution: USA - April 19-May 16, 1996.

Wa9630

Wa9609

Wa9609 Wa9602

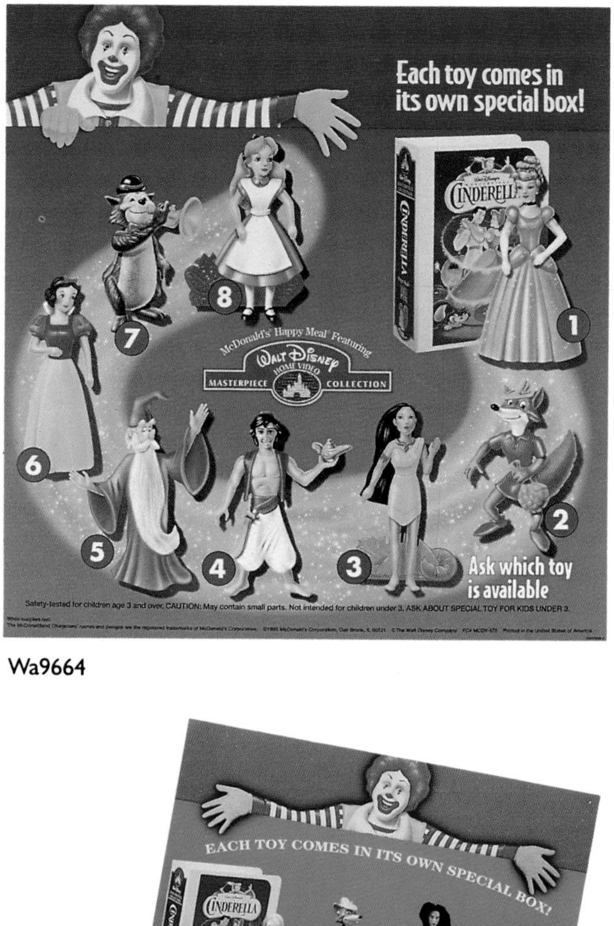

Wa9664

Left to right: Wa9604, Wa9603, Wa9602, Wa9601

Left to right: Wa9608, Wa9607, Wa9605, Wa9606

Sn9627

One Hundred and One Dalmatians Snow Domes Self-Liquidating Promotion, 1996

❑ ❑ USA Sn9610 **Snow Dome - Dog Sledding,** 1996, 2 Dogs on Red Sled with Dome Package. $4.00-6.00

❑ ❑ USA Sn9611 **Snow Dome - Dalmatian Celebration,** 1996, 101 Log with Dogs in "O". $4.00-6.00

❑ ❑ USA Sn9612 **Snow Dome - Snowman's Best Friend,** 1996, Frosty Type Snowman with Dogs in Center. $4.00-6.00

❑ ❑ USA Sn9613 **Snow Dome - Snow Furries,** 1996, Dogs in Snow with Yel Ribbon Around Dome/Red Base. $4.00-6.00

❑ ❑ USA Sn9626 **Display**: Snow Domes with 4 domes. $20.00-35.00

❑ ❑ USA Sn9627 **Color Card.** $1.00-2.00

Comments: National Distribution: USA/Canada/Mexico - November 27-December 26, 1996 as a self-liquidator. Snow domes were sold for $1.99 each with a food purchase and $2.99 without purchase in the USA. Each snow dome included came packed in a color gift box.

Sn9626

Space Jam Looney Tunes Characters Promotion, 1996

❑ ❑ USA Lo9601 **Lola Bunny,** 1996, Lady Basketball Player with Pnk Bag/Stuffed. $3.00-4.00

❑ ❑ USA Lo9602 **Bugs Bunny,** 1996, with Basket Ball/Stuffed. $3.00-4.00

❑ ❑ USA Lo9603 **2 Nerdlucks,** 1996, 1 Purp 4" Standing Char with Yel Tie/1 Brn/Yel 4" Standing with Grn Tie/Stuffed. $3.00-4.00

❑ ❑ USA Lo9604 **Daffy Duck,** 1996, Blk/Org Daffy with 2p Blu/Wht Outfit/Stuffed. $3.00-4.00

❑ ❑ USA Lo9605 **Tasmanian Devil,** 1996, Standing with Blu/Wht 2p Outfit/Stuffed. $3.00-4.00

❑ ❑ USA Lo9606 **Monstar/Blanko,** 1996, Turq/Black Player Wearing Blk Shoes/Stuffed. $3.00-4.00

Comments: National Distribution: USA/Canada/Mexico: November 1-26, 1996 in conjunction with Space Jam Happy Meal. Each stuffed character was sold for $2.99 with a food purchase or $3.49 without.

Top row, left to right: Lo9602, Lo9604, Lo9606
Bottom row, left to right: Lo9605, Lo9601, Lo9603

USA Generic Promotions, 1996

❑ ❑ USA Ge9601 **Booklet - Ronald McDonald in the Hm Workshop,** 1995, Paper. $.50-1.00
❑ ❑ USA Ge9602 **Booklet - Ronald McDonald and the Lost Dog,** 1995, Paper. $.50-1.00

❑ ❑ USA Ge9603 **Book Marker - Ron on Bike,** Nd, with Peel off Stickers. $.25-.50
❑ ❑ USA Ge9604 **Book Marker - Ron on Roller Coaster,** Nd, with Peel off Stickers. $.25-.50

❑ ❑ USA Ge9605 **Hot Spot Travel Wheels - Who's Hiding Where?/"M"**, 1996. $.25-.50
❑ ❑ USA Ge9606 **Hot Spot Travel Wheels - True or False?/ Hamburglar**, 1996. $.25-.50
❑ ❑ USA Ge9607 **Hot Spot Travel Wheels - What's the Joke?/ Birdie**, 1996. $.25-.50
❑ ❑ USA Ge9608 **Hot Spot Travel Wheels - I Didn't Know That!/Ronald**, 1996. $.25-.50

❑ ❑ USA Ge9609 **Post Cards/2 with Stickers - Grim with Kite/Ron Watering Flowers.** $.50-1.00
❑ ❑ USA Ge9610 **Post Cards/2 with Stickers - Ron with Surf Board/Ron Undersea.** $.50-1.00

❑ ❑ USA Ge9611 **FTM: Special Issue: Fire Safety Activity Book.** $.25-.50
❑ ❑ USA Ge9612 **FTM: 1996-Issue 1 Search For Treasure.** $.50-1.00
❑ ❑ USA Ge9613 **FTM: 1996-Issue 2 Pets! Pets! Pets!** $.50-1.00
❑ ❑ USA Ge9614 **FTM: 1996-Issue 3 Summer Fun.** $.50-1.00
❑ ❑ USA Ge9615 **FTM: 1996-Issue 4 It's Game Time!** $.50-1.00
❑ ❑ USA Ge9616 **FTM: 1996-Issue 5 Halloween - It's a Scream.** $.50-1.00
❑ ❑ USA Ge9617 **FTM: 1996-Issue 6 Lights! Camera! Action!** $.50-1.00

❑ ❑ USA Ge9618 **1996 Calendar: Ronald McDonald & Friends World Records/Fun Facts.** $1.00-1.25
❑ ❑ USA Ge9619 **1996 Calendar: Ronald McDonald a Celebration of the Spirit of Children.** $2.00-3.00

❑ ❑ USA Ge9620 **Plate: Easter - Ronald/Grimace with Easter Bunny.** $3.50-4.00

❑ ❑ USA Ge9622 **Plate: Zoo - Ronald.** $3.00-4.00
❑ ❑ USA Ge9623 **Plate: Zoo - Birdie.** $3.00-4.00
❑ ❑ USA Ge9624 **Plate: Zoo - Grimace.** $3.00-4.00
❑ ❑ USA Ge9625 **Plate: Zoo - Hamburglar.** $3.00-4.00
❑ ❑ USA Ge9626 **Plate: Olympics.** $3.00-4.00
❑ ❑ USA Ge9627 **Plate: Olympics with "Atlanta" on flag.** $7.00-10.00

Comments: Regional Distribution: USA - 1996 as Fun Times Magazine promotion and/or sold in McDonald's stores.

In 1996, Ronald McDonald Houses and Ronald McDonald Children's Charities combined operations. The 13th National O/O Convention met in New Orleans, Louisiana with the theme of "QSC and Me."

Ge9618

Top left to bottom right: Ge9622, Ge9623, Ge9625, Ge9624

Ge9626

ORDER TODAY FOR HALLOWEEN & CHRISTMAS SALES
• Two new 9-inch kid's collector's plates for the holidays.
• Proven built-in appeal that generates steady traffic.
• Free point-of-purchase displays hold 20 plates each.
FRIGHTFULLY FUN
Dishwasher Safe
Break Resistant
2700 S. Westmoreland Ave.
Dallas, TX 75233
(800) 634-2554 FAX (214) 337-7428

SEASONS
GREETINGS
Sun Coast
PMC Consumer Products Division
SEASONS GREETINGS
Dishwasher Safe
Break Resistant
ORDER TODAY FOR HALLOWEEN & CHRISTMAS SALES

Sun Coast
PMC Consumer Products Division
2700 S.Westmoreland Ave.
Dallas, TX 75233
(800) 634-2554
FAX (214) 337-7428
CELEBRATE SPRING
Dishwasher Safe
Break Resistant
NEW: Celebrate Spring Collector Plates
• Proven built-in appeal that generates steady traffic. • Free point-of-purchase displays hold 20 plates each.

Ge9620

COMING AUGUST 1, 1996
PETTING ZOO FUN
10 oz. Mug
New 3-Item Program:
Petting Zoo Fun.
Includes 8" melamine plate, 10 oz. thermoplastic mug, and 16 oz. melamine bowl. Break-resistant and dishwasher safe for years of enjoyment. Order each item separately to develop a program customized to your needs. Free point of purchase display when you order six or more cases of product.
Petting Zoo Fun 3-Item program available August 1, 1996.
8" Plate
16 oz. Bowl
FREE POINT OF SALE DISPLAYS

1997

Animal Pals Happy Meal, 1997
Barbie/Hot Wheels VIII Happy Meal, 1997
BeetleBorgs Metallix Happy Meal, 1997
Fisher-Price Toddler Toys for U-3
Hercules I Happy Meal, 1997
Hunchback of Notre Dame Happy Meal, 1997
Jungle Book II/Halloween '97 Happy Meal, 1997
Little Mermaid II Happy Meal, 1997
Mighty Ducks the Animated Series Happy Meal, 1997
101 [One Hundred and One] Dalmatians The Series [Flipcars] Happy Meal III, 1997
Sky Dancers (Spinning) and Micro Machines HM, 1997
Sleeping Beauty Happy Meal, 1997
Tangle Twist-A-Toid (Nickelodeon) Happy Meal, 1997
Teenie Beanie Babies I Happy Meal, 1997
(Teenie) Beanie Babies Promotional Contest for All 77 Full Size Beanie Babies, 1997
Walt Disney Home Video Masterpiece Collection II HM (Act II), 1997
USA Generic Promotions, 1997

- **"My McDonald's" logo used**
- **25th year of serving breakfast celebrated**
- **"did somebody say McDonald's?" jingle**
- **McDonald's & Disney's "Flubber - Flubberman" is introduced**
- **Teenie Beanie Babies Happy Meal promotion is a sellout!**

Animal Pals Happy Meal, 1997

Bags:

❑ ❑ USA An9730 **Hm Bag: Animal Pals Love to Play Games/ Bear & Moose,** 1997. $.25-.50
❑ ❑ USA An9731 **Hm Bag: Animal Pals have Gone Fishing!/ Moose, Yak & Gorilla,** 1997. $.25-.50

Premiums:

❑ ❑ USA An9701 **#1 Panda**, 1997, Blk/White Stuffed Bear. $1.00-1.50
❑ ❑ USA An9702 **#2 Rhinoceros**, 1997, Grey Rhino with White Horn/Stuffed. $1.00-1.50
❑ ❑ USA An9703 **#3 Yak**, 1997, Brn Yak with Wht Horns/Stuffed. $1.00-1.50
❑ ❑ USA An9704 **#4 Moose**, 1997, Tan Moose with Wht Antlers/Stuffed. $1.00-1.50
❑ ❑ USA An9705 **#5 Brown Bear**, 1997, Brown Small Baby Bear/Stuffed. $1.00-1.50
❑ ❑ USA An9706 **#6 Gorilla**, 1997, Blk Gorilla with Wht Eyes/ Nose/Mouth/Stuffed. $1.00-1.50

❑ ❑ USA An9726 **Display/Premiums**, 1997, with 6 Premiums. $10.00 -15.00
❑ ❑ USA An9743 **Crew Reference Sheet**, 1997, Blk/Wht Pic. $.50-1.00
❑ ❑ USA An9744 **Crew Poster**, 1997. $1.00-2.00
❑ ❑ USA An9764 **Translite/Sm**, 1997. $2.00-3.00

Comments: National Distribution: USA - August 1-August 24, 1997. U-3 Fisher-Price toddler toys Case #F was distributed to children under the age of three. Happy Meal was delayed a week in distribution due to overstocking of Hercules toys.

An9730 An9731

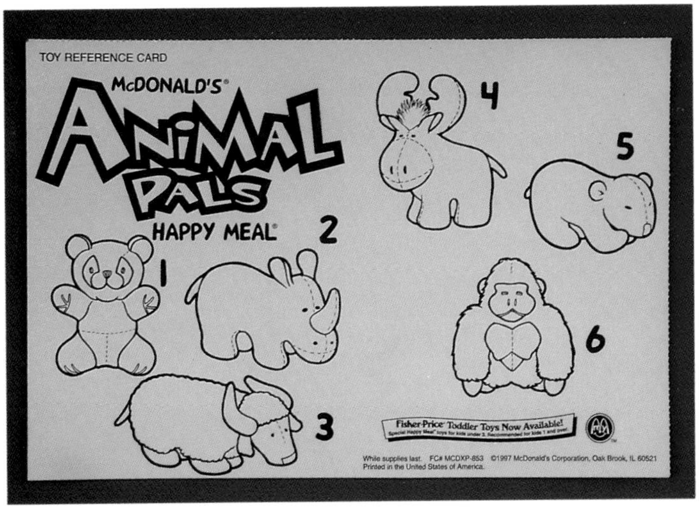

An9743

Top row, left to right: An9701, An9704, An9706
Bottom row, left to right: An9703, An9705, An9702

An9764

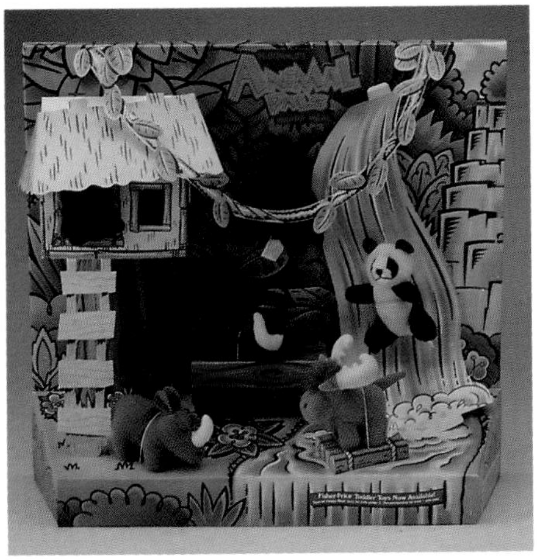

An9726

Barbie/Hot Wheels VIII Happy Meal, 1997

Boxes:

❑ ❑ USA Ba9710 **Hm Bag - 2 Barbie dolls pictured: Rapunzel & Blossom Beauty.** $.25-.50

❑ ❑ USA Ba9711 **Hm Bag - 3 Barbie dolls pictured: Blossom Beauty Barbie & Friends.** $.25-.50

Premiums: Barbie Dolls

❑ ❑ USA Ba9701 **#1 Wedding Bride Rapunzel Barbie** - White Cloth Wedding Dress With Gold Trim, White Hair, Wht Heart Doll Stand/2p. $1.50-2.50

❑ ❑ USA Ba9702 **#2 Rapunzel Barbie** - Pink Cloth Long Dress, Cinderella Sleeves, Gold Trim, White Hair, Grey Circle Doll Stand/2p. $1.50-2.50

❑ ❑ USA Ba9703 **#3 Angel Princess Barbie** - White Long Dress with Wht/Pnk/Blue Accents with White Petal Shaped Wings, White Hair, Pnk Doll Stand/2p. $1.50-2.50

❑ ❑ USA Ba9704 **#4 Happy Holidays Barbie** - Red/White Long Dress with Gold Trim, Long Brown Hair, Grn Doll Wreath Doll Stand/2p. $1.50-2.50

☐ ☐ USA Ba9705 **#5 Blossom Beauty Barbie** - African American Barbie in Pink/Yel/Blue Floral Long Dress, Long Brn Hair, Yellow Flower Petal Doll Stand/2p. $1.50-2.50

Left to right: Hw9706, Hw9707, Hw9708, Hw9709, Hw9710

Premiums: Hot Wheels Vehicles

☐ ☐ USA Hw9706 **#6 Tow truck** - Dark Blue Tow Truck with Yellow Lift & Bumper, 1994. $1.00-1.50

☐ ☐ USA Hw9707 **#7 Taxi car** - Yellow Taxi with Black Spoiler, 1994. $1.00-1.50

☐ ☐ USA Hw9708 **#8 Police car** - Black/White Police Car with 1968 Gold Star On Hood, 1993. $1.00-1.50

☐ ☐ USA Hw9709 **#9 Ambulance van** - White Ambulance with Red Flashing-Type Lights with Red Cross Symbol On Side, 1994. $1.00-1.50

☐ ☐ USA Hw9710 **#10 Fire truck** - Red Fire Truck with Grey Extension Hose on Top, 1994. $1.00-1.50

☐ ☐ USA Ba9726 **Display/Premiums**, 1997, with 10 Premiums. $25.00-40.00

☐ ☐ USA Ba9743 **Crew Reference Sheet**, 1995, Blk/Wht Pic. $.50-1.00

☐ ☐ USA Ba9744 **Crew Poster**, 1997. $1.00-2.00

☐ ☐ USA Ba9764 **Translite/Sm**, 1997. $3.00-4.00

Comments: National Distribution: USA October 24-November 27, 1997. Dolls #Ba9701-03 were distributed in Japan [1997] prior to USA distribution. Hot Wheels vehicles marked: "Hot Wheels 1994 (or 1993) Mattel, Inc. China KH Chine." Barbie dolls marked: "Made for McDonald's. 1996 Mattel, Inc. China SW Chine."

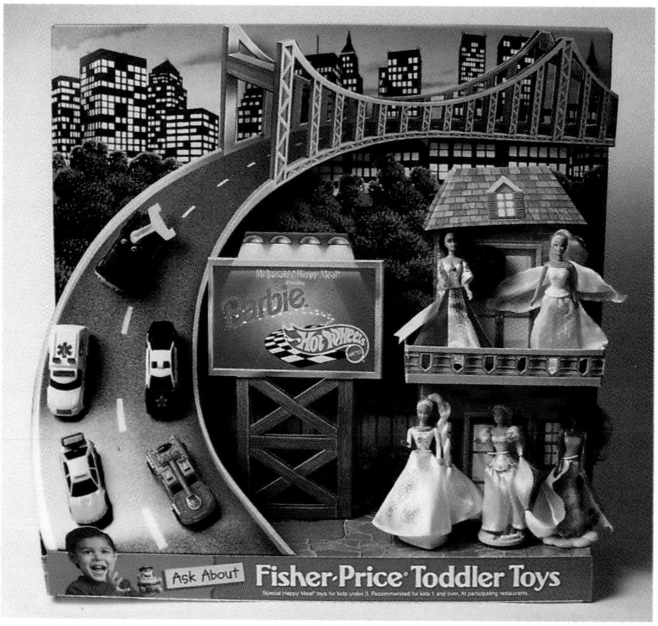

Ba9726

Ba9710

Left to right: Ba9701, Ba9702, Ba9703, Ba9704, Ba9705

Color Card

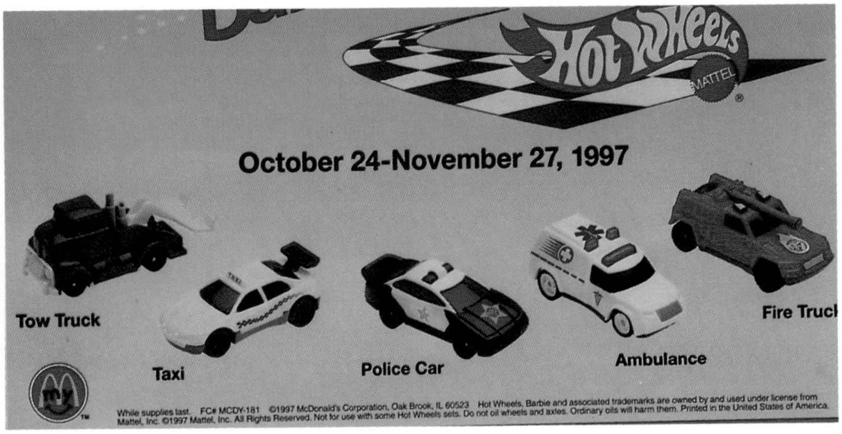

BeetleBorgs Metallix Happy Meal, 1997

Bags:

❑ ❑ USA Be9730 **Hm Bag: A Flab-ulous Birthday!,** 1997. $.25-.50

❑ ❑ USA Be9731 **Hm Bag: Poof!,** 1997. $.25-.50

Premiums:

❑ ❑ USA Be9701 **#1 Beetle Bonder,** 1996, Gry/Blk with Blk Claws, Wings Flip Out. $1.00-1.50

❑ ❑ USA Be9702 **#2 Chromium Gold Beetleborg Covert Compact,** 1996, Gold/Blue Compact with Blk Cord/Opens/with Adv Booklet. $1.00-1.50

❑ ❑ USA Be9703 **#3 Hunter Claw**, 1996, Gry/Blk Beetle Shaped with Orange Claws/Top flips Up. $1.00-1.50

❑ ❑ USA Be9704 **#4 Platinum Purple Beetleborg Covert Compact**, 1996, Purp/Red Compact with Clasp/Opens. $1.00-1.50

❑ ❑ USA Be9705 **#5 Stinger Drill**, 1997, Blue/Blk Drill/Cone Shape with Crank. $1.00-1.50

❑ ❑ USA Be9706 **#6 Titanium Silver Beetleborg Covert Compact Wristband**, 1996, Bright Silver Compact with Silver Claws/Opens. $1.00-1.50

❑ ❑ USA Be9726 **Display/Premiums**, 1997, with 6 Premiums. $10.00-15.00

❑ ❑ USA Be9743 **Crew Reference Sheet**, 1997, Blk/Wht Pic. $.50-1.00

❑ ❑ USA Be9744 **Crew Poster**, 1997. $1.00-2.00

❑ ❑ USA Be9764 **Translite/Sm**, 1997. $2.00-3.00

Comments: National Distribution: USA - August 15-September 4, 1997. U-3 Fisher-Price toddler toys were distributed to children under the age of three (box "F").

Be9730 Be9731

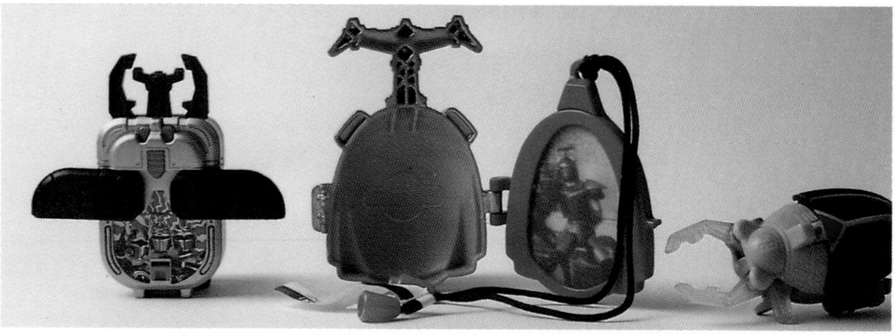

Left to right: Be9701, Be9702, Be9703

Be9764

Left to right: Be9704, Be9705, Be9706

Be9726

Fi9713 Fi9715 Fi9714 Fi9716

Fisher-Price Toddler Toys for U-3, 1997

Group G:
- ❑ ❑ USA Fi9701 **Ronald in a Green/Purple Boat.** $2.00-2.50
- ❑ ❑ USA Fi9702 **Hamburglar in a Burgermobile Walker with Blue Wheels.** $2.00-2.50
- ❑ ❑ USA Fi9703 **Boy Pilot with Orange Scarf in White/Red Airplane.** $2.00-2.50
- ❑ ❑ USA Fi9704 **Farmer boy with Yellow Hat in Red Tractor with Green Wheels.** $2.00-2.50

Group H:
- ❑ ❑ USA Fi9705 **Rolling Ball/Green with White/Orange Rolling Face.** $2.00-2.50
- ❑ ❑ USA Fi9706 **Ring Toss/White Base with Yellow & Blue Rings/3p.** $2.00-2.50
- ❑ ❑ USA Fi9707 **Phone/White/Blue Cell Phone with Purp/Green/Orange/Yellow Push Knobs.** $2.00-2.50
- ❑ ❑ USA Fi9708 **Radio/Red/Yellow Square Radio with Blue Dial.** $2.00-2.50

Group I:
- ❑ ❑ USA Fi9709 **Train Engineer/Blue in Blue Train Engine** $2.00-2.50
- ❑ ❑ USA Fi9710 **Grimace in Store Doorway with Revolving Door** $2.00-2.50
- ❑ ❑ USA Fi9711 **Hamburglar in Flat Hamburger Magnet.** $2.00-2.50
- ❑ ❑ USA Fi9712 **Lawn Mower Push Toy with Character Pictured with Musical Instruments Rolling On Red Wheels.** $2.00-2.50

Group J:
- ❑ ❑ USA Fi9713 **Car with Dog/Spotted White/Black on Roller Ball** $2.00-2.50
- ❑ ❑ USA Fi9714 **Dog/Blue with Blue Collar with Yellow Bell** $2.00-2.50
- ❑ ❑ USA Fi9715 **Elephant Rolling Car/Grey with White Baby Elephant Car.** $2.00-2.50
- ❑ ❑ USA Fi9716 **Camera/Blue/Red/White with Red/Yellow Dial.** $2.00-2.50

Group K:

❑ ❑ USA Fi9715 **Silo/Red/Yellow/Blue.** $2.00-2.50

❑ ❑ USA Fi9716 **Taxi/Yellow with "Taxi" On Door.** $2.00-2.50

❑ ❑ USA Fi9717 **Dog in White Car with Blue Rolling Figure.** $2.00-2.50

❑ ❑ USA Fi9718 **Cow.** $2.00-2.50

Group L:

❑ ❑ USA Fi9721 **Chicken McNuggets in Box** $2.00-2.50

❑ ❑ USA Fi9722 **Soft Drink Cup With Straw.** $2.00-2.50

❑ ❑ USA Fi9723 **Apple Pie in Red Box.** $2.00-2.50

❑ ❑ USA Fi9724 **French Fries in White Package.** $2.00-2.50

❑ ❑ USA Fi9727 **Color Card** with picture of all 24 FP toys. $3.00-5.00

Comments: Distribution: USA - September 1997 - August 1998. Following the distribution of twenty-four Fisher-Price toys (Groups A-F) for kids under three, McDonald's and Fisher-Price distributed a second set of twenty-four additional toddler toys. Packages were marked, "Under-3 Toy." Toys marked, "1996 Fisher-Price, Inc."

Left to right: Fi9709, Fi9710, Fi9711, Fi9712

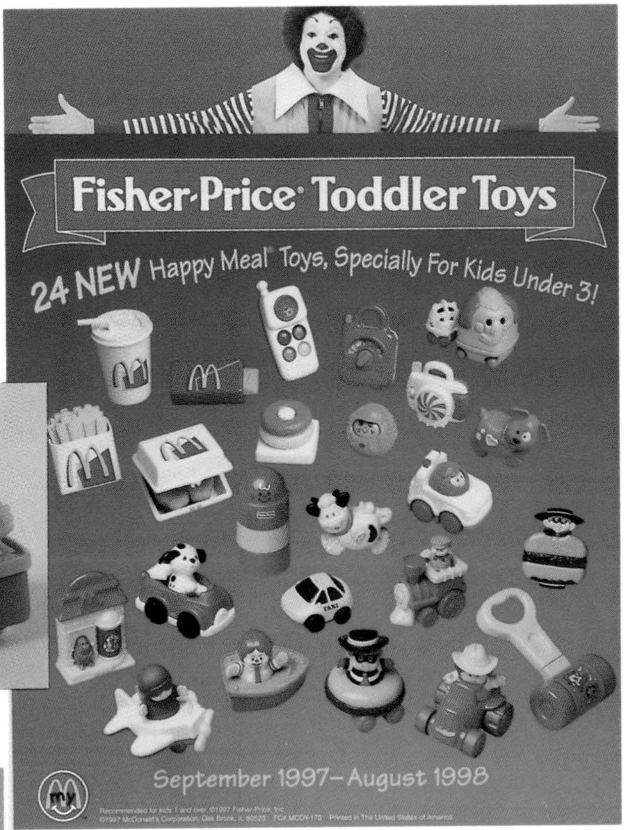

Fi9727

Left to right: Fi9702, Fi9703, Fi9704, Fi9701

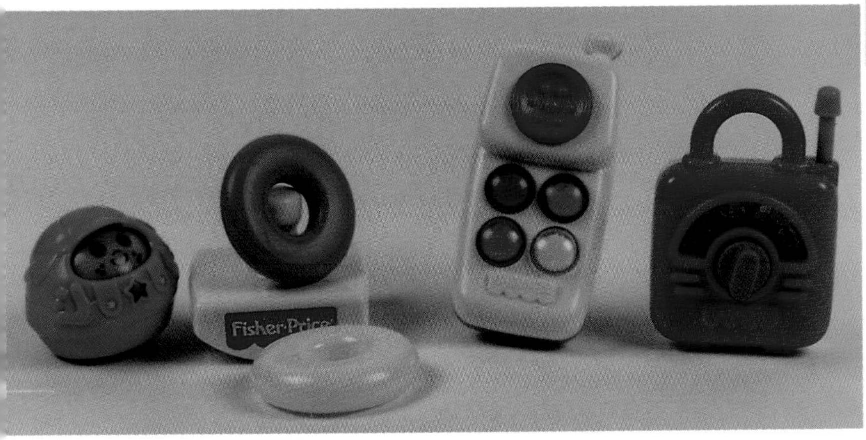

Left to right: Fi9705, Fi9706, Fi9707, Fi9708

Hercules I Happy Meal, 1997

Bags:

❑ ❑ USA He9730 **Hm Bag: My Herc-Story,** 1997. $.10-.25
❑ ❑ USA He9731 **Hm Bag: Hercules & Pegasus,** 1997. $.10-.25

Premiums:

❑ ❑ USA He9701 **#1 Wind Titan & Hermes - Blue Figure with Grey Case/3p.** $1.00-1.50
❑ ❑ USA He9702 **#2 Rock Titan & Zeus - Org/Purple Fig with Brown Case/3p.** $1.00-1.50
❑ ❑ USA He9703 **#3 Hydra & Hercules - Brown/Tan Fig with Gold Shield with Purple Case/3p.** $1.00-1.50
❑ ❑ USA He9704 **#4 Lava Titan & Baby Pegasus - White/ Blue Baby Horse with Red Case** $1.00-1.50
❑ ❑ USA He9705 **#5 Cyclops & Pain - Purple Fig with Lg White Teeth With Cream Case/3p.** $1.00-1.50
❑ ❑ USA He9706 **#6 Fates & Panic - Turq Fig with Wht Eye-ball with Grey Case/3p.** $1.00-1.50
❑ ❑ USA He9707 **#7 Pegasus & Megara - Female Fig with Purp Dress with Long Hair with Wht/Blu Horse Case/ 3p.** $1.00-1.50
❑ ❑ USA He9708 **#8 Ice Titan & Calliope - Female Fig with Purp Dress with Short Brn Hair with Clear Case/3p.** $1.00-1.50
❑ ❑ USA He9709 **#9 Nessus & Phil - Tan/Org Figure with Dark Purp Case/3p.** $1.00-1.50
❑ ❑ USA He9710 **#10 Cerberus & Hades - Blue/Grey Fig with Blk Red Eye with 3 Headed Case/3p.** $1.00-1.50

❑ ❑ USA He9726 **Display/Premiums**, 1997, with 10 Premiums. $15.00 -20.00
❑ ❑ USA He9728 **Hercules Comic: An Insider's LOOK AT THE MOVIE.** $.50-1.00
❑ ❑ USA He9729 **Hercules Poster:** Help Our HERO! $1.00-1.50
❑ ❑ USA He9730 **Hercules Decal: "HEY, I'M AN ACTION FIGURE!"** $.50-1.00
❑ ❑ USA He9743 **Crew Reference Sheet**, 1997, Blk/Wht Pic. $1.00-2.00
❑ ❑ USA He9744 **Crew Poster**, 1997. $2.00-3.00
❑ ❑ USA He9764 **Translite/Sm**, 1997. $2.00-4.00

Comments: National Distribution: USA - June 20-July 24, 1997. U-3 Fisher-Price toys were distributed to children under the age of three. Six Hercules plates were sold for $1.99 along with the Happy Meal promotion, with the purchase of any value meal, and/or with any large sandwich or Happy Meal. Separately, the plates were sold for $2.99 each without a purchase. During the first two weeks of the promotion either a Hercules poster, small magazine, or decal was given to children under the age of twelve.

Left to right: He9703, He9708, He9701, He9702, He9707

He9707 He9706 He9708

Left to right: He9709, He9706, He9707

Top row, left to right: He9702, He9701, He9710
Bottom row, left to right: He9708, He9705, He9704

He9703 He9704

He9728

He9709 He9706 He9704 He9705

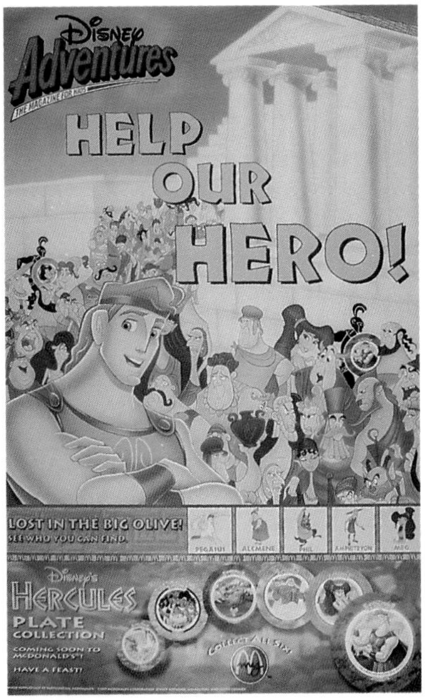

He9729

He9726

He9730

He9743

He9726

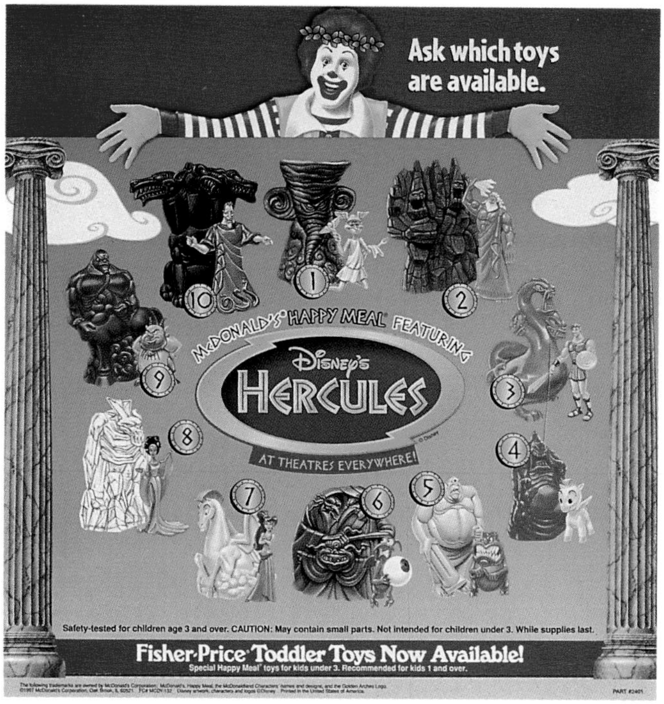

He9764

Hercules Plate Promotion, 1997

❑ ❑ USA He9711 **Plate: Hercules.** $4.00-5.00
❑ ❑ USA He9712 **Plate: Zeus.** $4.00-5.00
❑ ❑ USA He9713 **Plate: Megara.** $4.00-5.00
❑ ❑ USA He9714 **Plate: Pegasus.** $4.00-5.00
❑ ❑ USA He9715 **Plate: Phil.** $4.00-5.00
❑ ❑ USA He9716 **Plate: Muses.** $4.00-5.00

❑ ❑ USA He9726 **Display**: Holding 1 plate. $4.00-5.00

Comments: National Distribution: USA - June 20-July 3, 1997. Six plates were sold, separately from the Happy Meal, for $1.99 each (with additional purchase) or $2.99 (without additional purchase) plus tax.

Hunchback of Notre Dame Happy Meal, 1997

Bags:

❑ ❑ USA Hu9730 **Hm Bag: What A Crowd/Help Esmeralda find Djali,** 1996. $.25-.50

❑ ❑ USA Hu9731 **Hm Bag: The Notre Dame Cathedral is Over 833 Years Old,** 1996. $.25-.50

Premiums:

❑ ❑ USA Hu9701 **#1 Esmeralda Amulet -** Necklace: Tan Amulet Hanging on Purp Cord. $1.00-1.50

❑ ❑ USA Hu9702 **#2 Scepter -** Org/Red Scepter with Push **Button**/Quasimodo Appears Inside. $1.00-1.50

❑ ❑ USA Hu9703 **#3 Clopin Mask** - Purp/Pnk Mask on Purple Pole. $1.00-1.50

❑ ❑ USA Hu9704 **#4 Hugo Horn -** Hugo/Grey Blowing Purple/Yel Whistle/Horn. $1.00-1.50

❑ ❑ USA Hu9705 **#5 Juggling Balls -** 3 Grey Rubber Balls/Faces on Balls/3p. $1.00-1.50

❑ ❑ USA Hu9706 **#6 Drum -** Jester with Purp Hat on Top of Purp/Pnk Drum with Base. $1.00-1.50

❑ ❑ USA Hu9707 **#7 Quasimodo Bird Catcher -** Quasimodo in Green Shirt with Blue Bird in Brn Dish. $1.00-1.50

❑ ❑ USA Hu9708 **#8 Tambourine -** Blue/Orange with 2 Green Ribbons. $1.00-1.50

❑ ❑ USA Hu9726 **Display/Premiums**, 1997, with 8 Premiums. $10.00 -15.00

❑ ❑ USA Hu9728 **Color Card** with picture 8 toys. $2.00-3.00

❑ ❑ USA Hu9743 **Crew Reference Sheet**, 1997, Blk/Wht Pic. $.50-1.00

❑ ❑ USA Hu9744 **Crew Poster**, 1997. $2.00-3.00

❑ ❑ USA Hu9764 **Translite/Sm**, 1997. $2.00-4.00

Comments: National Distribution: USA - March 7-April 3, 1997. U-3 Fisher-Price toys were distributed to children under the age of three, on request. Series consists of eight premiums designed to support the video release of Disney's *Hunchback of Notre Dame* animated movie. The premiums are designed for children to re-enact the Festival of Fun scene from the movie. Toys are not marked with a date or McDonald's logo, they are marked "Disney/China."

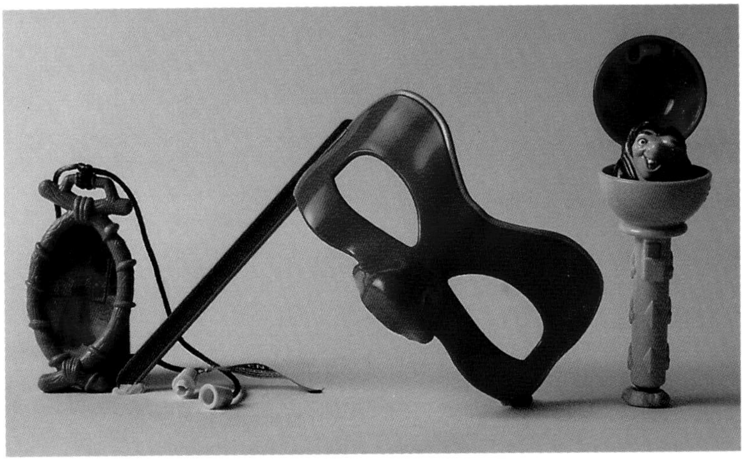

Hu9701 Hu9703 Hu9702

Hu9704 Hu9706 Hu9705

Hu9708 Hu9707

Hu9730 Hu9731

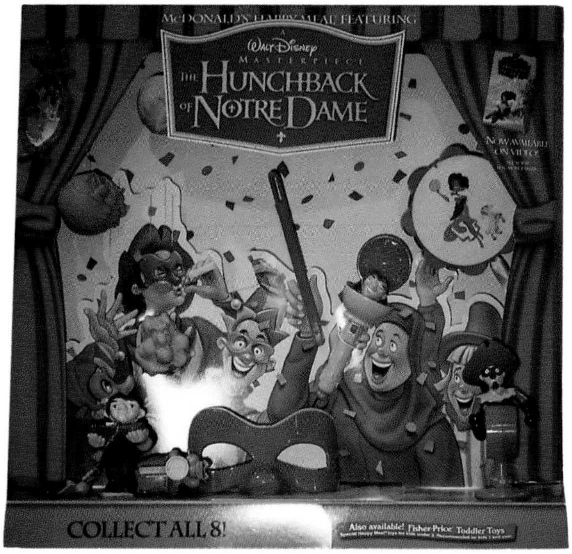

Hu9726

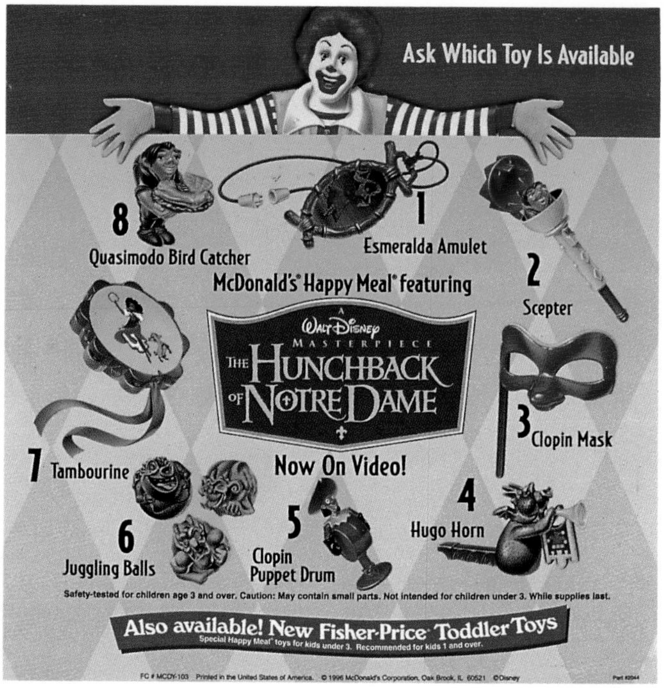

Hu9764

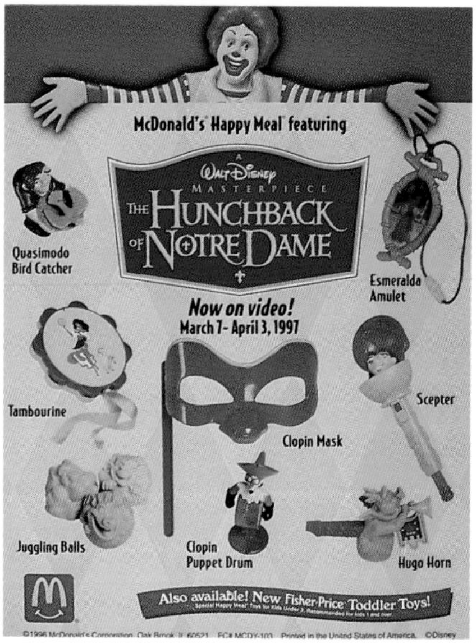

Hu9728

Hu9743

Jungle Book II/Halloween '97 Happy Meal, 1997

Boxes:

❑ ❑ USA Ju9710 **Hm Box: Can you count 10 coconuts?/Baloo dancing,** 1997. $.25-.50

❑ ❑ USA Ju9711 **Hm Box: Can you find another jungle flower?/Mowgli with Baloo & Bagheera,** 1997. $.25-.50

Premiums: Figurines with Nerds Candy Packet (MIP)

❑ ❑ USA Ju9701 **#1 Baloo - Bear Holding Yellow Bunch of Bananas**, 1997, Grey Bear with Grape Nerds Candy. $1.50-2.00

❑ ❑ USA Ju9702 **#2 Junior - Elephant**, 1997, Grey Elephant with Cherry Nerds Candy. $1.50-2.00

❑ ❑ USA Ju9703 **#3 Bagheera - Cheetah**, 1997, Grey Cheetah with Rainbow Nerds Candy. $1.50-2.00

❑ ❑ USA Ju9704 **#4 King Louie - Monkey**, 1997, Orange Monkey with Rainbow Nerds Candy. $1.50-2.00

❑ ❑ USA Ju9705 **#5 Kaa - Snake on Palm Tree**, 1997, Grey/Tan Snake Around Palm Tree with Watermelon Nerds Candy. $2.50-4.00

❑ ❑ USA Ju9706 **#6 Mowgli - Boy with coconuts**, 1997, Boy with Coconuts on Palm Island with Strawberry Nerds Candy. $1.50-2.00

❑ ❑ USA Ju9726 **Display/Premiums**, 1997, with 6 Premiums. $15.00-25.00

❑ ❑ USA Ju9727 **Banner,** 1997, with 6 Premiums Displayed. $15.00-25.00

❑ ❑ USA Ju9743 **Crew Reference Sheet**, 1997, Blk/Wht Pic. $.50-1.00

❑ ❑ USA Ju9744 **Crew Poster**, 1997. $2.00-3.00

❑ ❑ USA Ju9764 **Translite/Sm**, 1997. $3.00-5.00

❑ ❑ USA Ju9775 **Wal-Mart: 4 Face Masks:** Bagheera, Baloo, Shere Khan & Mowgli. Set of 4. $4.00-6.00

Comments: National Distribution: USA - October 3-23, 1997. A blue colored package of Nerds candy accompanied each toy distributed. The candy packages were not marked McDonald's; they contained red, green, purple, and mixed candy colors. Toys are marked: "MFG, FOR McD CORP, CHINA WM CHINE, DISNEY." U-3 Fisher-Price toys were distributed to children under the age of three and above the age of one. Jungle Book II was considered the Halloween '97 Happy Meal. Kaa - Snake on Palm Tree was recalled mid-way through the promotion. The majority of #5 Kaa - Snake on Palm Tree were distributed in the stores prior to the recall.

Ju9711 Ju9710

Ju9701 Ju9702 Ju9703

Ju9704 Ju9705 Ju9706

Ju9775

Ju9775

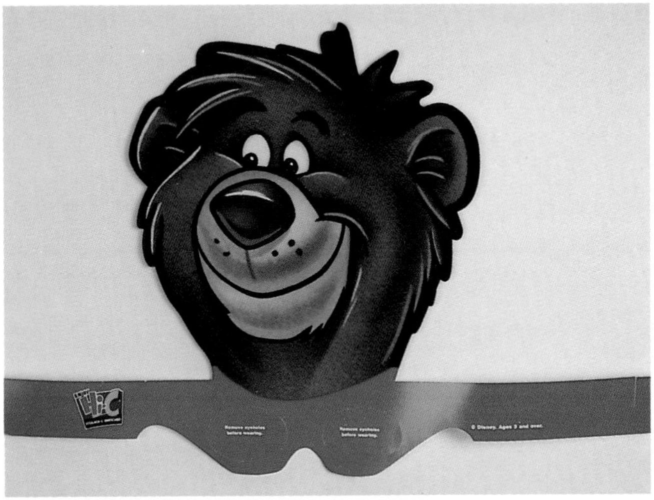

Ju9775

Little Mermaid II Happy Meal, 1997

Boxes:

❑ ❑ USA Li9710 **Hm Box: Mermaid punch out.** $.50-1.00
❑ ❑ USA Li9711 **Hm Box: Sebastian punch out.** $.50-1.00

Premiums:

❑ ❑ USA Li9701 **Ursula - Black/Purple Ursula Blowup Floater with Grey Ring/2p.** $2.00-3.00
❑ ❑ USA Li9702 **Flounder - Yellow/Blue Fish Floater.** $2.00-3.00
❑ ❑ USA Li9703 **Scuttle - White Bird with Orange Feet/ Windup Floater.** $2.00-3.00
❑ ❑ USA Li9704 **Ariel - Mermaid with Red Hair Holding Seahorse/Floater.** $2.00-3.00
❑ ❑ USA Li9705 **Max - Grey Sea Animal with 2 Arms/Floater.** $2.00-3.00
❑ ❑ USA Li9706 **Glut - Grey Shark/Floater.** $2.00-3.00
❑ ❑ USA Li9707 **Eric - Prince Eric in Boat/Floater.** $2.00-3.00
❑ ❑ USA Li9708 **Sebastian - Red Crab/Floater.** $2.00-3.00

❑ ❑ USA Li9709 **Gold Ursula** - Black/Purple Ursula Blowup Floater with Gold Ring/2p. $4.00-5.00
❑ ❑ USA Li9710 **Gold Flounder** - Gold Fish Floater. $4.00-5.00
❑ ❑ USA Li9711 **Gold Scuttle** - Gold Windup Floater. $4.00-5.00
❑ ❑ USA Li9712 **Gold Ariel** - Gold Mermaid Floater. $4.00-5.00
❑ ❑ USA Li9713 **Gold Max** - Gold Sea Animal with 2 Arms/ Floater. $4.00-5.00
❑ ❑ USA Li9714 **Gold Glut** - Gold Shark/Floater. $4.00-5.00
❑ ❑ USA Li9715 **Gold Eric** - Gold Prince Eric in Boat/Floater. $4.00-5.00
❑ ❑ USA Li9716 **Gold Sebastian** - Gold Crab/Floater. $4.00-5.00

❑ ❑ USA Li9726 **Display/Premiums**, 1997, with 10 Premiums (8 regular plus gold Flounder and Ariel). $35.00-65.00
❑ ❑ USA Li9743 **Crew Reference Sheet**, 1997, Blk/Wht Pic. $1.00-1.50
❑ ❑ USA Li9744 **Crew Poster**, 1997. $1.00-2.00
❑ ❑ USA Li9764 **Translite/Sm**, 1997. $3.00-4.00
❑ ❑ USA Li9775 **Wal-Mart: Little Mermaid CD.** $2.00-3.00
❑ ❑ USA Li9776 **Wal-Mart: Phone Card: The Santa Hotline.** $2.00-3.00

Comments: National Distribution: USA - November 28-December 25, 1997. One of every ten toys distributed was reported to be one of the "Gold Set." Set consists of a series of eight toys designed to support the re-release of Disney's movie, *The Little Mermaid.* All toy designs float in water. Ten per cent of the toys in each design were painted gold and randomly distributed in opaque blue polybags. Order forms were provided in the stores for ordering the "Gold Set" from McDonald's for $12.99 plus postage, valid until January 15, 1998. The Gold Set came boxed in a specially designed carrying case (gold cardboard box).

Wal-Mart discount stores, in conjunction with McDonald's restaurants, began distributing Little Mermaid CDs along with the Happy Meal purchase for an additional $.49. The CD-Rom preview features a look at Ariel's Story Studio, one month free access to Disney's Daily Blast (an online service for children), a free month of the Microsoft Network Internet, the song "Les Poissons" along with the Little Mermaid soundtrack, and a preview of Disney's picture *The Little Mermaid.* Also distributed during the holiday season were the Santa Hotline Phonecards. Children could call an 800 number and tell Santa what they wanted for Christmas.

Li9711 Li9710

Left to right: Li9703, Li9701, Li9702, Li9704

Left to right: Li9705, Li9706, Li9707, Li9708

Li9712 Li9710

Li9726

Top: Li9727
Top row, left to right: Li9712, Li9715, Li9711
Center row, left to right: Li9709, Li9716
Bottom row, left to right:'Li9713 Li9714 Li9710

Gold Set

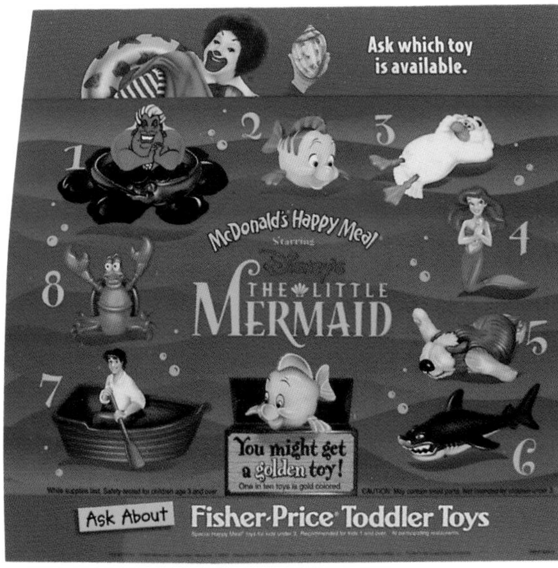

Li9764

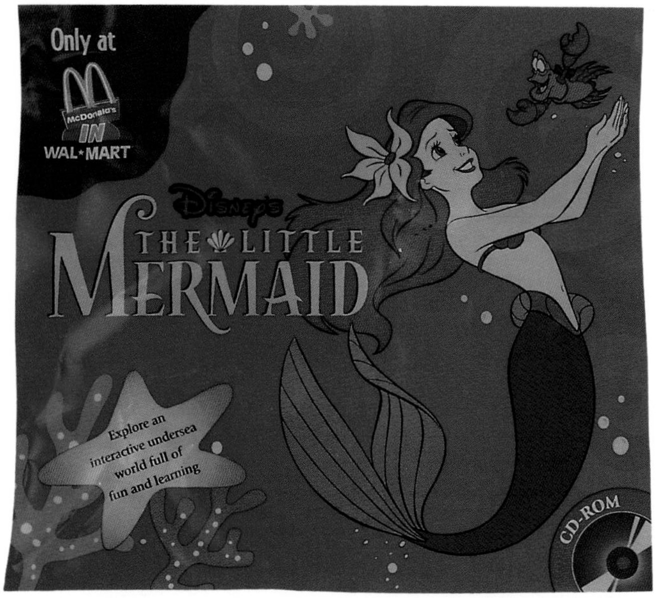

Li9775

Gift certificate envelope.

Wal-Mart ad for Little Mermaid CD.

Mighty Ducks the Animated Series Happy Meal, 1997

Boxes:

❑ ❑ USA Mi9710 **Hm Box: One Duck with Spaceship**, 1996. $.25-.50

❑ ❑ USA Mi9711 **Hm Box: Three Ducks with Hockey Sticks,** 1996. $.25-.50

Premiums: Hockey Pucks

❑ ❑ USA Mi9701 **#1 Wildwing - Black Hockey Puck,** 1997, White Beak Duck. $1.00-1.50

❑ ❑ USA Mi9702 **#2 Nosedive - Purple Hockey Puck**, 1997, Orange Beak Duck. $1.00-1.50

❑ ❑ USA Mi9703 **#3 Mallory - Yellow Hockey Puck** , 1997, Female Duck/Org Beak. $1.00-1.50

❑ ❑ USA Mi9704 **#4 Duke L'orange - Blue Hockey Puck** , 1997, Orange Beak. $1.00-1.50

❑ ❑ USA Mi9726 **Display/Premiums**, 1997, with 4 Premiums. $10.00-15.00

❑ ❑ USA Mi9727 **Color Card.** $2.00-3.00

❑ ❑ USA Mi9743 **Crew Reference Sheet**, 1997, Blk/Wht Pic. $.50-1.00

❑ ❑ USA Mi9744 **Crew Poster**, 1997. $2.00-3.00

❑ ❑ USA Mi9764 **Translite/Sm**, 1997. $2.00-4.00

Comments: National Distribution: USA - February 7-March 6, 1997. U-3 Fisher-Price toys were distributed as U-3 toys. Series consists of four sliding puck Happy Meal toys. The toys are based on the Disney animated TV series in the USA.

Mi9711 Mi9710

Top row, left to right: Mi9701, Mi9702
Bottom row, left to right: Mi9703, Mi9704

Mi9726

Mi9764

Mi9727

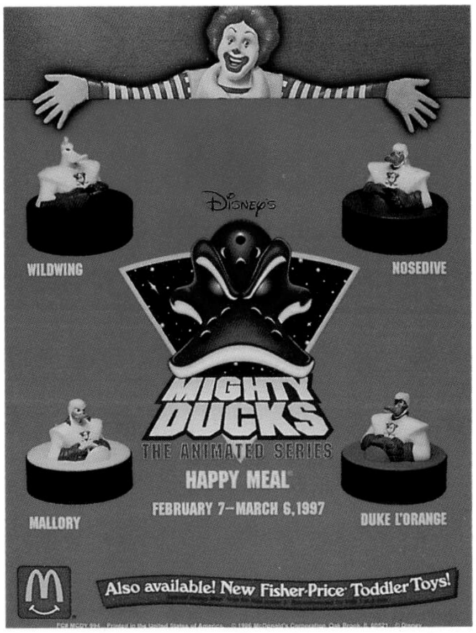

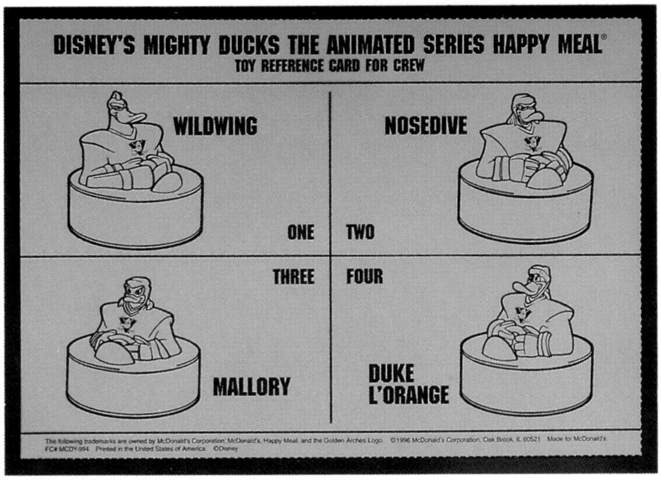

Mi9743

---

101 [One Hundred and One] Dalmatians The Series [Flipcars] Happy Meal III, 1997

Bags:

❑ ❑ USA On9710 **Hm Bag: De Vil's Car.** $.25-.50

❑ ❑ USA On9711 **Hm Bag: Two Dalmatians with Bone/Farm scene.** $.25-.50

Premiums:

❑ ❑ USA On9701 **Toy #1 Grey Dalmatian Char in Orange/Blue Flip Car with Pink Wheels.** $1.00-1.50

❑ ❑ USA On9702 **Toy #2 White Dalmatian with 2 Blk Ears in Yellow/Purp Flip Car with Blk/Org Wheels.** $1.00-1.50

❑ ❑ USA On9703 **Toy #3 White Dalmatian with 2 Blk Ears/Red Collar in Grey/Org Flip Car with Blk/Grn Wheels.** $1.00-1.50

❑ ❑ USA On9704 **Toy #4 White Dalmatian with Spotted Ears/Blue Collar in Light Purple/Grey Flip Car with Org/Blue Wheels.** $1.00-1.50

❑ ❑ USA On9705 **Toy #5 Green Dalmatian Char in Blu/Purp/Grn Flip Car with Yellow/Org Wheels.** $1.00-1.50

❑ ❑ USA On9706 **Toy #6 Pink Dalmatian Char in Org/Green Flip Car with White/Blue Wheels.** $1.00-1.50

❑ ❑ USA On9707 **Toy #7 White Dalmatian with Blue Collar in Blue/Yellow Flip Car with Grn/Purp Wheels.** $1.00-1.50

❑ ❑ USA On9708 **Toy #8 Grey Dalmatian Char in Yellow/Purple Flip Car with Red/Tan Wheels.** $1.00-1.50

❑ ❑ USA On9726 **Display/Premiums**, 1997, with 8 Premiums. $15.00-25.00

❑ ❑ USA On9727 **Color Card.** $2.00-3.00

❑ ❑ USA On9728 **Banner**, 1997, with 8 Premiums illustrated. $20.00-35.00

❑ ❑ USA On9743 **Crew Reference Sheet**, 1997, Blk/Wht Pic. $.50-1.00

❑ ❑ USA On9744 **Crew Poster**, 1997. $1.00-2.00

❑ ❑ USA On9764 **Translite/Sm**, 1997. $3.00-4.00

❑ ❑ USA On9775 **Wal—Mart Straws: Set of 4 Dalmatian Straws:** Cadpig, Rolly, Cruella, and Lucky. Set of 4.
$10.00-15.00

Comments: National Distribution: USA - December 26, 1997-January 22, 1998. Series consists of eight free-wheeling flipcar vehicles featuring sixteen characters from the *101 Dalmatians* TV program. Each flipcar features two vehicles and two characters from the show. When the character is pushed and the vehicle is turned over the new character and vehicle appear. Fisher-Price U-3 toys were distributed for children under the age of three. The toys do not have names. On the polybags, the toys were distinguished by the number in the upper right hand corner and the line art drawings of the toys.

Wal-Mart discount stores, with McDonald's restaurants inside, began offering drinking straws with an attached Dalmatian disc for an additional $.49 with the Happy Meal. Set consists of four straws with McDonald's sticker inside the disc; decal marked, "Disney."

On9726

On9727

On9710

On9711

Left to right: On9701, On9702, On9703, On9704

Left to right: On9705, On9706, On9707, On9708

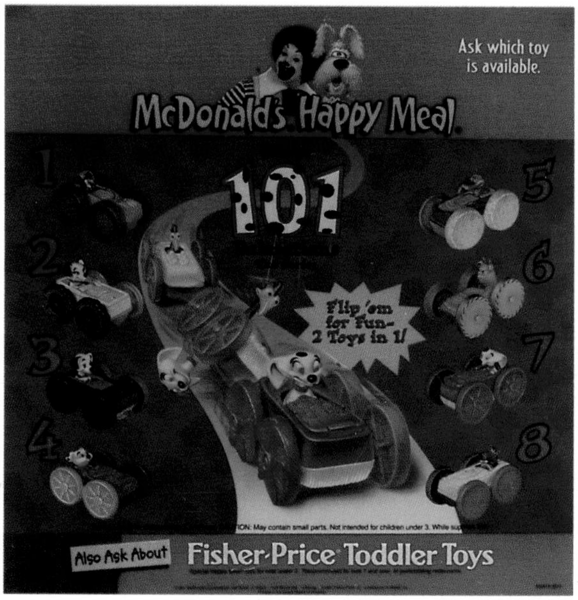

On9764

Sky Dancers (Spinning) and Micro Machines Happy Meal, 1997

Bags:

❑ ❑ USA Sk9710 **Hm Bag: Do You Know What's at The End of the Rainbow?**, 1997. $.25-.50

❑ ❑ USA Sk9711 **Hm Bag: Find Two Stars that Match**, 1997. $.25-.50

Premiums For Girls: Dancing Dolls

❑ ❑ USA Sk9701 **#1 Swan Shimmer - Elegant Ballerina, Nd, Brn Face, Org Wings/Body with Lt Blue Base/2p.** $1.00-1.50

❑ ❑ USA Sk9702 **#2 Rosemerry - Rosemarie, Nd, Red Hair, Wht Face, Lime Green Wings with Dk Purp Base/2p.** $1.00-1.50

❑ ❑ USA Sk9703 **#3 Flutterfly - Luciole, Nd, Pnk Hair, Wht Face, Lt Yel Wings with Turq Base/2p.** $1.00-1.50

❑ ❑ USA Sk9704 **#4 Princess Pegus - Princess Pivoine, Nd, Yel Hair, Wht Face, Pnk Wings with Lt Purp Base/2p.** $1.00-1.50

Premiums For Boys: Vehicles

❑ ❑ USA Sk9705 **#5 Evac Copter, 1996, Gold Helicopter Body/Blk Wings/Red Base.** $1.00-1.50

❑ ❑ USA Sk9706 **#6 Polar Explorer Vehicle, 1996, Lt Purp/Silver Body with Red/Blue Front Bumper/Antennae on Roof.** $1.00-1.50

❑ ❑ USA Sk9707 **#7 Deep Sea Hunter - Sea Crane, 1996, Grey Crane/Metallic Org Body/Blu Base.** $1.00-1.50

❑ ❑ USA Sk9708 **#8 Ocean Flyer Airplane - Sea Plane, 1996, Silver Body/Blk Prop/Red Base.** $1.00-1.50

❑ ❑ USA Sk9726 **Display/Premiums**, 1997, with 8 Premiums. $15.00 -20.00

❑ ❑ USA Sk9743 **Crew Reference Sheet**, 1997, Blk/Wht Pic. $.50-1.00

❑ ❑ USA Sk9744 **Crew Poster**, 1997. $1.00-2.00

❑ ❑ USA Sk9764 **Translite/Sm**, 1997. $2.00-3.00

Comments: National Distribution: USA - May 30-June 19, 1997 (a three week promotion instead of the regular four weeks). U-3 Fisher-Price toys were distributed as U-3 toys. Sky Dancer's base marked, "© A.g.e., Inc. China/Chine Wh3-5." Micro Machines's base marked, "© '96 Lgt, China/Chine Sv 2-10." Toys are not marked McDonald's. Along with this promotion, McDonald's sold Disney CD's and/or tapes (3) featuring songs from several Disney movies. CD's were priced at $3.99 and tapes were priced at $3.79.

Left to right: Sk9701, Sk9702, Sk9703, Sk9704

Left to right: Sk9705, Sk9706, Sk9707, Sk9708

Sk9726

Sk9764

Sleeping Beauty Happy Meal, 1997

Boxes:

- ❑ ❑ USA SI9710 **Hm Box - Maleficent has put Sleeping Beauty in a trance**, 1997. $.50-1.00
- ❑ ❑ USA SI9711 **Hm Box - The Princess is fast asleep**, 1997. $.50-1.00

Premiums:

- ❑ ❑ USA SI9701 **#1 Sleeping Beauty - Pencil Cap & Eraser**, 1997, SB with long blue dress with yel spinning wheel eraser/2p. $2.00-3.00
- ❑ ❑ USA SI9602 **#2 Maleficent - Ruler & Stencil**, 1997, black cape Maleficent with green ruler/stencil/2p. $1.00-1.50
- ❑ ❑ USA SI9703 **#3 Prince Philip - Paint Brush and Palette**, 1997, grey/black Prince holding blue shield with paper palette with grey sword(brush)/3p. $1.00-1.50
- ❑ ❑ USA SI9704 **#4 Flora - Paper-Punch**, 1997, orange/grey roly poly Flora with inset paper punch. $1.00-1.50
- ❑ ❑ USA SI9705 **#5 Dragon - Ink Pen**, 1997, black/grey/purple dragon with inset ink pen. $1.00-1.50
- ❑ ❑ USA SI9706 **#6 Raven - Book Clip**, 1997, black raven with wings as clip. $1.00-1.50

- ❑ ❑ USA SI9726 **Display/Premiums**, 1997, with 6 Premiums. $25.00-40.00
- ❑ ❑ USA SI9727 **Banner**, 1997, with 6 Premiums Displayed. $20.00-25.00
- ❑ ❑ USA SI9743 **Crew Reference Sheet**, 1997, Blk/Wht Pic. $.50-1.00
- ❑ ❑ USA SI9744 **Crew Poster**, 1997. $3.00-4.00
- ❑ ❑ USA SI9764 **Translite/Sm**, 1997. $4.00-5.00

Comments: National Distribution: USA - September 12 - October 2, 1997.

Left to right: SI9701, SI9702, SI9703, SI9704, SI9705, SI9706

SI9726

SI9764

Tangle Twist-A-Toid (Nickelodeon) Happy Meal, 1997

Bags:

- ❑ ❑ USA Ta9730 **Hm Bag: Which One of Us Did You Get?**, 1996. $.25-.50
- ❑ ❑ USA Ta9731 **Hm Bag: Twisted Adventure**, 1996. $.25-.50

Premiums:

- ❑ ❑ USA Ta9701 **#1 - Purple/Pink 3-Legged Creature** with 2 Long Pink/2 Short Pink Twists/5p. $.50-1.00
- ❑ ❑ USA Ta9702 **#2 - Lime Green Creature** with 2 Long Orange/2 Short Orange Twists/5p. $.50-1.00
- ❑ ❑ USA Ta9703 **#3 - Red Body/Gold Eyed Headed Standing Creature** with 2 Long Purple/2 Short Purple Twists/5p. $.50-1.00
- ❑ ❑ USA Ta9704 **#4 - Gold Body Creature with 3 legs** with 2 Lime Grn/1 Blue/1 Orange Twist/5p. $.50-1.00
- ❑ ❑ USA Ta9705 **#5 - Purple Body Creature with Lime Green Eyes** with 1 Long Grn/1 Short Grn/1 Gold Short/1 Pnk Short Twist/5p. $.50-1.00
- ❑ ❑ USA Ta9706 **#6 - Orange Body/Purple Legged Creature** with 1 Long Gold/1 Short Gold/1 Long Grn/1 Purple Short Twist/5p. $.50-1.00
- ❑ ❑ USA Ta9707 **#7 - Green Body Creature** Standing with 1 Long Purple/1 Short Purple/1 Short Grn/1 Short Purple/5p. $.50-1.00
- ❑ ❑ USA Ta9708 **#8 - Blue Blow Fish Creature** with 1 Long Org/1 Short Org/1 Long Blue/1 Short Purp/5p. $.50-1.00

❑ ❑ USA Ta9726 **Display/Premiums**, 1997, with 8 Premiums. $10.00-15.00
❑ ❑ USA Ta9727 **Color Card.** $1.00-2.00
❑ ❑ USA Ta9743 **Crew Reference Sheet**, 1997, Blk/Wht Pic. $.50-1.00
❑ ❑ USA Ta9744 **Crew Poster**, 1997. $2.00-3.00
❑ ❑ USA Ta9764 **Translite/Sm**, 1997. $2.00-4.00

Comments: National Distribution: USA - January 10-February 6, 1997. U-3 Fisher-Price toys (third set of four toys — USA Fp9609-12) were distributed to children under the age of three, on request. The Tangle Twist-A-Toid toys were not named, only numbered in the original package. Once removed from the package, the parts were designed to be intermingled together.

Ta9726

Left: Ta9730
Right: Ta9731

Ta9727

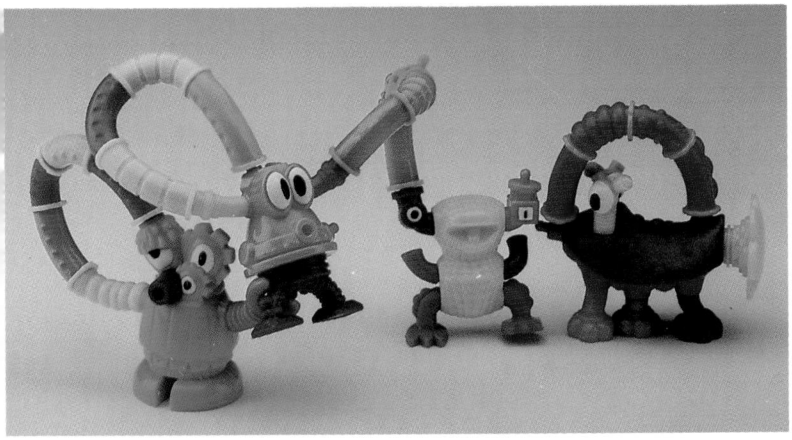

Left to right: Ta9707, Ta9706, Ta9702, Ta9701

Ta9764

Left to right: Ta9708, Ta9705, Ta9704, Ta9703

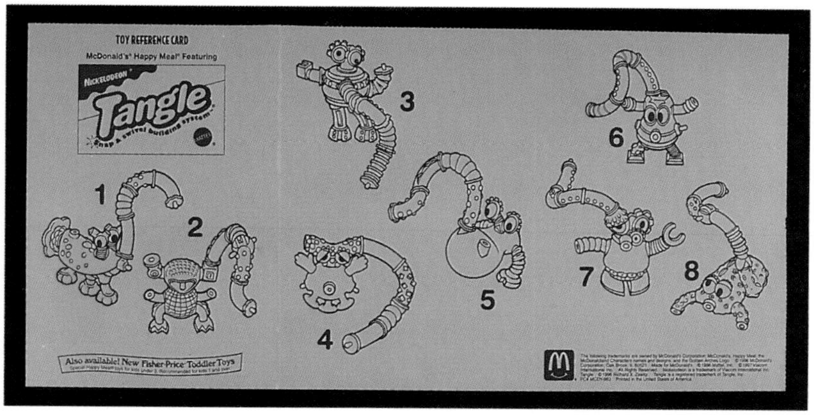

Ta9743

Teenie Beanie Babies I Happy Meal, 1997

Bags:

❑ ❑ USA Ty9730 **Hm Bag: Hi! Best Fishes!/Boy Holding Bookbag,** 1997. $1.50-3.00+

❑ ❑ USA Ty9731 **Hm Bag: Lunch Is on Me!/Girl Holding Cheeseburger,** 1997. $1.50-3.00+

Premiums:

❑ ❑ USA Ty9701 **#1 Patti Platypus - Purple Stuffed Platypus with Gold Beak/Feet.** $15.00-20.00+

❑ ❑ USA Ty9702 **#2 Chops Lamb - White Stuffed Lamb with Black Face.** $8.00-12.00+

❑ ❑ USA Ty9703 **#3 Goldie Goldfish - Gold Goldfish with Red Tale Stripe.** $8.00-10.00+

❑ ❑ USA Ty9704 **#4 Seamore Seal - White Seal with Black Eyes.** $8.00-10.00+

❑ ❑ USA Ty9705 **#5 Quacks Duck - Yellow Duck with Gold Beak/Feet.** $7.00-15.00+

❑ ❑ USA Ty9706 **#6 Pinky Flamingo - Pink Flamingo with Gold Beak.** $15.00-20.00+

❑ ❑ USA Ty9707 **#7 Chocolate Moose - Brown Moose with Gold Antlers.** $8.00-15.00+

❑ ❑ USA Ty9708 **#8 Speedy Turtle - Green Turtle with Brown Shell.** $10.00-15.00+

❑ ❑ USA Ty9709 **#9 Snort Bull - Red Bull with White Hoofs.** $10.00-15.00+

❑ ❑ USA Ty9710 **#10 Lizzy Lizard - Blue Lizard with Black Spots/Gold Stomach.** $8.00-10.00+

❑ ❑ USA Ty9726 **Display/Premiums**, 1997, with 10 Premiums. $175.00-275.00+

❑ ❑ USA Ty9727 **Color Card** with picture of all 10 Teenie Beanie Babies. $20.00-25.00+

❑ ❑ USA Ty9729 **Contest Display** with 77 Beanie Babies. $800.00-1000.00+

❑ ❑ USA Ty9743 **Crew Reference Sheet**, 1997, Blk/Wht Pic. $8.00-15.00+

❑ ❑ USA Ty9744 **Crew Poster**, 1997. $8.00-20.00+

❑ ❑ USA Ty9764 **Translite/Sm**, 1997. $10.00-25.00+

Ty9731 Ty9730

Top row: Ty9703
Bottom row, left to right: Ty9705, Ty9702, Ty9704

Top row: Ty9706
Center row, left to right: Ty9710 Ty9708 Ty9707
Bottom row: Te9701

Original artwork by Rich Seidelman. $25-40+

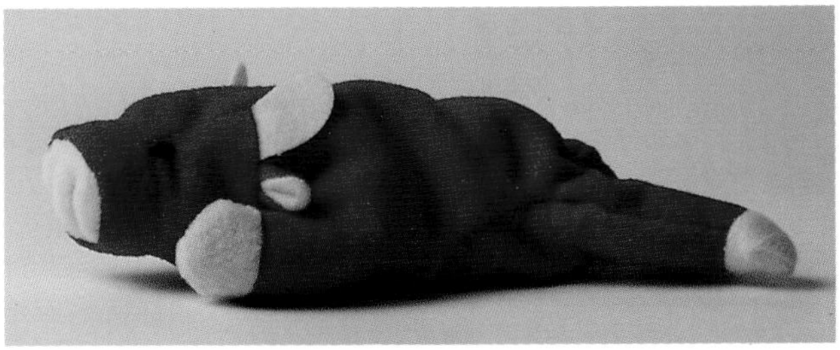

TY9709

Ty9726

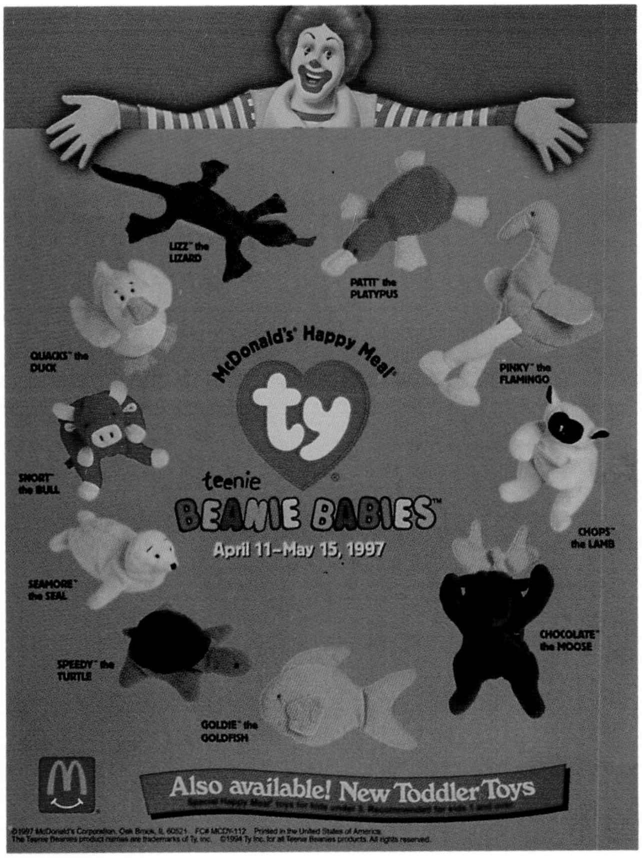

Ty9727

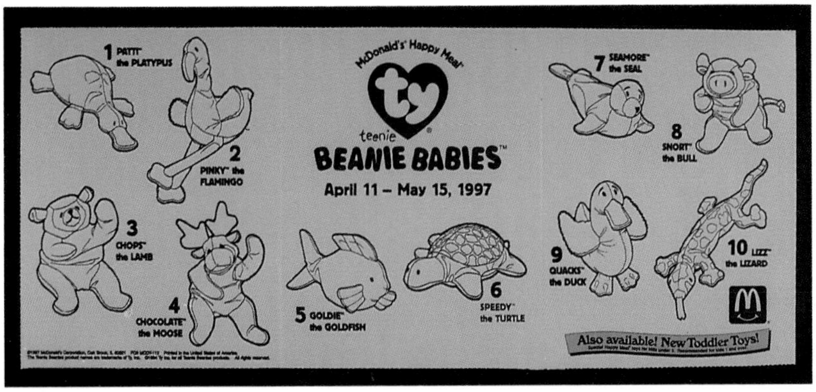

Ty9743

Teenie Beanie Babies layout pre-production drawings. $25-40 each.

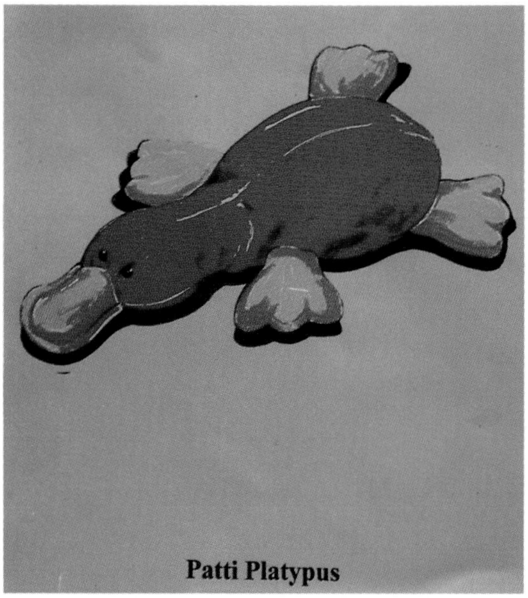

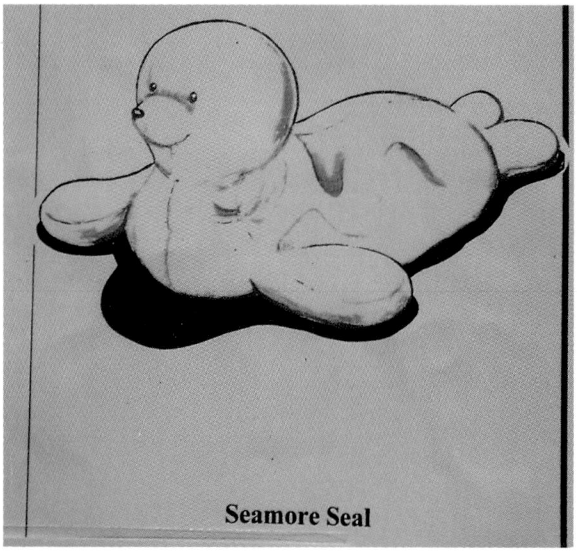

Pinky Flamingo

Speedy Turtle

Snort

~~Tabasco Red Bull~~

Chocolate Moose

Lizzy Lizard

Ty9744

Original storyboard art by Rich Seidelman. $25.00-$40.00+

Ty9764

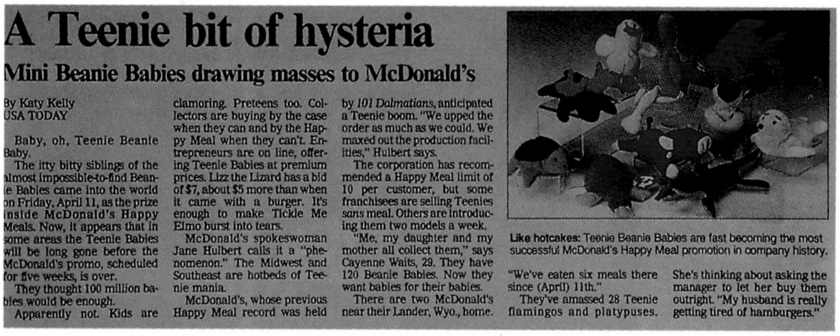

A Teenie bit of hysteria

Mini Beanie Babies drawing masses to McDonald's

By Katy Kelly
USA TODAY

Baby, oh, Teenie Beanie Baby.

The itty bitty siblings of the almost impossible-to-find Beanie Babies came into the world on Friday, April 11, as the prize inside McDonald's Happy Meals. Now, it appears that in some areas the Teenie Babies will be long gone before the McDonald's promo, scheduled for five weeks, is over.

They thought 100 million babies would be enough.

Apparently not. Kids are clamoring. Preteens too. Collectors are buying by the case when they can and by the Happy Meal when they can't. Entrepreneurs are on line, offering Teenie Babies at premium prices. Lizz the Lizard has a bid of $7, about $5 more than when it came with a burger. It's enough to make Tickle Me Elmo burst into tears.

McDonald's spokeswoman Jane Hulbert calls it a "phenomenon." The Midwest and Southeast are hotbeds of Teenie mania.

McDonald's, whose previous Happy Meal record was held by *101 Dalmatians*, anticipated a Teenie boom. "We upped the order as much as we could. We maxed out the production facilities," Hulbert says.

The corporation has recommended a Happy Meal limit of 10 per customer, but some franchisees are selling Teenies *sans* meal. Others are introducing them two models a week.

"Me, my daughter and my mother all collect them," says Cayenne Waits, 29. They have 120 Beanie Babies. Now they want babies for their babies.

There are two McDonald's near their Lander, Wyo., home. "We've eaten six meals there since (April) 11th."

They've amassed 28 Teenie flamingos and platypuses. She's thinking about asking the manager to let her buy them outright. "My husband is really getting tired of hamburgers."

Like hotcakes: Teenie Beanie Babies are fast becoming the most successful McDonald's Happy Meal promotion in company history.

USA. Today newspaper article.

Comments: National Distribution: USA - April 11-May 15, 1997. Prices are very volatile on the Teenie Beanie Babies and Ty Beanie Babies. U-3 Fisher-Price toys were provided. Series consists of ten brightly colored beanbag stuffed animal toys that are miniature versions of the popular Ty, Inc. "Beanie Babies" retail line. Each Happy Meal premium came with a heart shaped name tag like on the retail toys. In many areas of the USA, the demand for the Teenie Beanie Babies outpaced the supply. In some areas the Teenie Beanie Babies were distributed in only five days or less, leaving the stores to distribute clean-up premiums during this time period. One hundred million Teenie Beanie Babies were distributed. Demand on the east coast of the USA exceeded demand on the west coast.

Media presentation box.

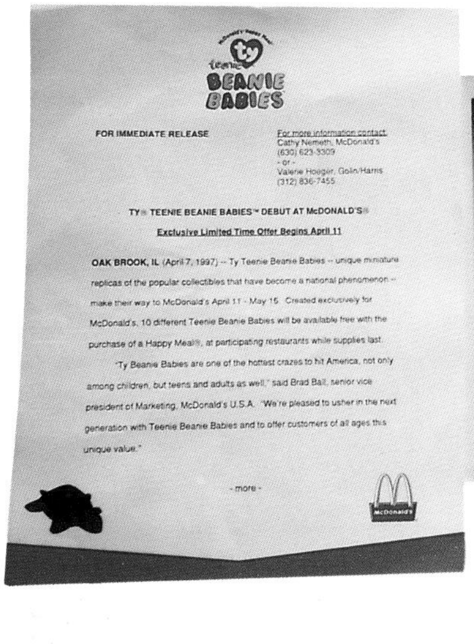
teenie
BEANIE
BABIES

FOR IMMEDIATE RELEASE

For more information contact:
Cathy Nemeth, McDonald's
(630) 623-3309
- or -
Valerie Hoeger, Golin/Harris
(312) 836-7455

TY® TEENIE BEANIE BABIES™ DEBUT AT McDONALD'S®

Exclusive Limited Time Offer Begins April 11

OAK BROOK, IL (April 7, 1997) -- Ty Teenie Beanie Babies -- unique miniature replicas of the popular collectibles that have become a national phenomenon -- make their way to McDonald's April 11 - May 15. Created exclusively for McDonald's, 10 different Teenie Beanie Babies will be available free with the purchase of a Happy Meal®, at participating restaurants while supplies last.

"Ty Beanie Babies are one of the hottest crazes to hit America, not only among children, but teens and adults as well," said Brad Ball, senior vice president of Marketing, McDonald's U.S.A. "We're pleased to usher in the next generation with Teenie Beanie Babies and to offer customers of all ages this unique value."

- more -

McDonald's

THE CRAZE CONTINUES -- Ty® Teenie Beanie Babies™, miniature replicas of the popular collectibles, will be available exclusively at McDonald's® restaurants nationwide starting April 11. The collection includes: Chocolate™ the Moose, Snort™ the Bull, Pinky™ the Flamingo, Patti™ the Platypus, Chops™ the Lamb, Goldie™ the Goldfish, Speedy™ the Turtle, Seamore™ the Seal, Quacks™ the Duck and Lizz™ the Lizard.

(Teenie) Beanie Babies Promotional Contest for All 77 Full Size Beanie Babies, 1997

❑ ❑ USA Bb9701 **Ally the Alligator (R).** $25.00-40.00
❑ ❑ USA Bb9702 **Bernie the St. Bernard.** $8.00-10.00
❑ ❑ USA Bb9703 **Bessie the Cow (R).** $40.00-50.00
❑ ❑ USA Bb9704 **Blackie the Bear.** $8.00-10.00

❑ ❑ USA Bb9705 **Bones the Dog.** $8.00-10.00
❑ ❑ USA Bb9706 **Bongo the Monkey.** $10.00-15.00
❑ ❑ USA Bb9707 **Bubbles the Fish (R).** $80.00-125.00
❑ ❑ USA Bb9708 **Bucky the Beaver (R).** $25.00-30.00

❑ ❑ USA Bb9709 **Chocolate the Moose.** $10.00-20.00
❑ ❑ USA Bb9710 **Congo the Gorilla.** $8.00-10.00
❑ ❑ USA Bb9711 **Crunch the Shark.** $8.00-10.00
❑ ❑ USA Bb9712 **Cubbie the Bear (R).** $25.00-40.00

❑ ❑ USA Bb9713 **Curly the Bear.** $15.00-35.00
❑ ❑ USA Bb9714 **Daisy the Cow.** $8.00-10.00
❑ ❑ USA Bb9715 **Derby the Horse.** $15.00-25.00
❑ ❑ USA Bb9716 **Digger the Crab.** $80.00-100.00

❑ ❑ USA Bb9717 **Doby the Doberman.** $15.00-25.00
❑ ❑ USA Bb9718 **Ears the Bunny.** $7.00-10.00
❑ ❑ USA Bb9719 **Flash the Dolphin (R).** $75.00-100.00
❑ ❑ USA Bb9720 **Fleece the Lamb.** $8.00-10.00
❑ ❑ USA Bb9721 **Flip the Cat (R).** $35.00-40.00
❑ ❑ USA Bb9722 **Floppity the Bunny.** $10.00-15.00
❑ ❑ USA Bb9723 **Freckles the Leopard.** $7.00-10.00

❑ ❑ USA Bb9724 **Garcia the Bear (R).** $100.00-150.00
❑ ❑ USA Bb9725 **Goldie the Goldfish (R).** $25.00-35.00
❑ ❑ USA Bb9726 **Gracie the Swan.** $7.00-10.00

❑ ❑ USA Bb9727 **Grunt the Razorback (R).** $150.00-175.00
❑ ❑ USA Bb9728 **Happy the Hippo.** $7.00-10.00
❑ ❑ USA Bb9729 **Hippity the Bunny.** $10.00-15.00
❑ ❑ USA Bb9730 **Hoppity the Bunny.** $10.00-15.00

❑ ❑ USA Bb9731 **Hoot the Owl (R).** $25.00-35.00
❑ ❑ USA Bb9732 **Inch the Worm.** $7.00-10.00
❑ ❑ USA Bb9733 **Inky the Octopus.** $7.00-10.00
❑ ❑ USA Bb9734 **Legs the Frog (R).** 25.00-35.00

❑ ❑ USA Bb9735 **Lizzy the Lizard (R).** $25.00-40.00
❑ ❑ USA Bb9736 **Lucky the Ladybug.** $7.00-10.00

❑ ❑ USA Bb9737 **Magic the Dragon (R).** $50.00-60.00
❑ ❑ USA Bb9738 **Manny the Manatee (R).** $150.00-175.00
❑ ❑ USA Bb9739 **Mel the Koala.** $8.00-10.00

❑ ❑ USA Bb9740 **Mystic the Unicorn.** $50.00-60.00
❑ ❑ USA Bb9741 **Nip the Cat (R).** $30.00-40.00
❑ ❑ USA Bb9742 **Nuts the Squirrel.** $7.00-10.00

❑ ❑ USA Bb9743 **Patti the Platypus.** $10.00-15.00
❑ ❑ USA Bb9744 **Peanut the Elephant.** $7.00-10.00

❑ ❑ USA Bb9745 **Pinchers the Lobster.** $10.00-15.00

❑ ❑ USA Bb9746 **Pinky the Flamingo.** $15.00-20.00

❑ ❑ USA Bb9747 **Pouch the Kangaroo.** $8.00-10.00
❑ ❑ USA Bb9748 **Quackers the Duck.** $8.00-10.00
❑ ❑ USA Bb9749 **Radar the Bat (R).** $150.00-175.00
❑ ❑ USA Bb9750 **Ringo the Raccoon.** $7.00-10.00

❑ ❑ USA Bb9751 **Rover the Dog.** $7.00-10.00
❑ ❑ USA Bb9752 **Scoop the Pelican.** $7.00-10.00
❑ ❑ USA Bb9753 **Scottie the Terrier.** $7.00-10.00

❑ ❑ USA Bb9754 **Seamore the Seal (R).** $150.00-175.00
❑ ❑ USA Bb9755 **Seaweed the Otter.** $7.00-10.00
❑ ❑ USA Bb9756 **Sly the Fox.** $7.00-10.00

❑ ❑ USA Bb9757 **Snip the Cat.** $8.00-10.00
❑ ❑ USA Bb9758 **Snort the Bull.** $8.00-10.00
❑ ❑ USA Bb9759 **Sparky the Dalmatian (R).** $125.00-140.00

❑ ❑ USA Bb9760 **Speedy the Turtle (R).** $25.00-35.00
❑ ❑ USA Bb9761 **Splash the Whale (R).** $90.00-100.00
❑ ❑ USA Bb9762 **Spooky the Ghost (R).** $50.00-75.00

❑ ❑ USA Bb9763 **Spot the Dog (R).** $40.00-50.00

❑ ❑ USA Bb9764 **Spike the Rhinoceros.** $8.00-10.00

❑ ❑ USA Bb9765 **Squealer the Pig.** $8.00-10.00
❑ ❑ USA Bb9766 **Stinky the Skunk.** $8.00-10.00

❑ ❑ USA Bb9767 **Stripes the Tiger.** $8.00-10.00
❑ ❑ USA Bb9768 **Tank the Armadillo (R).** $60.00-75.00
❑ ❑ USA Bb9769 **Teddy the Bear (R).** $50.00-75.00
❑ ❑ USA Bb9770 **Twigs the Giraffe.** $8.00-10.00

❑ ❑ USA Bb9771 **Valentino the Bear.** $15.00-25.00
❑ ❑ USA Bb9772 **Velvet the Panther (R).** $25.00-35.00

❑ ❑ USA Bb9773 **Waddle the Penguin.** $8.00-10.00

❑ ❑ USA Bb9774 **Weenie the Dog.** $8.00-10.00

❑ ❑ USA Bb9775 **Wrinkles the Dog.** $8.00-10.00

❑ ❑ USA Bb9776 **Ziggy the Zebra.** $8.00-10.00
❑ ❑ USA Bb9777 **Zip the Cat.** $8.00-10.00
❑ ❑ USA Bb9778 **Full Set of 77 Full Size Beanie Babies.** $2,000-2,800+

Left to right: Bb9701, Bb9702 , Bb9731, Bb9704

Comments: The full collection of 77 Beanie Babies (full size) were raffled off at over 2,000 McDonald's in the USA. Beanie Babies are marked: Ty Inc. Distribution: April 11-May 15, 1997, with the raffle concluding on May 15, 1997.

Left to right: Bb9706, Bb9707, Bb9705, Bb9708

Left to right: Bb9709, Bb9712, Bb9710, Bb9711

Left to right: Bb9713, Bb9714, Bb9715, Bb9716

Left to right: Bb9717, Bb9718 , Bb9719

Left to right: Bb9720, Bb9721, Bb9722, Bb9723

Left to right: Bb9724, Bb9725, Bb9726

Left to right: Bb9731, Bb9732, Bb9733, Bb9734

Left to right: Bb9727, Bb9728, Bb9729, Bb9730

Left to right: Bb9735, Bb9736

Left to right: Bb9737, Bb9738, Bb9739

Left to right: Bb9744, Bb9745, Bb9746, Bb9743

Left to right: Bb9740, Bb9741, Bb9742

Left to right: Bb9747, Bb9748, Bb9749, Bb9750

Left to right:
Bb9751, Bb9752,
Bb9753

Left to right: Bb9754, Bb9755, Bb9756

Left to right: Bb9757, Bb9758, Bb9759

Left to right: Bb9760, Bb9761, Bb9762

Left to right: Bb9763, Bb9765, Bb9766

Left to right: Bb9767, Bb9768, Bb9769, Bb9770

Left to right: Bb9771, Bb9772, Bb9764

Left to right: Bb9775, Bb9773

Left to right: Bb9774, Bb9776, Bb9777

Walt Disney Home Video Masterpiece Collection Happy Meal (Act II), 1997

Bags:

❑ ❑ USA Wa9730 **Hm Bag: Bambi/Walt Disney Home Video Masterpiece Collection,** 1997. $.25-.50

❑ ❑ USA Wa9730 **Hm Bag: The Three Caballeros/ Walt Disney Home Video Masterpiece Collection,** 1997. $.25-.50

Premiums:

❑ ❑ USA Wa9701 **#1 Bambi (Bambi),** 1996, Moveable Legs. $2.00-2.50

❑ ❑ USA Wa9702 **#2 Simba (The Lion King),** 1996, Moveable Legs. $2.00-2.50

❑ ❑ USA Wa9703 **#3 Elliott (Pete's Dragon),** 1996, Green Dragon with Purple Wings. $2.00-2.50

❑ ❑ USA Wa9704 **#4 Dodger (Oliver & Company),** 1996, White Dog with Brn Face/Red Ribbon on Neck. $2.00-2.50

❑ ❑ USA Wa9705 **#5 Princess Aurora (Sleeping Beauty),** 1996, Blue Dress with Gold Locket/Moveable Arms. $2.00-2.50

❑ ❑ USA Wa9706 **#6 Woody (Toy Story),** 1996, Brn Hat/Boots with Gold Shirt/Blue Pants/Moveable Arms/2p. $2.00-2.50

❑ ❑ USA Wa9707 **#7 Donald (Duck) - (The Three Caballeros),** 1996, Brn Mexican Hat with Blanket on Moveable Arms. $2.00-2.50

❑ ❑ USA Wa9708 **#8 Tigger (The Many Adventures of Winnie the Pooh),** 1996, Org Tiger with White Face/Moveable Legs. $2.00-2.50

❑ ❑ USA Wa9726 **Display/Premiums**, 1995, with 8 Premiums. $20.00-35.00

❑ ❑ USA Wa9727 **Color Card**. $2.00-3.00

❑ ❑ USA Wa9743 **Crew Reference Sheet**, 1995, Blk/ Wht Pic. $.50-1.00

❑ ❑ USA Wa9744 **Crew Poster**, 1995. $2.00-3.00

❑ ❑ USA Wa9764 **Translite/Sm**, 1995. $4.00-6.00

Comments: National Distribution: USA - originally scheduled for May 16-June 12, 1997. These toys were distributed ahead of schedule, April 25-May 21, 1997 due to overwhelming demand for the previous Happy Meal toys (Teenie Beanie Babies).

Wa9701 Wa9703

Wa9702 Wa9708 Wa9704 Wa9705

Left: Wa9707
Right: Wa9706

Wa9727

Wa9743

Wa9764

USA Generic Promotions, 1997

❑ ❑ USA Ge9701 **Silly Face Spinner Game,** 1997, Paper. $.50-1.00

❑ ❑ USA Ge9702 **Magic Touch Color Card - Ronald,** 1997. $.25-.50

❑ ❑ USA Ge9703 **Magic Touch Color Card - Grimace,** 1997. $.25-.50

❑ ❑ USA Ge9704 **Magic Touch Color Card - Hamburglar,** 1997. $.25-.50

❑ ❑ USA Ge9705 **Magic Touch Color Card - Birdie,** 1997. $.25-.50

❑ ❑ USA Ge9706 **Comic Book - Ronald Goes Camping**/3 1/2" x 7". $.50-1.00

❑ ❑ USA Ge9707 **Sticker Games - Ronald's Picnic Puzzle/Ronald's Outdoor Bingo**, 1997. $.50-1.00

❑ ❑ USA Ge9708 **Sticker Games - Ronald's Memory Game/Ronald's Treasure Trip**, 1997. $.50-1.00

❑ ❑ USA Ge9709 **Ronald's Rainbow Painter Pad - Purple,** 1997. $.25-.50

❑ ❑ USA Ge9710 **Ronald's Rainbow Painter Pad - Green,** 1997. $.25-.50

❑ ❑ USA Ge9711 **Little Pocket Press - Red Ronald/Grimace,** 1997. $.25-.50

❑ ❑ USA Ge9712 **Little Pocket Press - Purple Ronald/Birdie,** 1997. $.25-.50

❑ ❑ USA Ge9713 **Little Pocket Press - Yellow Ronald/Grimace,** 1997. $.25-.50

❑ ❑ USA Ge9714 **Little Pocket Press - Green Ronald/Birdie,** 1997. $.25-.50

❑ ❑ USA Ge9715 **FTM: 1997-1: Crafty Artists,** 1997. $.25-.50

❑ ❑ USA Ge9716 **FTM: 1997-2: It's a Wild Life!,** 1997. $.25-.50

❑ ❑ USA Ge9717 **FTM: 1997-Road Safety Activity Book,** 1997. $.25-.50

❑ ❑ USA Ge9718 **FTM: 1997-3: Think Big!,** 1997. $.25-.50

❑ ❑ USA Ge9719 **FTM: 1997-4: Silly Day,** 1997. $.50-1.00

❑ ❑ USA Ge9720 **FTM: 1997-5 It's a ...HALLOWEEN,** 1997. $.25-50

❑ ❑ USA Ge9721 **FTM: 1997-6: Here Come The Holidays!,** 1997. $.25-50

❑ ❑ USA Ge9722 **1997 Calendar: Ronald McDonald A Celebration of the Spirit of Children.** $2.00-3.00

Comments: Regional Distribution: USA - 1997 as Fun Times Magazine Promotions and alternatives.

Teenie Beanie Babies Happy Meal, 1997 sold out to millions, 100 million in fact! The demand for the Teenie Beanie Babies far exceeded the supply. The "collectors" swamped the stores for the Teenie Beanie Babies stuffed toys, forcing the collector demand for toys and products to be fully recognized.

McDonald's teamed with Disney for a ten year period. Purchasing plates, stuffed animals, and/or glasses along with food items seemed right in step with the "in a hurry" '90s generation. On the other hand, customer reaction to the Arch Deluxe multi-million dollar promotion was not in step with the tastes and desires of the aging population. McDonald's changed pace with a management change and an advertising agency switch. Many Happy Meal promotions were reduced from a four or five week promotion to a three week promotion in an attempt to keep the Happy Meal promotions "fresh." Americans were increasingly making several trips per week for fast food and expected something "new" at their [My McDonald's] McDonald's. The latest "My McDonald's" logo and "did somebody say McDonald's" jingle simplified the selection process during the "Magic Moment."

Disney introduced its newest character - Flubber. "Flubberman" is a jolly looking, green character with a sometimes white smile on his round, ever-changing body dimensions. His appearance resembles a cross between an early Grimace and Uncle O'Grimacey, except that he appears to be a "bouncing character." This was McDonald's latest attempt to add "zip and bounce" to its year ending promotions.

1998

Animal Kingdom Happy Meal, 1998
Barbie/Hot Wheels IX Happy Meal, 1998 [Projected*]
A Bug's Life Happy Meal, 1998 [Projected*]
Fisher-Price Toys for U-3, 1998/1999 [Projected*]
Halloween '98 Happy Meal, 1998 [Projected*]
Hercules II Happy Meal, 1998
The Legend of Mulan Happy Meal, 1998 [Projected*]
McDonaldland Happy Meal, 1998 [Projected*]
My Little Pony II/Transformers Beast Wars Transmetals II Happy Meal, 1998
Peter Pan Happy Meal, 1998
Simba's Pride Happy Meal, 1998 [Projected*]
Tamagotchi Happy Meal, 1998 [Projected*]
Teenie Beanie Babies II Happy Meal, 1998 [Projected*]
USA Generic Promotions, 1998 [Projected*]

* Projected Happy Meal information obtained from the Internet.

- **14th National O/O Convention**
- **"did somebody say McDonald's?" (Repeated)**
- **"Where the World's Best Come Together" (Olympics 1998)**
- **"Made for You"**
- **"Made for You...At the Speed of McDonald's"**
- **"Iam Hungry" character introduced (computer animated)**
- **"the value of GOLD"**

Animal Kingdom Happy Meal, 1998

Boxes:

❑ ❑ USA An9821 **Hm Box - Gorilla Falls**

❑ ❑ USA An9822 **Hm Box - Elephant/Harambe, Africa**

❑ ❑ USA An9831 **Hm Box - Animal Kingdom - Only at Restaurantosaurus**! (Dinoland Walt Disney, Orlando, Fla.) $5.00-8.00

Premiums: 12 Figurines + 1 Wal-Mart Figurine

❑ ❑ USA An9801 **#1 Triceratops** - Grn/Lt Grn Triceratops with 2 White Horns/Figurine. $.50-1.00

❑ ❑ USA An9802 **#2 Toucan** - Yel/Org/Grn Beak Bird Figurine/Talks When Head is Bent/Figurine. $.50-1.00

❑ ❑ USA An9803 **#3 Gorilla & Baby Gorilla On Pole** - Blk Gorilla Holding Baby on Tan Pole/Figurine. $.50-1.00

❑ ❑ USA An9804 **#4 Elephant** - Grey Elephant with Tusks Figurine. $.50-1.00

❑ ❑ USA An9805 **#5 Ring Tail Lemur** - Brn with Wht Head & Blk Striped Velvet Tail/Figurine. $.50-1.00

❑ ❑ USA An9806 **#6 Dragon** - Purp Dragon with Lg Purple Plastic Wings/Figurine/Pressing Chest Moves Wings. $1.00-1.50

❑ ❑ USA An9807 **#7 Iguanodon** - Grn/Lavender Iguana/Figurine/Moving Tail Open/Closes Mouth $.50-1.00

❑ ❑ USA An9808 **#8 Zebra** - Blk/Wht Striped/Figurine/White Knob Wind-Up. $.50-1.00

❑ ❑ USA An9809 **#9 Lion** - Yellowish/Brn Lion Figurine/Moving Right Leg/Moves Mouth. $.50-1.00

❑ ❑ USA An9810 **#10 Cheetah** - Lt Yellow/Blk Cheetah Figurine. $.50-1.00

❑ ❑ USA An9811 **#11 Crocodile** - Greenish Crocodile with Open Mouth/Figurine/Pressing Back Opens Mouth. $.50-1.00

❑ ❑ USA An9812 **#12 Rhino** - Grey Rhino with 2 Horns. $.50-1.00

❑ ❑ USA An9813 **#13 Tortoise - Wal-Mart Special** - Greenish Turtle. $2.00-4.00

❑ ❑ USA An9826 **Display/Premiums**, 1998, with 12 Premiums. $25.00-40.00

❑ ❑ USA An9843 **Crew Reference Sheet**, 1998, Blk/Wht Pic.

❑ ❑ USA An9844 **Crew Poster**, 1998.

❑ ❑ USA An9864 **Translite/Sm**, 1998.

❑ ❑ USA An9827 **Banner.**

❑ ❑ USA An9876 **Disney World Orlando: Restaurantosaurus - Tyrannosaurus Rex Squirter**. $5.00-8.00

❑ ❑ USA An9877 **Disney World Orlando: Restaurantosaurus - Squirter.** $5.00-8.00

Comments: National Distribution: USA - April 24-May 21, 1998. The thirteenth premium was ONLY given out at Wal-Mart stores having a McDonald's. Additionally, the McDonald's Restaurant (Restaurantosaurus) in the Dinoland section of Disney's newest theme park located in Walt Disney World in Orlando, Florida, distributed the two water squirters in a specially designed box. One is a water gun shaped like a T-Rex, 4 1/2" x 1 3/4". The T-Rex is blue with green accents and a yellow trigger. T-Rex is marked, "Disney's ANIMAL KINGDOM, MFG. FOR McD CORP., 1998, McDonald's Corp., Disney China, MT." Squirter comes mint in a package. The Happy Meal box has dinosaur pictures and facts as well as a punch-out post card that can be filled out, stamped, and mailed home, with Disney Animal Kingdom logo and McDonald's logo. Box also states, "ONLY AT RESTAURANTOSAURUS! and Welcome to DINOLAND U.S.A."

An9831

An9826

Left to right:
An9801, An9802,
An9803, An9804

Left to right:
An9805, An9806,
An9807, An9808

Left to right: An9809, An9810, An9811, An9812

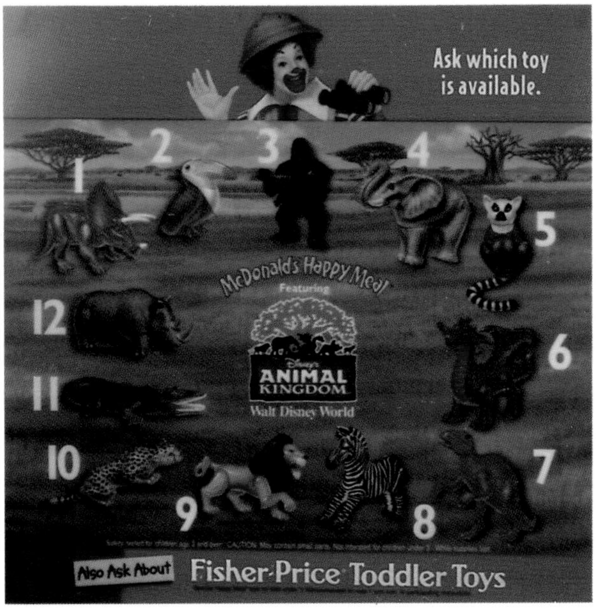

An9864

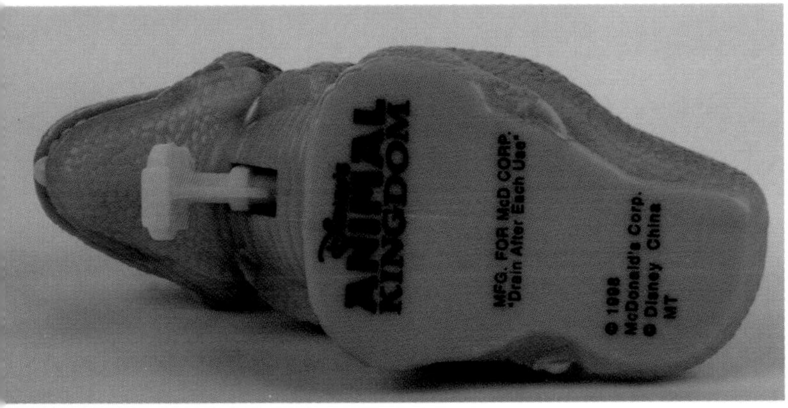

Disney toy from McDonald's in Orlando.

Disney toy package.

An9813

Barbie/Hot Wheels IX Happy Meal, 1998 [Projected]

Bags or Boxes:
❑ ❑ USA Ba9810 **Hm Barbie/Hot Wheels.**
❑ ❑ USA Ba9811 **Hm Barbie/Hot Wheels.**

Premiums: 5 Barbie Dolls
❑ ❑ USA Ba9801 **#1**
❑ ❑ USA Ba9802 **#2**
❑ ❑ USA Ba9803 **#3**
❑ ❑ USA Ba9804 **#4**
❑ ❑ USA Ba9805 **#5**

Premiums: 5 Hot Wheels Vehicles
❑ ❑ USA Hw9806 **#6**
❑ ❑ USA Hw9807 **#7**
❑ ❑ USA Hw9808 **#8**
❑ ❑ USA Hw9809 **#9**
❑ ❑ USA Hw9810 **#10**

❑ ❑ USA Ba9826 **Display/Premiums,** 1998, with 10 Premiums.
❑ ❑ USA Ba9843 **Crew Reference Sheet**, 1998, Blk/Wht Pic.

❑ ❑ USA Ba9844 **Crew Poster**, 1998.
❑ ❑ USA Ba9864 **Translite/Sm**, 1998.
❑ ❑ USA Ba9875 **Wal-Mart**:

Comments: Projected National Distribution: USA - August 14-September 10, 1998.

A Bug's Life Happy Meal, 1998 [Projected]

Bags or Boxes:
❑ ❑ USA Bu9810 **Hm B**
❑ ❑ USA Bu9811 **Hm B**

Premiums: Insect Changeable Figurines
❑ ❑ USA Bu9801 **#1**
❑ ❑ USA Bu9802 **#2**
❑ ❑ USA Bu9803 **#3**
❑ ❑ USA Bu9804 **#4**
❑ ❑ USA Bu9805 **#5**
❑ ❑ USA Bu9806 **#6**
❑ ❑ USA Bu9807 **#7**
❑ ❑ USA Bu9808 **#8**

❑ ❑ USA Bu9826 **Display/Premiums**, 1998, with 8 Premiums.
❑ ❑ USA Bu9843 **Crew Reference Sheet,** 1998, Blk/Wht Pic.

❑ ❑ USA Bu9844 **Crew Poster,** 1998.
❑ ❑ USA Bu9864 **Translite/Sm,** 1998.
❑ ❑ USA Bu9875 **Wal-Mart**:

Comments: Projected National Distribution: USA - November 20-December 17, 1998.

Fisher-Price Toddler Toys for U-3, 1998 - 1999 [Projected]

Group M:
❑ ❑ USA Fi9801
❑ ❑ USA Fi9802
❑ ❑ USA Fi9803
❑ ❑ USA Fi9804

Group N:
❑ ❑ USA Fi9805
❑ ❑ USA Fi9806
❑ ❑ USA Fi9807
❑ ❑ USA Fi9808

Group O:
❑ ❑ USA Fi9809
❑ ❑ USA Fi9810
❑ ❑ USA Fi9811
❑ ❑ USA Fi9812

Group P:
❑ ❑ USA Fi9813
❑ ❑ USA Fi9814
❑ ❑ USA Fi9815
❑ ❑ USA Fi9816

Group Q:
❑ ❑ USA Fi9815
❑ ❑ USA Fi9816
❑ ❑ USA Fi9817
❑ ❑ USA Fi9818

Group R:
❑ ❑ USA Fi9821
❑ ❑ USA Fi9822
❑ ❑ USA Fi9823
❑ ❑ USA Fi9824

❑ ❑ USA Fi9827 **Color Card with Picture of All 24 Fisher Price Toys.** $3.00-5.00

Comments: Distribution: USA - September 1998 - August 1999. Following the distribution of forty-eight Fisher-Price toys (Groups A-L) for kids under three, McDonald's and Fisher-Price distributed a third set of twenty-four more Toddler Toys. Packages were marked, "Under-3 Toy." Toys marked, "1997 Fisher-Price, Inc."

Halloween '98 Happy Meal [Projected]

Hercules II Happy Meal, 1998

Boxes:
❑ ❑ USA He9810 **Hm Box: Megara & Hercules on Pegasus.** $.50-1.00
❑ ❑ USA He9811 **Hm Box: Pegasus, Hercules & Phil.** $.50-1.00

Hercules Happy Meal crew buttons.

He9810

Left to right: He9808, He9806, He9802, He9804
He9807

He9811

He9826

Left to right: He9805, He9801, He9803

He9864

Premiums:

❑ ❑ USA He9801 **#1 Zeus Football - Orange Mini Football with Zeus' Face in White.** $1.00-1.50

❑ ❑ USA He9802 **#2 Hades Stopwatch - Blue/Grey/Yellow Plastic Clock Shaped Stopwatch.** $1.00-1.50

❑ ❑ USA He9803 **#3 Hercules Sports Bottle - Blue Column Shaped Bottle with Herc Picture.** $1.00-1.50

❑ ❑ USA He9804 **#4 Eyes of Fates Foot Bag - White Bean Bag with Eye Imprint.** $1.00-1.50

❑ ❑ USA He9805 **#5 Pegasus Whistling Discus - Silver Disc.** $1.00-1.50

❑ ❑ USA He9806 **#6 Pain and Panic Sound Baton - Purple Column Shaped Sound Stick.** $1.00-1.50

❑ ❑ USA He9807 **#7 Hercules Medal - Silver/Black Locket Hercules.** $1.00-1.50

❑ ❑ USA He9808 **#8 Phil Megaphone - Purple/Blue/Beige Megaphone.** $1.00-1.50

❑ ❑ USA He9826 **Display/Premiums**, 1998, with 8 Premiums. $15.00 -20.00

❑ ❑ USA He9827 **Color Card** with picture 8 toys. $2.00-3.00

❑ ❑ USA He9843 **Crew Reference Sheet**, 1998, Blk/Wht Pic. $1.00-2.00

❑ ❑ USA He9844 **Crew Poster**, 1998. $2.00-3.00

❑ ❑ USA He9864 **Translite/Sm**, 1998. $2.00-4.00

❑ ❑ USA He9875 **Wal-Mart: McGoody Bag.** $1.00-2.00

Comments: National Distribution: USA - January 30-February 26, 1998. The promotion was a tie-in with the global Winter Olympic Games in Nagano, Japan. U-3 Fisher-Price toys "H" were distributed to children under the age of three.

My Little Pony II/Transformers Beast Wars II Happy Meal, 1998

Bags:

❑ ❑ USA My9810 **Hm Bag - Clouds with Rainbow/Soft as a Pony's Smile.** $.50-1.00

❑ ❑ USA My9811 **Hm Bag - Bridge with Rainbow/Ponies Love Flowers.** $.50-1.00

Premiums: My Little Pony

❑ ❑ USA My9801 **#1 Ivy - Turquoise Pony with Pink Tail and Purple Mane.** $2.00-3.00

❑ ❑ USA My9802 **#2 Sundance - Pink Pony with Pink Tail and Yellow Sunburst on Rump, Blue/Pink Mane.** $2.00-3.00

❑ ❑ USA My9803 **#3 Light Heart - White Pony with Pink Heart on Rump, Purple/Beige Tail.** $2.00-3.00

Premiums: Transformers

❑ ❑ USA My9804 **#4 Scorponok - Purp/Blue/Grey Crablike Figure with Crab Claws.** $1.00-1.50

❑ ❑ USA My9805 **#5 Blackarachnia - Purple Body/Blue Mask/Org Claws Forming a Beetlelike Figure.** $1.00-1.50

❑ ❑ USA My9806 **#6 Dinobot - Blue/Silver/Green Serpentlike Figure with Green Head Mask.** $1.00-1.50

❑ ❑ USA My9826 **Display/Premiums**, 1998, with 6 Premiums. $35.00-50.00

❑ ❑ USA My9827 **Color Card** with picture 6 toys. $2.00-5.00

❑ ❑ USA My9843 **Crew Reference Sheet**, 1998, Blk/Wht Pic. $2.00-3.00

❑ ❑ USA My9844 **Crew Poster,** 1998. $7.00-10.00

❑ ❑ USA My9864 **Translite/Sm**, 1998. $7.00-10.00

❑ ❑ USA My9875 **Wal-Mart:**

Comments: National Distribution: USA - March 27-April 17, 1998. Series consists of toys based on Hasbro's line of retail toys. This three week Happy Meal featured two toys per week: one My Little Pony and one Transformer Beast Wars figure.

My9810

My9801 My9802 My9803

My9804 My9805 My9806

My9827

My9826

My9864

The Legend of Mulan Happy Meal, 1998 [Projected]

Boxes:
❑ ❑ USA Mu9810 **Hm Box**
❑ ❑ USA Mu9811 **Hm Box**

Premiums:
❑ ❑ USA Mu9801 **#1 Shun-Yu** - Evil Warrior with Eagle and Sword Blue/Blk Outfit. $.50-1.00
❑ ❑ USA Mu9802 **#2 Mulan** - Samuri Warrior with Blue/Blk Armour. $.50-1.00
❑ ❑ USA Mu9803 **#3 Khan** - Black Horse with Yellow Saddle/ Figurine/Grn Knob Windup. $.50-1.00

❑ ❑ USA Mu9804 **#4 Shang-Li** - Male Samuri Warrior in White Jacket/Red Belt. $.50-1.00
❑ ❑ USA Mu9805 **#5 Chien-Po, Ling, Yao** - Summo Wrestler with Figurine on Neck with sm. Figurine attachedon Rope/ 2p. $.50-1.00
❑ ❑ USA Mu9806 **#6 Cri-Kee** - Beetle Dark Blue Legs/Blue Body/Figurine. $.50-1.00

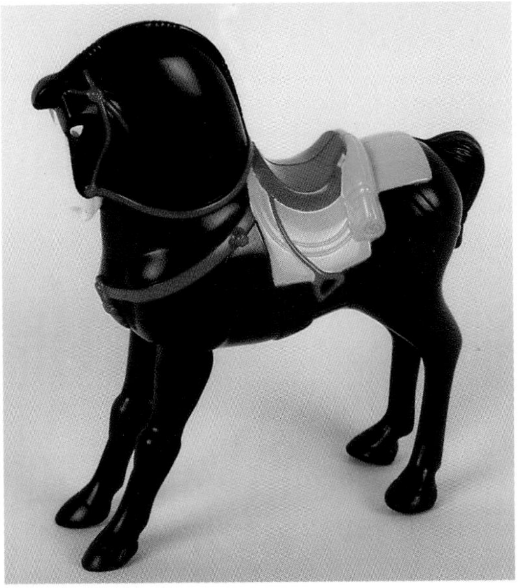

Mu9803

❑ ❑ USA Mu9807 **#7 Little Brother -** White Dog with Black Nose/Begging Pose. $.50-1.00
❑ ❑ USA Mu9808 **#8 Mushu -** Red/Yellow Dragon beating on Gong/Figurine. $.50-1.00
❑ ❑ USA Mu9826 **Display/Premiums**, 1998, with 8 Premiums. $20.00-$35.00
❑ ❑ USA Mu9843 **Crew Reference Sheet,** 1998, Blk/Wht Pic. $1.00-1.50
❑ ❑ USA Mu9844 **Crew Poster**, 1998. $1.00-2.00
❑ ❑ USA Mu9864 **Translite/Sm**, 1998. $1.00-2.00

Comments: Projected National Distribution: USA - June 19-July 16, 1998. The first McDonald's Happy Meal distributed globally; that is, at the same approximate time around the world. Distribution coincides with the global release of Disney's movie, *The Legend of Mulan*.

Mu9826

McDonaldland Happy Meal, 1998 [Projected]

Boxes:
❑ ❑ USA Mc9810 **Hm Box**
❑ ❑ USA Mc9811 **Hm Box**

Premiums:
❑ ❑ USA Mc9801 **#1 Birdie Toy Sound Maker** $.50-1.00
❑ ❑ USA Mc9802 **#2 Grimace Toy Sound Maker** $.50-1.00
❑ ❑ USA Mc9803 **#3 Hamburglar Toy Sound Maker** $.50-1.00
❑ ❑ USA Mc9804 **#4 Ronald Toy Sound Maker** $.50-1.00

Comments: Regional Distribution: USA - 1998 during cleanup weeks following Teenie Beanie Babies II Happy Meal sell out.

Peter Pan Happy Meal, 1998

Bags:
❑ ❑ USA Pe9810 **Hm Bag - Captain Hook has Two Enemies.** $.25-.50
❑ ❑ USA Pe9811 **Hm Bag - Help Peter Pan lead Wendy, John & Michael to Never Land!** $.25-.50

Premiums:
❑ ❑ USA Pe9801 **#1 Peter Pan Glider** - Peter Pan Fig With Green Clothes Attached to White Wings. $1.00-1.50
❑ ❑ USA Pe9802 **#2 Tick Tock Crocodile Compass** - Crocodile/Green with Compass in Fliptop Mouth. $1.00-1.50
❑ ❑ USA Pe9803 **#3 Captain Hook Spyglass** - Red Spyglass with Capt Hook's Head/Arm on Handle. $1.00-1.50
❑ ❑ USA Pe9804 **#4 Wendy & Michael Magnifier** - Wendy & Michael Figures Imprinted on Green Magnifier. $1.00-1.50
❑ ❑ USA Pe9805 **#5 Peter Pan Activity Tool** - Brown Knifelike Tool with Green Crocodile/Purple Tool/Red Tool Attached. $1.00-1.50
❑ ❑ USA Pe9806 **#6 Tinker Bell Lantern** - Tinker Bell inside Red/Yellow/Blue Sm Lantern. $1.00-1.50
❑ ❑ USA Pe9807 **#7 Smee Light** - Man in Brown Barrel with Red Flashlight Effect. $1.50-2.50

❑ ❑ USA Pe9826 **Display/Premiums,** 1998, with 7 Premiums. $35.00-45.00
❑ ❑ USA Pe9827 **Color Card** with picture of 7 toys. $2.00-4.00
❑ ❑ USA Pe9843 **Crew Reference Sheet**, 1998, Blk/Wht Pic. $1.00-2.00
❑ ❑ USA Pe9844 **Crew Poster**, 1998. $1.50-3.00
❑ ❑ USA Pe9864 **Translite/Sm**, 1998. $4.00-6.00

❑ ❑ USA Pe9875 **Wal-Mart: Peter Pan Coloring Booklet/ Little Golden Book style without crayons.** $1.00-1.50

Comments: National Distribution: USA - February 27-March 26, 1998. Peter Pan Happy Meal coincided with the 45th Anniversary of Walt Disney's *Peter Pan* movie re-release. The series of seven adventure toys was designed to support the video re-release of Disney's classic animated film. Toys featured key characters from the movie. USA Pe9805 Peter Pan Activity Tool was distributed twice, making the distribution two toys per week for four weeks (seven different toys). Cases "H" and "I" Fisher-Price U-3 toys accompanied the distribution. The Smee light is a flashlight in a barrel.

Pe9810

Pe9801 Pe9802 Pe9803

Pe9827

Left to right: Pe9804, Pe9805, Pe9806, Pe9807

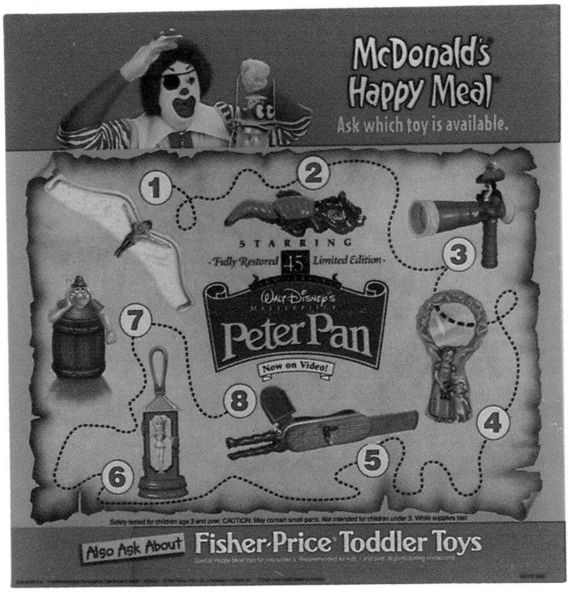

Pe9864

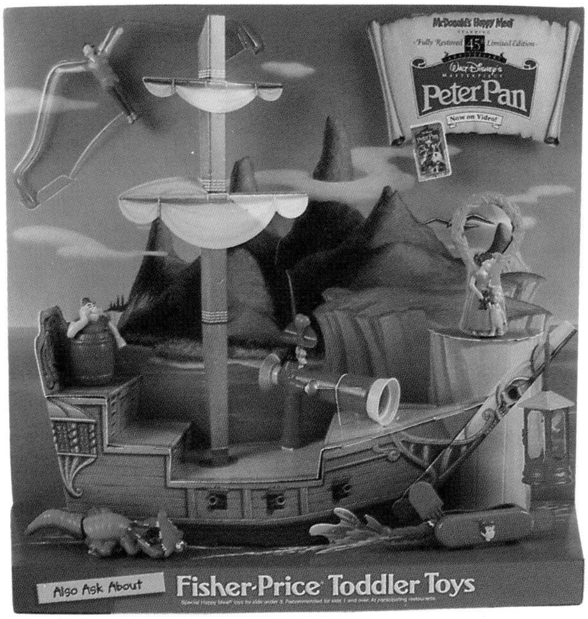

Pe9826

Pe9875

Simba's Pride Happy Meal, 1998 [Projected]

Bags or Boxes:
❑ ❑ USA Si9830 **Hm B**
❑ ❑ USA Si9831 **Hm B**

Premiums:
❑ ❑ USA Si9801 **#1**
❑ ❑ USA Si9802 **#2**
❑ ❑ USA Si9803 **#3**
❑ ❑ USA Si9804 **#4**
❑ ❑ USA Si9805 **#5**
❑ ❑ USA Si9806 **#6**
❑ ❑ USA Si9807 **#7**
❑ ❑ USA Si9808 **#8**

❑ ❑ USA Si9826 **Display/Premiums**, 1998, with 8 Premiums.
❑ ❑ USA Si9843 **Crew Reference Sheet**, 1998, Blk/Wht Pic.
❑ ❑ USA Si9844 **Crew Poster**, 1998.
❑ ❑ USA Si9864 **Translite/Sm**, 1998.
❑ ❑ USA Si9875 **Wal-Mart**:

Comments: Projected National Distribution: USA. U-3 Fisher-Price toys will be provided.

Tamagotchi Happy Meal, 1998 [Projected]

Bags or Boxes:
❑ ❑ USA Ta9830 **Hm Bag**
❑ ❑ USA Ta9831 **Hm Bag**

Premiums:
❑ ❑ USA Ta9801 **#1 Yellow Key Chain Case** $.50-1.00
❑ ❑ USA Ta9802 **#2 Purple Key Chain Case with Yellow/Grn Dog Figurine**/2p Looks Like the "Real Tomagotchi" Version. $.50-1.00
❑ ❑ USA Ta9803 **#3 Green Key Chain Case** $.50-1.00
❑ ❑ USA Ta9804 **#4 Red Key Chain Case** $.50-1.00
❑ ❑ USA Ta9805 **#5 Blue Key Chain Case** - with yellow figurine/2p $.50-1.00
❑ ❑ USA Ta9806 **#6 White Key Chain Case** - with red/blk figurine/2p $.50-1.00
❑ ❑ USA Ta9807 **#7 Orange Key Chain Case** $.50-1.00
❑ ❑ USA Ta9808 **#8 Blue Key Chain Case** $.50-1.00
❑ ❑ USA Ta9809 **#9 Wal-Mart Toy** $3.00-4.00

❑ ❑ USA Ta9826 **Display/8 Premiums**, 1998 $15-20.00
❑ ❑ USA Ta9843 **Crew Reference Sheet**, 1998 $1.00-2.00
❑ ❑ USA Ta9844 **Crew Poster**, 1998. $1.00-2.00
❑ ❑ USA Ta9864 **Translite/Sm**, 1998. $2.00-3.00

Comments: Projected National Distribution: USA July 17-August 13, 1998. U-3 Fisher-Price toys will be provided.

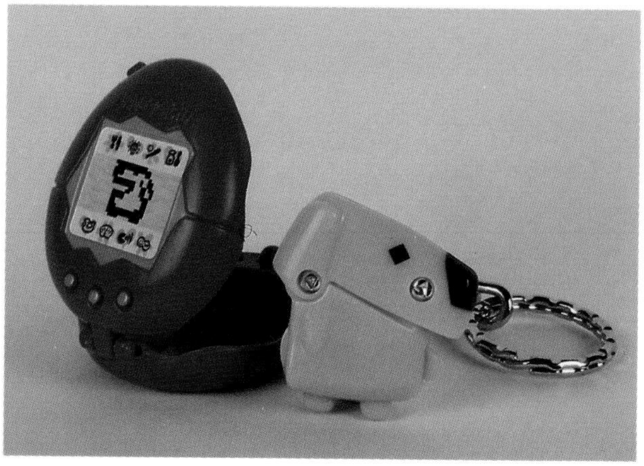

Teenie Beanie Babies II Happy Meal, 1998

Bags or Boxes:
❑ ❑ USA Ty9830 **Hm Bag:**
❑ ❑ USA Ty9831 **Hm Bag:**

Premiums:
❑ ❑ USA Ty9801 **#1 Doby the Doberman -** $10.00-15.00
❑ ❑ USA Ty9802 **#2 Bongo the Monkey -** $10.00-15.00
❑ ❑ USA Ty9803 **#3 Twigs the Giraffe -** $15.00-20.00
❑ ❑ USA Ty9804 **#4 Inch the Worm -** $5.00-8.00
❑ ❑ USA Ty9805 **#5 Pinchers the Lobster -** $5.00-8.00
❑ ❑ USA Ty9806 **#6 Happy the Hippo -** $5.00-8.00
❑ ❑ USA Ty9807 **#7 Mel the Koala -** $5.00-8.00
❑ ❑ USA Ty9808 **#8 Scoop the Pelican -** $8.00-10.00
❑ ❑ USA Ty9809 **#9 Bones the Dog -** $5.00-8.00
❑ ❑ USA Ty9810 **#10 Zip the Cat -** $5.00-8.00
❑ ❑ USA Ty9811 **#11 Waddle the Penguin -** $5.00-8.00
❑ ❑ USA Ty9812 **#12 Peanut the Elephant -** $8.00-10.00

❑ ❑ USA Ty9826 **Display/Premiums**, 1998, with 12 Premiums. $225.00-350.00
❑ ❑ USA Ty9843 **Crew Reference Sheet**, 1998, Blk/Wht Pic. $4.00-5.00
❑ ❑ USA Ty9844 **Crew Poster**, 1998. $7.00-10.00
❑ ❑ USA Ty9864 **Translite/Sm**, 1998. $15.00-25.00

Comments: National Distribution: USA - May 22-June 18, 1998. Production figures indicate that over 188 million toys were distributed during the 2-3 week promotion. This is an 88 per cent increase over the 1997 promotion. U-3 Fisher-Price toys will be provided. According to McDonald's press release dated February 19, 1998: "....Happy Meal features an all new collection of Ty Beanie Babies available only at McDonald's." Cleanup weeks featured toys from past promotions and a set of McDonaldland Band toy instruments (whistles)

Left to right: Ty9801, Ty9802, Ty9803, Ty9804

Left to right: Ty9807, Ty9808, Ty9806, Ty9805

Left to right: Ty9810, Ty9812, Ty9811, Ty9809

Ty9826

USA Generic Promotions, 1998 [Projected]

❑ ❑ USA Ge9801 **January/December 1997/8 - Magic Paint Greeting Card,** 1997, Paper. $.50-1.00

❑ ❑ USA Ge9802 **January/December 1997/8 - Magic Paint Greeting Card,** 1997. $.25-.50

❑ ❑ USA Ge9803 **February - Fun Times Magazine 1998-1: Friends Are The Best,** 1997. $.25-.50

❑ ❑ USA Ge9804 **March - Prismatic Foil Sticker - Ronald, 3" x 3"**, 1997. $.25-.50

❑ ❑ USA Ge9805 **March - Prismatic Foil Sticker - Birdie, 3" x 3"**, 1997. $.25-.50

❑ ❑ USA Ge9806 **March - Prismatic Foil Sticker - Hamburglar, 3" x 3"**, 1997. $.50-1.00

❑ ❑ USA Ge9807 **March - Prismatic Foil Sticker - Grimace, 3" x 3"**, 1997. $.50-1.00

❑ ❑ USA Ge9808 **April - Fun Times Magazine 1998-2: Green Detectives**, 1997. $.50-1.00

❑ ❑ USA Ge9809 **April - Fun Times Magazine 1998 - Road Safety Activity Book,** 1997. $.25-.50

❑ ❑ USA Ge9810 **May - Poster: Get Fit With Ronald Games & Poster,** 1998. $.25-.50

❑ ❑ USA Ge9811 **June - Fun Times Magazine 1998-3: Hooray for Summer,** 1998. $.25-.50

❑ ❑ USA Ge9812 **July - Magic Reveal Storybooks**, 1998. $.50-1.00

❑ ❑ USA Ge9813 **August - Fun Times Magazine 1998-4: Countdown to School**, 1998. $.50-1.00

❑ ❑ USA Ge9814 **September - Award Chart: You're A Star!**, 1998. $.50-1.00

❑ ❑ USA Ge9815 **September - Fun Times Magazine 1998-Fire Safety Activity Book,** 1998. $.25-.50

❑ ❑ USA Ge9816 **October - Fun Times Magazine 1998-5: Jeepers, Creepers, It's Halloween!,** 1998. $.25-.50

❑ ❑ USA Ge9817 **November - Mini Book: Surprise Inside**, 1998. $.50-1.00

❑ ❑ USA Ge9818 **December - Fun Times Magazine 1998-6: Here Come The Holidays!,** 1998. $.25-.50

Comments: Projected Regional Distribution: USA - 1998 as Fun Times Magazine promotions and alternatives.

The "Iam Hungry" computer animated and computer generated character is a flying green furball creature with orange arms and a huge mouth with a purple tongue. In February 1998 commercials, he is seen constantly attacking Ronald McDonald for his food and appears not to take "No" for an answer. This hungry and aggressive furball creature demonstrates an attitude problem, while being disgusting and downright rude in manners (all in a fun-provoking way). This is a departure from McDonald's positive attitude approach in its previous cast of characters, but these early encounters lead to some very exaggerated slapstick humor. It is humor, after all, along with fun that captivates the attention of the viewing audience and results in a positive image rating for McDonald's!

The Happy Meal toys of the nineties were primarily designed by M B Sales in Westmont, Illinois, and Simon Marketing in Oak Brook Terrace, Illinois. M B Sales also designed some of the international toys. It is the efforts of the top designers at these two agencies which generate the smiles in children around the world as well as in the child that lives inside all of us!

Lastly, two score and three plus have passed since Ray Kroc opened his first McDonald's restaurant in Des Plaines, Illinois in 1955. McDonald's has grown from 1 to over 23,000 restaurants in over 109 countries. Incredible as it sounds, the McDonald's Corporation is today just beginning to settle into its #1 market — the American market — while it aggressively expands worldwide. The McDonald's barrel of fun continues to roll and create an exciting thunder of laughter heard 'round the world. We hope you enjoyed our tour of Happy Meal toys from the nineties!

Left to right: Ge9805, Ge9804, Ge9807, Ge9806

For additional information on Happy Meal toys and pre-Happy Meal toys, see Joyce and Terry Losonsky's additional books:

McDonald's Pre-Happy Meal Toys from the Fifties, Sixties, and Seventies and ***McDonald's Happy Meal Toys from the Eighties,*** which trace the history of McDonald's toys and promotions from the earliest beginnings in the 1950s through 1989.

McDonald's Happy Meal Toys Around the World, which traces the history of Global Happy Meal toys from the beginning through June 1995.

McDonald's Collectors Club information:

Membership Secretary: Charlie Wichmann, 255 New Lenox Road, Lenox, Massachusetts, 01240 USA. E-mail: charmarmcd@aol.com
President: Sharon Iranpour, 24 San Rafael Drive, Rochester, New York 14618 USA. E-mail: siranpour@aol.com
Membership Year: January - December

Index